OFF-BROADWAY:
The Prophetic Theater

Also by the Author

THE PLAYMAKERS
(WITH ARTHUR CANTOR)

Off-Broadway:

The Prophetic Theater
by
Stuart W. Little

COWARD, McCANN & GEOGHEGAN, INC.

NEW YORK

For the many theater friends whose diligent self-promotion tutored me and especially for those rare few—including Richard Barr, Julian Beck and Judith Malina, Gene Frankel, Theodore Mann, Jose Quintero, and Joseph Papp—who put theater above self and made off-Broadway the advance post of the American theater.

Contents

Illustrations follow pages 68, 100, 132, 164, 228, 260

One

In 1952 Sheridan Square, the busy, commercial hub of Greenwich Village, was not yet known as a center of theater. The cobblestone thoroughfare of Seventh Avenue South carried the uptown traffic down through the square to the Holland Tunnel and out to New Jersey. Before Jack Delaney's Restaurant stood the islanded IRT subway entrance with its overburdened newsstand, a rock around which swirled streams of Villagers and visitors hurrying to homes and shops. The side streets radiated outward in bewildering traffic patterns that soon became lost among back alleys and hidden blocks crowded with small Italian groceries, bead and button shops, family-run restaurants, and one-window art galleries at sidewalk level. On Perry Street in a line of nineteenth century red-brick houses with stoops stood the four-story studio-home of Alfred Frueh, for years a fixture on the drama page of *The New Yorker*. Down Christopher Street toward the river was the handsome new Theater de Lys. In the quiet crook of Commerce Street nestled the Cherry Lane in a building dating from Colonial times. To the Broadway sophisticate they were mere dollhouse theaters busying themselves with amateur theatricals. But they were the beginning of off-Broadway.

Off-Broadway is a state of mind, a set of production conditions, a way of looking at theater at every point at odds with

Broadway's patterns. But one thinks of it first in geographical terms. In the Actors' Equity rulebook off-Broadway is defined in an exclusion clause that relegates its under-300-seat theaters to areas of the city outside the borders of the regular Times Square theater district. One thinks of the clusters of small, dusty theaters above and below street level stretching in three bands across Manhattan at the level of Eighth Street: some theaters in Sheridan Square, more theaters farther east along Macdougal and Bleecker streets, and more still farther east on Second Avenue. Later they were to spread up and across town, into the Eighties along Broadway, into the Seventies on the upper East Side.

But off-Broadway, for historical purposes, may be said to have begun in Sheridan Square on the evening of April 24, 1952, when *Summer and Smoke* with Geraldine Page opened at Circle in the Square and became the first major theatrical success below Forty-second Street in thirty years. If one were to try to reconstruct that evening, a starting point would be Louie's Bar, next door to the theater, where Jose Quintero, the director, had decided to sit out the performance and try to detach himself from the play, to put out of his mind the too-familiar lines and cadences of his actors. For him to stand in the back of the theater, as many directors did, with one eye on the audience, the other nervously on the stage, worrying over every unrehearsed pause on the part of the actors or the littlest stirring of audience inattention, was an exercise in futility.

Nor did Quintero anticipate anything very different about this opening night. Since its inception, Circle in the Square had produced seven plays. Each opening night meant simply the finish of one intensive work period, the prelude to another. Circle openings were never burdened by critics from uptown, and opening-night audiences, while occasionally moved to self-conscious applause at curtain rise, were not demonstrative. The Circle company worked mainly to please themselves. After a few beers at Louie's, Quintero sauntered back to the theater just at the moment the play was ending. He was not prepared for the scene that followed. He did not know that Brooks Atkinson was in the audience for the *Times*. No one could have anticipated that in a few hours Atkinson's words in type in the *Times* would give this particular evening an importance immeasurably greater than the size of their stage and their ambition seemed to warrant.

His first suspicion that anything out of the ordinary had occurred came when his normally undemonstrative partner, Theodore Mann, walking up the aisle to meet him, embraced Quintero and kissed him on the forehead. "It's beautiful, Jose," he said. The play was over, and the applause broke out. In that moment, Quintero was awakened to a totally new experience in the theater. From all sides bravos rang out for Geraldine Page. The new actress appeared diffidently and took a bow. In earlier Circle productions there was never any demand for repeated curtain calls. Quintero had never rehearsed the actors in more than one call. He hurried backstage to find Miss Page standing paralyzed and uncertain. "Go out, they want you!" he said sharply, shocked himself at the force of the reaction. But Miss Page was hesitant. "Should I really?" she asked. The applause called her back to the stage again and again and again.

It was in this moment, as we look back, that Circle in the Square became a theater—a theater of respected professionals instead of a studio for out-of-work actors and hopeful theater artists. In this moment, in the larger sense, the off-Broadway theater was born. Off-Broadway is defined by the variety of its uses. It is a showcase for new actors and directors, a place where new talent can be discovered. It is a place to revive Broadway failures and restore the reputations of playwrights who may have been ill served in the regular commercial theater. It provides the means of encouraging the growth of theaters that exist in time and so engage the loyalties of talented professionals that they can develop continuity of production and a consistent artistic policy.

All these aspects of off-Broadway are implicit in Circle in the Square's fortunate choice of Tennessee Williams' *Summer and Smoke*, a disappointing failure on Broadway four years earlier, and in the Circle's casting of Geraldine Page to play Alma Winemiller, the ardent spinster of Glorious Hill, whom the reviews now proclaimed the new actress in town to watch. The production also showed off the brilliant but as then unproved directorial talents of Jose Quintero. If there was no need to "restore" the playwriting reputation of Williams, the Circle production at least assured *Summer and Smoke* a place as one of the four or five major works on which his reputation as a dramatist rests. And, lastly, the success and public attention created by the production gave an ongoing life to Circle in the Square, afterward one of the finest and certainly one of the most durable of off-Broadway institutions. The success of *Summer and Smoke* made theater off-Broadway a realizable goal for promising young actors, directors, designers, and aspiring producers who felt shut out of the Broadway commercial theater and judged it anyway to be hostile to new theater ideas and untested talent. To a postwar generation *Summer and Smoke* opened the door.

The Circle's first hit resulted from the lucky convergence at the beginning of their careers of three individuals of very diverse talents: Page, Quintero, and Mann. Quintero, the catalytic agent, met Mann in Woodstock, New York, in summer theater and joined forces with him in New York in the fall of 1950 to establish the Circle. Quintero met Page in Chicago at the Goodman Theater School in the mid-1940's. They were casual acquaintances, Page, theatrically, being much more advanced than he. She had been acting since she was seventeen. By the time she reached New York in the late 1940's she had the accumulated experience of four summers of stock at the Lake Zurich Playhouse, outside Chicago, which she helped run. In her own mind a veteran, in her mid-twenties, she was determined to find the right part in

New York, although she was half-resigned to being offered only character roles because of her five-foot-seven height. One day she heard that Julian Beck and Judith Malina, who had recently started up their own Living Theater and were putting on avant-garde plays at the Cherry Lane, were casting a play about Alexander the Great. She begged them to give her one small part left with a brief scene in the last act. During rehearsal, the leading actress, afraid of damaging her voice, refused to let out a piercing scream in the opening scene. In the best tradition of the understudy, Miss Page volunteered. "I'll do it!" she said. "I'll do the scream." At stage left in the narrow Cherry Lane was a small scooped-out area that once served as a wine cellar. Here, crouching down on all fours, she delivered the leading lady's scream at the opening of the play. There was no crossover out of view of the audience, so she had to remain there, doubled over, for the rest of the act.

Shortly after this episode, by chance she met Quintero on the street for the first time since Chicago. They stopped and talked, and he described the little theater group he and some friends were starting up to do poetry readings, dance recitals, and good plays. All very worthy, but Miss Page felt she had been through this phase already in Chicago. Soon she would have to have her teeth fixed and would need some sensible employment to meet the dentist's bills. To join Quintero's group would be just one more delaying indulgence. She forgot their talk until one day, in her routine theatergoing, she dropped in on a performance of *Dark of the Moon* without realizing that it was Quintero's. She was struck by the intensity of the actors. This was unusual for off-Broadway, where the players were generally so busy calling attention to themselves from the stage, in case anyone in the audience might want to hire them for something better, that the play itself suffered. The real message of the evening was making its desperate cry heard: "Look at me! Look at what I can do. Hire me!" This was off-Broadway showcasing at its self-defeating worst. These actors, in contrast, seemed so absorbed and involved as to be unaware of the audience. All the more was the audience fascinated with what they were doing.

Miss Page took to hanging about the theater, watching, listening, observing rehearsals, not saying very much herself but hoping that Quintero would find a part for her. In the early days a company policy was in effect at the Circle. The large parts went to the older members, the smaller ones to newcomers. Just now they were casting Lorca's *Yerma*, and Quintero offered Page a small character role with one or two lines. The pay was $10 a week. In the tedious scramble to make a substitute living in New York until a good acting job came along, Gerry Page had found employment in the garment business, working at first in a thread company for $21 a week. Her friends advised her to try modeling; that was where the money was. With her long legs she never seemed the proper size for modeling until she tried a nightgown shop on Madison Avenue. But the employment there seemed no more certain than the theater. The woman who ran the shop was always firing Gerry during the day and rehiring her before quitting time. Gerry later discovered she was getting $5 under the going rate for lingerie models of $50 a week, which was very likely the reason for her boss' second thoughts. Balancing the *Yerma* offer against this weekly check, Gerry Page turned Quintero down. Then, just as *Yerma* was to go into rehearsal in March, 1952, she was fired for good, a victim of the seasonal nature of the garment trade. The part was still open. Officially she joined the Circle company.

Her role was that of the pagan crone, an eighty-year-old woman who has one scene seated alone toward the end of the play and takes a bite out of an apple. Geraldine Page made this tiny part unforgettable. To this day Theodore Mann says he can still hear the crunch of the apple as she bit into it. Unknown, of course, to herself, Geraldine Page became the obvious choice for Alma in *Summer and Smoke*, the next Circle production.

The play was not the first choice to follow *Yerma*. The Circle wanted to do *The Children's Hour*, but Lillian Hellman, hoping to arrange a Broadway revival, withheld permission. There were other rights problems over *Winesburg, Ohio*, leaving them with nothing, and then one day Quintero burst into the theater clutching the script of *Summer and Smoke*. "I've found the play!" he shouted. Williams had worked on this play while he wrote *A Streetcar Named Desire*. The themes of the two plays ran parallel, and the principal characters in both plays shared certain personality traits, Williams in both plays setting off female gentility against male brutishness. The late Margo Jones first put the play on in Dallas in her theater-in-the-round, following up with a Broadway production under her sponsorship and direction in October, 1948, while *Streetcar* was still running. The play never got over. From her own recollection of the production, Geraldine Page felt cuts in the script were partly to blame. Possibly in the interests of getting the commuters home on time, the prologue and one of the scenes in the first act were eliminated, and the rest of the play, she felt, was rushed. In Jo Mielziner's setting, which followed the playwright's explicit instructions, the stone statue of the angel, which lends symbolism to the opening and closing of the play, took on too obtrusive a presence. Except when Anne Jackson was on stage as the young girl, the Broadway production had seemed ponderous. In contrast, the spread-out playing areas in the Circle's production, simply designed by Keith Cuerden, the reduction of the statue to less dominant dimensions, and the restoration of the cuts seemed to free the play and give it life. Director and cast had no thought but to do the work. The convenience of commuters never entered their heads. Sometimes the curtain did not come down until after midnight when Gerry Page practiced some of her longer acting pauses.

She had not expected to get the part of Alma. Reading the script, she rather imagined the lead would go to Kathleen Murray, who had been longer with the company but was really too young for the role and was later more suitably cast in the Anne Jackson part. For herself she expected to be given the part of Alma's eccentric mother with her embarrassing weakness for ice cream. The ice cream would be a kind of consolation for Gerry's not getting Alma. But at this point the company system, with its recognition of seniority, was beginning to disintegrate. There was no question in Jose's mind but that Geraldine should play Alma. From the one part he had seen her perform Quintero could sense in the girl enormous acting confidence, but like so many very good actresses, she seemed two persons, her offstage self a shrunken and fainter facsimile of the greater-than-life presence she showed onstage. The director's eye took inventory of her physical attributes—the long, lovely legs, the neat ankles, the very small wrists and exquisite hands. Her hair was piled up wildly on her head like eagles' nests. There was the potato nose and the funny, high-pitched squeaky voice like that of a peevish child. But onstage, in her role, the voice deepened and became as rich and responsive as a chamber ensemble. Onstage she became a breathtakingly beautiful woman, and sometimes, in offstage conversation, when she slipped casually into the dramatic reconstruction of some happening, the complete transformation took place right before one's eyes.

Quintero at the time did not look at Geraldine Page in any objective critical sense and say to himself, as he later would, she is a great actress, a very great actress. Instinctively, he understood her talent. In common with almost everyone then working at the Circle he felt the excitement of Page onstage, and he was sure she could perform the role. As he later said, "I knew it in the back of my head but not in the front of my head." Whatever self-doubts and hesitancies Miss Page may have felt offstage, she, too, was confident of her acting ability. Ever since her first theater experience at the age of seventeen, she has felt secure before an audience and has been a self-confessed admirer of her own work.

The role of Alma Winemiller seemed exactly right for her:

the minister's daughter, a little careful, a little proud, but hopelessly in love with the young, worldly, traveled doctor who lived next door, who indulged his senses while she guarded her soul. Gerry Page judged precisely the firmness in Alma's character when a gossipy neighbor delivered the crushing news that Dr. John was planning to marry Rosa Gonzales, the flirtatious daughter of the local Mafioso who ran the gambling casino at the edge of town. In directing the scene Quintero had Miss Page walking up and down the room. Miss Page felt the movement was wrong, out of key with the character.

"Remember, she's a fighter," Quintero said. "She won't give up."

But Gerry Page was unconvinced. "Even a fighter has to stop and take a breath." Alma, she felt, would receive the news absolutely still, and the stillness at the center would only heighten the storm. "If Williams had wanted Alma to show some reaction," she argued, "he would have written it into the part." The scene was played her way, and it worked. Walter Kerr was later to write in the Sunday New York *Herald Tribune*, "The performance is as moving as anything you are likely to encounter in a whole season of playgoing." One had to remember that neither Miss Page nor Lee Richardson, as Dr. John, was at all known, that the young director was without credits of any standing, that the Circle had gone largely unreviewed, and that in these performances a Tennessee Williams play that had seemed unremarkable on Broadway suddenly was revealed, in Kerr's words, as "a thoroughly mature and deeply satisfying work."

The two characters played by Page and Richardson were near relatives of Blanche DuBois and Stanley Kowalski of *Streetcar*, gentler, more muted, more refined, but violently attracted to each other and sharply divided. The peculiar characteristic of Geraldine Page's performance was spontaneity, and the evening was filled with declarations and retractions, involvements and withdrawals. To call attention merely to the breathlessness and the pauses that were part of her special style was to give only a crude notation of how she *thought* her way into the character. William Hawkins was to write in the *World-Telegram and Sun:* "Every word and move seems inspired by the moment's inspiration. . . . She seems constantly to be conceiving of her next remark just as she says it."

Quintero, self-conscious about his accent but one of the most voluble of directors, listening to Page deliver Williams' lines, felt that he was hearing English the way it should be spoken. Page could break a one-syllable word like "cool" in half until it sounded like a breeze stirring or spread the vowels of a word such as "failed" into a lament. He was as enchanted as a child with her reading of lines such as "The Gulf wind has failed us this year, disappointed us dreadfully this summer. We used to be able to rely on the Gulf wind to cool the nights off for us, but this summer has been an exceptional season."

Quintero worked intuitively on the essence of each scene. One evening, rather late, he was working with Page and Richardson on what they referred to as "the chart scene." The stone angel standing in the fountain in the town square expressed the spiritual nature of Alma. In the doctor's office in the Buchanan house hung an anatomy chart which Dr. John, in a chilling speech, uses to force Alma to recognize the physical hungers of man. They had done this scene and were quitting for the night. Quintero sat for a moment longer on the set, replaying the action in his head. He called them back.

"Now I've got it," he said. "Instead of pulling away from the chart to show your fear of the body," he told Gerry Page, "you should go up to it and fight it." Quintero stepped to the chart. "There's the heart! There's the stomach! There's the sex!" He stabbed his finger savagely at the diagrammed parts of the body. "Fight it! Fight it! Fight it!" He grew more and more incoherent as he worked revulsion and attraction into the moment. Then Page and Richardson ran the scene again, going counter to the indicated emotion, deliberately playing opposite the intention. The essential emotion was released, and the scene flowered.

At no time did Quintero conceive of his role in relation to Page in authoritarian terms. One does not "direct" an actress of genius. Quintero assumed that his job, like that of the cast, was to help interpret and perhaps illuminate the text. Williams, in his directions, had indicated that the play should open with a gesture of violence and end with a gesture of salute. At the end Alma is a soul doubly lost. She has lost Dr. John to the younger girl who had been her least promising singing pupil, and she has cast off the refinement of principle that had originally repelled him. In the final scene Alma stands before the stone angel in the fountain. Quintero puzzled over the function of the fountain in relation to the dying moments of the play. All parks are built around a monument of some kind; all love is, too. Having lost all, Alma turns bitterly and faces the angel with upraised fist. Quintero told Miss Page to hold the gesture there, and he asked her to remember that this angel had looked down when she and the doctor as children had written their names with water on the fountain rim. Remembering, Alma slowly lowers her arm, and the gesture of defiance dissolves into a reluctant salute. In this closing gesture the beginning and the end of the play are joined; childhood and middle age, hope and abandonment, and the merging meanings are frozen into timelessness like the stone statue.

As the play ended, no one was prepared for the volume of applause. After the curtain calls Quintero sat down with Gerry Page in her dressing room for a long time while she took off her makeup. They talked quietly together about almost everything but the play and the performance. They talked about her job, his parents in Panama, their days in Chicago at Goodman, what play they would do next. They never mentioned *Summer and Smoke*. Then they walked out into the semidark theater lit only by the single work light. In the forlorn darkness Gerry saw the empty seats which so recently had been filled with applauding, cheering people. Looking out, with a cry of surprise, she said, "They've all gone home." Not at once did Quintero understand what she meant. The play was over; of course the audience had gone home.

Ted Mann had taken the subway to Times Square to buy the morning paper. He had never done that before. The Circle didn't expect reviews, and he hardly knew where to find the early morning edition. The freshly printed *Times* carried half a column on their evening. Mann announced to the gathered cast, "We're a hit!" No one could take seriously the Broadway terminology applied to something of theirs. He opened the paper and read out Brooks Atkinson's review:

Nothing has happened for quite a long time as admirable as the new production at the Circle in the Square—in Sheridan Square to be precise. Tennessee Williams' *Summer and Smoke* opened there last evening in a sensitive, highly personal performance. . . . Geraldine Page's portrait of the lonely, panicky spinster of Glorious Hill, Mississippi, is truthful, perceptive and poignant. And Lee Richardson's portrait of the wayward young doctor is the exact counterpart, assured, callous and boorish. Although *Summer and Smoke* was acted beautifully uptown four years ago, the Sheridan Square production is more intimate and penetrating.

The following morning the phones started ringing in the box office. Other critics began coming down, alerted by Atkinson's review. Circle productions were usually limited to five weeks. But this play was sure to run. Challenging off-Broadway custom, it would even outlast the hot summer. The absence of air conditioning caused dead faints in the audience on the hotter nights. In July Mann arranged to have a twenty-five-ton unit brought into the theater, but it was so noisy it could be run only intermittently, in certain scenes, not in others. Theater professionals showed up to see the new actress, the reclaimed Williams play, the work of the brilliant young Panamanian director. The Circle began to count the celebrities out front. One night, looking into the audience, Geraldine Page recognized Marlene Dietrich in the second row. Stage light caught only the legs from the knees down. Even in her nearsightedness Miss Page knew who it was. Performing in front of famous people didn't worry her in the least. Having professionals out front only made her want to show the good things she was capable of doing, that she was putting into her performance, and to make them better. It challenged her best.

A few weeks into the run Williams himself came. Miss Page didn't realize he was in the house. At the end of the intermission she had to make her entrance through the audience from the bar in the lobby. The lights went down. Two late-returning members of the audience were right in her path trying to regain their seats. She was momentarily annoyed. Why hadn't the stage manager made sure the aisle was cleared? Only later did she learn it was Tennessee Williams and his friend Frank Merlo. After the curtain Williams went backstage and thanked everyone with great courtesy. He paid Geraldine Page the finest compliment of her career.

"That was the best performance of a female part in one of my plays since Laurette Taylor," he said.

Miss Page was then taking acting classes with Uta Hagen. Her friends urged her to repeat the Williams remark. Miss Hagen laughed and said, "You know, he says that to every actress in one of his plays. And to every male actor he says, 'That was the best performance of a male part in one of my plays since Marlon Brando.' And each time, of course, he means it."

That night Williams was carrying a cane. As they stood there in the crowded dressing room—Mann, Quintero, and some of the members of the cast—Williams' cane was pressed into Quintero's foot. Despite the agony, Quintero never moved or said a word.

The success of *Summer and Smoke* was to change their lives. Geraldine Page performed in the play through the summer and until the end of November, when she left to rehearse in *Mid-Summer* for her Broadway debut on January 21, 1953. She had already signed a seven-year movie contract. She was not again to be directed by Quintero until the Actors Studio production of *Strange Interlude* on Broadway in 1963. Nor was she to appear again at Circle in the Square.

For Mann success meant the assurance of a working theater with a future. The play had put the Circle on the map. The public henceforth was to know where it was. Success, too, changed the life of Jose Quintero in subtle ways. He had left Panama seven years earlier as a somewhat rebellious boy. The father had little sympathy for the son's attempts to make a career for himself in the theater. On the day after *Summer and Smoke* opened, with the Atkinson review in hand, Quintero called home for the first time in seven years. He spoke to his father and mother in Panama, attempting to explain what the opening had been like and what the review had meant while Quintero's father tried to establish the rank and importance of the critic who had praised his son's work.

From now on everything would be different. Everything would in some way be measured and compared and weighed against this first great success. They were no longer outcasts or disowned children free to work out their own destinies as they chose, away from judges, critics, curious professionals, suddenly interested parents, expectant audiences. The Circle had come into being like a newborn baby whose first breath had been spanked into it and which had let out a cry of joy and pain. The beginning had been made, and the beginning was already the beginning of the end. They had felt the love that was the reward of their work, and at the same time they realized they would always have to work to make certain of the love. It was only later that Quintero came to understand those words Geraldine Page spoke as they walked together through the darkened theater on the night *Summer and Smoke* opened. "They have all gone home!" *They* would not always be present with their love. From then on Gerry Page would be running after the elusive audience, trying to catch them again.

Two

"Are You Trying to Kill Off-Broadway?"

For the origins of off-Broadway one really has to go back to the early 1900's and revisit two half-forgotten theater groups that enjoyed brief but brilliant careers in the Greenwich Village of the First World War. Differing though they did in aim and method, each bequeathed something of its spirit to modern off-Broadway, and indeed, most of the established theaters and movements of off-Broadway since then are in a real sense collateral, if not linear, descendants of one or the other of these pioneers.

The Washington Square Players, the earlier of the two, was begun by a group of literary-minded Villagers that included Lawrence Langner and under his leadership was soon to evolve into the Theater Guild and set standards of dramatic excellence that were to influence American theater for four decades. The Provincetown Players, the second group, in a sense a split-off from the more highly organized Washington Square Players, was to become famous for producing the first plays of Eugene O'Neill.

The Washington Square Players aspired to a vaunting professionalism and laid claim to the classics of drama, ancient and modern, that Broadway was unable or unwilling to tackle. In contrast, the Provincetown jealously guarded a spirit of amateurism and restricted itself to new writers and American writing. The Washington Square Players admired finished stagecraft, experienced acting, and existing theater literature. Its orientation was uptown, where it was to land four years after its start in Greenwich Village in 1914. The Provincetown's founders, George Cram Cook and Susan Glaspell, were determined their theater should remain small, anticommercial, close to the current writing. In this sense the Provincetown embodied more of the essential off-Broadway spirit and in its life-style prefigures modern off-Broadway. One might say that the Provincetown Players were the spiritual forerunners of the early Circle in the Square, which was to revive O'Neill, and, particularly in its spirit of amateurism, noncommercialism, and concern for new writing, the Living Theater, Richard Barr and Edward Albee's Theater 1960, and such off off-Broadway groups as Ellen Stewart's La Mama. By the same analogy, the Washington Square Players preceded the Phoenix Theater and Circle in the Square in its later phase.

A revolt of some sort against the established theater is at the root of all off-Broadway movements. A general air of revolt—literary, political, social, theatrical—pervaded the Greenwich Village of 1914 and 1915, when the earliest little theaters were established. Susan Glaspell, an ardent young writer out of the Middle West, spoke for a generation of emancipated artists when she described her contemporaries in *The Road to the Temple* (Ernest Burn, Ltd., 1926) as follows: "Most of us were from families who had other ideas —who wanted to make money, played bridge, voted the Republican ticket, went to church, thinking one should be like everyone else. And so, drawn together by the thing we really were, we were as a new family; we lent each other money, worried through illnesses, ate together when a cook left, talked about our work. Each would be himself, that was perhaps the real thing we did for each other." In one of her later plays, *The Verge*, she depicted the new feminist, dramatizing the modern woman's violent reaction against marriage conventions, motherhood, and wifely subservience and encouraging the submerged wish of a woman to seek her own meaning in her own way. Susan Glaspell's Claire Archer was at that time perhaps the most radical feminist ever to stride the American stage, carrying the declared emancipation of womanhood a step forward from Ibsen.

The climate of the day favored emancipation and self-expression. Freudian psychology was then coming into vogue among the intellectuals, teaching the release of inhibitions and laying the basis for a new sexual freedom the Villagers began to practice with zest. Liberal ideas were in the wind; full artistic expression was the cry. Uptowners were held in suspicion, and literary life centered on the Washington Square Book Shop on Macdougal Street, a block south of the square—the exact geographical center of the new bohemia.

In retrospect the pacesetters of this new free society seem a confident, self-assertive, and favored clique. The bookshop, established by Albert Boni and his brother Charles in 1913, was to spawn not only a theater but, with Horace Liveright, the most venturesome publishing house of the 1920's, Boni & Liveright, publisher of Theodore Dreiser, Ernest Hemingway, Hart Crane, E. E. Cummings, Sherwood Anderson, Anita Loos, Stark Young, Max Eastman, and, for the earliest plays, Eugene O'Neill.

Next door to the bookshop at 137 Macdougal Street in an adjoining brownstone was the Liberal Club. A door was cut through so that patrons and members could meet and exchange views with such Socialists, would-be poets, and radical writers and editors as John Reed, Emma Goldman, Margaret Sanger, Dreiser, and Eastman, the editor of *The Masses*. Inevitably theater came into the conversation. Eastman's wife, Ida Rauh, with other Liberal Club members and likeminded Villagers in the winter of 1914, conspired to put on a play, using a room of the bookstore as a makeshift theater. From a store shelf they pulled down a handy copy of Lord Dunsany's *The Glittering Gate* as a likely initial script. Joining Ida

Rauh in this earliest of off-Broadway plots were Lawrence Langner; Robert Edmond Jones; Floyd Dell; George Cram Cook and his wife, Susan Glaspell; Hutchins Hapgood and his wife, Neith Boyce; Eastman; Wilbur Daniel Steele, the short story writer; Reed; and Mary Heaton Vorse, whose wharf in Provincetown at the tip of Cape Cod was another outcropping of the new theater. Amateurs mostly, the group incorporated as the Washington Square Players and almost at once rejected the hole-in-the-wall facilities the Village offered in favor of the Bandbox Theater on East Fifty-seventh Street off Third Avenue in what is now the Times Square of the art cinema houses. The Players early adopted the procedure of a play selection committee, which was to anticipate the structural patterns of the Theater Guild and its board of managers, and a certain professionalism in the group could be attributed to the presence of the formidable and handsome actress Helen Westley.

The manifesto was written by Langner, who was assigned business functions, with the assistance of his artistic colleagues Edward Goodman and Philip Moeller: "We have only one policy in regard to the plays which we will produce— they must have artistic merit. Preference will be given to American plays, but we shall also include in our repertory the works of well-known European authors which have been ignored by the commercial managers." By day engaged in the practice of patent law, Langner wrote the one-act play *Licensed* about the ticklish moral question involved in the death, moments before the marriage was to be performed, of the fiancé of a young girl who is pregnant. With this play on the bill the Washington Square Players opened the Bandbox on February 19, 1915. They were to stay there two seasons, then move to Broadway to the Shubert-owned Comedy Theater on West Thirty-eighth Street, only to suspend operations in 1918 because of the war. By that time they had presented sixty-two one-act plays, mostly by new American writers, including O'Neill, and six full-length plays, mostly by well-known Europeans, including Shaw. The Washington Square Players were to return bigger and bolder after the war under the banner of the Theater Guild, a Broadway organization aspiring to become an art theater, with a founding board of managers consisting of Langner, Moeller, the banker Maurice Wertheim, Helen Westley, Theresa Helburn, and Lee Simonson. The first play was *Bonds of Interest* on April 19, 1919.

Almost from the start the Washington Square Players seemed to be moving in a direction contrary to the inclinations of George Cram Cook and Susan Glaspell. Iowa-born like his wife, Cook started out at a novelist, but his real art was in rallying and encouraging the talents of others. With the stimulus and example of the Washington Square Players, Cook and Susan Glaspell turned to playwriting and together produced *Suppressed Desires*, a one-act play on a then novel Freudian theme. The Players having turned the script down for production at the Bandbox, Cook and Glaspell in the summer of 1915 put it on informally for themselves and a few friends in Neith Boyce's house at Provincetown on Cape Cod. It was performed with her play *Constancy*. Along the waterfront other willing writers waited. Wilbur Daniel Steele had a play, Cook had a comedy, and he was urging others, especially Miss Glaspell, to sit down and produce scripts. Seeking a stage, they took over an abandoned fish house at the end of a wharf owned by their neighbor Mary Vorse and converted it into a theater. Some plays are written simply because the space for them exists; the form of the space itself guides the writing. Sitting in this wharf, imagining characters and visualizing action on the stage, Susan Glaspell wrote her first play alone.

The following summer they renovated the wharf to seat ninety or so persons on wooden benches and practiced theater more systematically. Susan Glaspell's *Trifles* was one of the two hits of the summer. The other made history. By now

Eugene O'Neill, also summering on the Cape, was aware of
the new theatrical activity and had brought along his play
Bound East for Cardiff. Play selection procedures had become somewhat more formal. In the living room of one
group member the play was read aloud while O'Neill
waited uncomfortably in the dining room for the verdict.
Cook and the others instantly recognized the talent of the
new playwright in their midst. O'Neill for the first time on
any stage was produced on the wharf that summer. If the
appropriateness of the first setting of a play influences its
reception, and if an initial success is the chief impetus to
an important career, the wharf at Provincetown was the
foundation stone of O'Neill's fame. For the initial performance of his sea play *Bound East for Cardiff*, as if contrived by
the set designer, the tide was in. The water washing against
the pilings could be heard through the lines of the play.
There was a fog, Susan Glaspell recalled, and a fog bell
sounding monotonously out in the harbor.

They decided to give themselves the name of the Provincetown Players. And in the fall Cook felt they were ready for
New York. O'Neill proposed as an alternate name the Playwrights' Theater, and it was under this banner in a brownstone at 139 Macdougal Street, next to the buildings that
housed the Washington Square Book Shop and the Liberal
Club, on November 3, 1916, that the first performance of the
Provincetown Players was given in New York. The opening
bill consisted of *Bound East for Cardiff*, Louise Bryant's *The
Game*, and Floyd Dell's *King Arthur's Socks*. The Provincetown, interested only in new American writing, aimed to
provide a place where the playwright himself, with the assistance of other artists and helpers, could work on every phase
of the production. Two weeks later the second bill opened,
consisting of *Suppressed Desires*, *Enemies* by Hutchins Hapgood and Neith Boyce (a second husband-and-wife playwriting team) , and John Reed's *Freedom*.

Fire violations—through the years the chief hazard facing

the off-Broadway manager—forced the Provincetown to seek new quarters a few doors down the block in a building that stands today as the Provincetown Playhouse. It was here on December 20, 1918, that O'Neill's second produced play was presented—*The Moon of the Caribbees*. Already O'Neill's reputation was spreading. Four months after the opening, Horace Liveright, paying an advance of $125, published the first volume of O'Neill's one-act plays (including *The Moon of the Caribbees, Bound East for Cardiff*, and five other sea plays). Success was beginning in strange ways to change the character of the theater George Cram Cook had created. Susan Glaspell quoted him as saying, "We have no ambition to go uptown and become 'a real theater.' We have a theater because we want to do our own thing in our own way." Cook liked to involve all sorts of artists in every phase of production regardless of their specific areas of competence, but a new group led by Edna St. Vincent Millay looked for a less haphazard, more professional way of operation, and in 1919 Cook and Glaspell turned the theater over to them and withdrew to Cape Cod. In the winter of 1920 Cook was to return to stage *The Emperor Jones*. The excitement caused by the script set off a search for the proper actor for the title role and produced a frenzy of activity at the theater. Cook, dipping heavily into the theater treasury, insisted upon constructing a dome, or semicircular concrete backing to the stage, as a background for the desperate wanderings of O'Neill's frightened Negro. For the title role of Brutus Jones, they were fortunate in finding Charles S. Gilpin, and the Provincetown Players opened their most famous production on November 1, 1920. It took a few days for the critics to come down, but recognition for O'Neill, Gilpin, and the Provincetown spread rapidly throughout the professional theater world. After two weeks the play was moved uptown for a regular commercial run. Later that season the Playwrights' Theater put on O'Neill's *Diff'rent*, and the season ended with Susan Glaspell's *Inheritors* with Ann Harding.

It became increasingly harder to hold the theater together as uptown success more and more drew off the working talent.

The last season of the Provincetown Players came in 1921–22. It opened with Susan Glaspell's feminist play *The Verge*. More and more the theater was being used as a stepping-stone to the commercial theater. Cook said what they really needed was not a bigger theater but a smaller one. Finally, letting the theater go its own way, Cook and Susan Glaspell set sail for Greece in March, 1922. Cook was to die in Delphi several years later. Afterward Miss Glaspell took to writing mostly novels and short stories, although her play *Alison's House* was to win the Pulitzer Prize in 1931. A new successor theater named the Experimental Theater, Incorporated, was established by O'Neill, Kenneth Macgowan, and Robert Edmond Jones with the following statement of aims: "Our playhouse is essentially a laboratory for artistic experiment. Our aims are special. We are not seeking to rival the theater uptown. We make no attempt to cater to the tastes of a general public. Our audience is intentionally a restricted one." In this form and with this policy the theater survived until *Winter Bound* closed on December 14, 1929. Among the plays produced were *The Ancient Mariner* by Stark Young, works by Strindberg and Schnitzler, and O'Neill's *The Hairy Ape, All God's Chillun Got Wings* (with Paul Robeson), and *Desire Under the Elms*. But by this time Eugene O'Neill was playing on a wider stage. His *Beyond the Horizon* won the Pulitzer Prize on Broadway in 1920. *Anna Christie* earned the same honor two years later.

In spite of a natural rivalry there was some interaction in the overlapping lives of the Provincetown Players and the Washington Square Players in the days before the latter turned into the Theater Guild. The founders and principal workers in both theaters came out of the same Village pool, with some duplication at least in the beginning. There was also some cross-producing of plays. After an initial rejection, the Washington Square Players did put on the Cooks' *Suppressed Desires,* and Lawrence Langner's *Matinata,* a slight domestic comedy overpowered by its companion piece, was on the same Provincetown bill with *The Emperor Jones.* It was perhaps preordained that the strong business head of Lawrence Langner would see to the survival in another form of the Washington Square Players and that the Provincetown as the artistic embodiment of George Cram Cook's esthetic ideals, lacking any firm financial base, should eventually pass out of existence.

There were other attempts to establish theaters away from Broadway before the beginnings of modern off-Broadway in the late 1940's and early 1950's. In 1915, just before the first bill at the Bandbox, Alice and Irene Lewisohn founded the Neighborhood Playhouse on Grand Street as an adjunct of the Henry Street Settlement House on New York's Lower East Side, then teeming with new immigrants. Arising out of a milieu unrelated to Village Bohemia, the theater concentrated almost exclusively on European plays. It had a lifespan of twelve years. Eva Le Gallienne began her famous Civic Repertory Theater in 1926 when she was an actress still in her twenties and in great demand by Broadway managers. After a first attempt to locate an uptown theater (the Broadway owners disapproved of her low-price ticket policy) she found a large theater on West Fourteenth Street. Her operation did not really fit the off-Broadway description although to some extent the Civic Repertory Theater of the 1920's suggests the Phoenix Theater of the 1950's. Miss Le Gallienne's experiment died in 1932, a victim of the Depression. Through the 1930's there were various workers' theaters of awakened social consciousness. One of the better known was Mordecai Gorelik's Theater Collective formed in 1931. The coming of the Second World War effectively put a stop to off-Broadway activity, and it was not really to resume until the late 1940's.

Theater is relatively untouched by technology under normal conditions. Yet the beginning of the postwar revival of off-Broadway in a curious way was tied to the rise of television. Some of the impetus of off-Broadway naturally came from familiar resentments against the commercialism of Broadway. Some could be attributed to the desire on the part of veterans for a fresh start after the end of the war and the return to civilian life. Yet the rise of television was also a significant factor in the planning of these returnees. In retrospect, of course, television as a revolutionary new medium that would overturn standard entertainment practices did not live up to its advance billing. But the enormous technological changes brought on by the war conditioned people to expect significant disruptions from the new medium. They regarded television as a threat to their professional careers unless they could adjust to its as yet unforeseen demands. One useful precaution that occurred to radio performers of the time was to attempt to get back onstage and try to restore a missing dimension to their acting before facing the television cameras. Live theater might offer a bridge between the aural-only medium of radio and many-sided television. A group of actors so motivated was to produce Sartre's *The Respectful Prostitute* in the winter of 1948. The formative months for this group came in the summer and fall of 1947 when David Heilweil, a former stage manager and theater technician, and Norman Rose, an actor, located a theater in a closed cinema house on Bleecker Street directly opposite the run-down Mills Hotel, the Village headquarters for derelicts. It is the same building occupied into the 1970's by Circle in the Square—one further bit of evidence of the geographical continuity of off-Broadway. Renaming the house New Stages, the two theater managers formed a stock company (in the financial sense) under that name. Morton Gottlieb, who functioned as a kind of general manager, helped raise funds from some 125 individuals, many of them well-known theater figures: Gertrude Lawrence and Richard Aldrich, whom

Gottlieb knew from having worked summers in Aldrich's Cape Playhouse, Garson Kanin and Ruth Gordon, and Beatrice Straight.

From the beginning their intention was to be totally professional, yet it was hard to place the group in any category recognized by the unions. They were neither stock nor Broadway, but Equity, represented by one of its officials, the late Ben Irving, on its initial cast, permitted actors to perform at below-Broadway scales. In actual fact for a time New Stages actors were paid in stock in the company rather than cash. All the other theatrical unions made similar concessions to help the new group get started. Gottlieb and his colleagues set to work remodeling the old cinema house. City fire and building regulations denied a license to any theater lacking a permanent proscenium and an asbestos curtain if it seated 300 persons or more. In order to circumvent this regulation Morton Gottlieb had all but 299 seats in the house ripped out. Ever since, the number 299 has defined the allowable maximum size of a theater under off-Broadway union rules.

In its credo New Stages gave itself ample latitude: "It is the policy of New Stages to select plays not likely to be produced on Broadway. These will include plays by new writers, revivals of classics not frequently seen, first American productions of foreign plays, and new or unproduced plays by established writers." The first was *The Lamp at Midnight*, a biographical treatment of Galileo by Barrie Stavis which opened on December 21, 1947. The all-professional cast of thirty-one—it included Martin Balsam and Peter Zeisler, who with Oliver Rea was later to found the Minnesota Theater Company in Minneapolis—brought the critics into unknown theatrical ground. The theater was situated in what was then, and still is, a predominantly Italian neighborhood. Nothing of Village life as we know it today, or even as experienced by Edna St. Vincent Millay and Eugene O'Neill, was then going on. Still, the San Remo, a restaurant frequented by O'Neill, was operating. Some of the best Italian food outside Mulberry Street could be had at the Grand Ticino on Thompson Street, and one could find a good cup of capuccino at the Excelsior. Next door to the theater a bar sold whiskey at ten cents a shot. Above the theater the local American Legion post agreed to hold down the noise while the play was in progress. At least one critic, Ward Morehouse, subwaying to the theater, got lost en route, and the curtain had to be held. The play had a good review from Brooks Atkinson, but since the uptown production of Brecht's *Galileo* had preceded this version and a snowstorm struck a few days after opening night, business was slow to the point of peril. As substitutes for members of cast and crew prevented by the snow from arriving at the theater on time, a number of volunteers rallied to the New Stages, including Felicia Montealegre, Maureen Stapleton, Paddy Chayefsky, and Arthur Cantor, then an apprentice press agent.

The next production, a double bill consisting of *Church Street* by Lenox Robinson and *The Respectful Prostitute*, was an immediate sensation. The title brought New Stages some preopening notoriety and, difficult as it is to believe today, aroused considerable moral indignation. But with the handsome Meg Mundy in the title role, the Sartre play took on all the trappings of a fashionable Broadway hit: lines to the box office, calls from ticket brokers, and theatergoers arriving in chauffeured limousines. For the first time since O'Neill days at the Provincetown, several blocks away, the Village was on the theatrical map. Six weeks after opening, the play was moved uptown to the Cort Theater, where it had an eight-month run. New Stages was not to repeat the success. The honest earnings of *The Respectful Prostitute* were lost the next season by *Blood Wedding* and Sartre's *The Victors*, adapted by Thornton Wilder (who was to return to the scene in the 1960's, when his *Plays for Bleecker Street* were put on in the same house by Circle in the Square). New Stages did not live to see another season. Gottlieb himself had left in May, 1948, when Gilbert Miller summoned him as a general manager potentially capable of handling the supposedly irascible Robert Morley in *Edward, My Son*. But the company has never been dissolved. The corporate seal and the list of stockholders are missing, but moneys from the subsidiary rights to the movie version of *The Respectful Prostitute* still accumulate in an otherwise dormant account.

Two other theater groups sprang up at about the same time New Stages was formed. The first was the Interplayers, which took over the Provincetown Playhouse in the summer of 1948. Kim Stanley had come east from the Pasadena Playhouse. Some of the others were Gene Saks, Michael Gazzo, Anthony Franciosa, Beatrice Arthur, and, on the business management side, Merle Debuskey, the press agent, all of whom became well known subsequently. Moving into the old Provincetown, they found the poured concrete cyclorama which George Cram Cook had installed for *The Emperor Jones*. Numerous special refracted lighting effects were possible with this cyc, but the Interplayers never learned how to use it properly. With a budget for the summer of about $600, they worked without salary and functioned as a cooperative sharing the work detail without discrimination on sex to the point where even Kim Stanley, their acknowledged star, took her turn cleaning out the men's lavatory. When they wanted to rid themselves of a weak member of the company, in order to spare feelings, they took a secret vote of elimination. In that summer they put on Cocteau's *The Infernal Machine*, O'Casey's *Within the Gates*, and E. E. Cummings' *Him*. Cummings, a local resident, would walk past the door while rehearsals were in progress, but he refused to go in. Because of the heat that summer, they were forced to improvise a Rube Goldberg-like air-conditioning system. At the rear of the house in a small cubicle above the box office, they affixed a tray to carry large cakes of ice. Beneath, a frame held excelsior, and behind electric fans were positioned. In theory the ice would drip cold water into the excelsior and the fans behind the excelsior tray would send cool air wafting over the audience. In practice the audience got sprayed with water instead. Later that year the Interplayers put on a mid-winter show. *The Dog Beneath the Skin* by W. H. Auden opened at the Carnegie Recital Hall. There was a split in the ranks the following year. Off-Broadway, Inc., was formed as an offshoot and that summer occupied the Cherry Lane, in the winter kept lit by its play-producing proprietors, Paul Gilmore and his daughter Virginia. Through a friend, La-mont Johnson, who knew Gertrude Stein, Off-Broadway, Inc., was able to get permission to do *Yes Is for a Very Young Man.* The critics were drawn by the American pre-miere of a Gertrude Stein work, and the superb notices that resulted lifted Kim Stanley out of obscurity. Never again would she appear on a stage anywhere without a sense of excitement and anticipation. Still the positive reception for the Stein piece could not assure any real continuity for a theater group that was able to produce only sporadically. When in August of that year they did another work, Robert Hivnor's *Too Many Thumbs,* none of the critics came. Through 1950, however, this group managed a remarkable variety of plays: *The Creditors,* in which George Roy Hill appeared, *Le Bourgeois Gentilhomme, Six Characters in Search of An Author, The Taming of the Shrew,* and *No Exit.* Peripherally, there were a few other similarly insubstan-tial off-Broadway groups functioning, one of which was Stu-dio 7 formed by ex-members of the Yale Drama School including Eugene Wolsk, now a Broadway manager, which put on Strindberg at the Provincetown.

In the summer of 1949, five such groups, unrecognized by the theater establishment and facing a threat from Actors' Equity, organized the Off-Broadway League of Theaters. Equity looked with disfavor on its members appearing with non-Equity performers in these experimental companies and moved to disallow it. The league stated its own position as follows: "The obvious inability of the existing commercial theater to provide a place for serious young theater people is generally recognized as being the precipitating factor for the off-Broadway theater movement." Equity was loath to consort with the downtown groups especially since the going rate ranged downward from $35 a week for *Yes Is for a Very Young Man* to nothing. During the summer, powerful Equity and the determined newcomers jockeyed for position. Leading the league's campaign, Merle Debuskey took his case to the press and was able to win a few column inches at the bottom of the theater page of the New York *Times*. In September Equity agreed to permit union members to constitute up to 49 percent of the cast so long as the nonunion players registered with Equity and a token payment of $5 a week was made. These were significant concessions. The league in effect had won its first battle—twenty years before it was to lose what some people said might be its last battle, in the actors' strike of the winter of 1970. It may be only a small historical point, but it was in that very first union-management skirmish in the summer of 1949 that a since familiar all-purpose battle cry, raised whenever trouble looms, was heard for the first time, "What are you trying to do—kill off-Broadway?"

Three

The Idea of a Theater

Nearly everyone who went off-Broadway in the early 1950's did so not simply to put on productions but to establish theaters and make a life in the theater. The newcomers were eager to sink roots in new soil removed from the commercial hothouse of Broadway. They understood the necessity of buying a building or signing a long-term lease in the marginal real estate districts of Greenwich Village around Sheridan Square or Washington Square, of hiring and keeping a dedicated staff whose energies would be wholly devoted to however impossible a project, of retaining a nucleus of committed and idealistic actors.

To go off-Broadway was an intended rebuke to Broadway, which hired actors only as needed for single productions and made no pretense to continuity in the work. The uptown producers were independent, free of any binding commitment either to a given geographical location or to any one group of artists, except possibly to a hit playwright reliably capable of delivering each time out. A stream of independently conceived productions flowed from their offices and were channeled into a number of nearly identical Shubert theaters to live or die on the carriage trade. Downtown, the new committed producers stood by the work, sought new audience, and strove for continuity. As Jose Quintero later was to say of his work at Circle in the Square, "We have a sense of belonging. . . . We have a base. We're not a migrant pack like Broadway producers."

Within a year or two of the birth of Circle in the Square, the Living Theater, the Phoenix Theater, and Joseph Papp's New York Shakespeare Festival were to be formed. Each has endured two decades of off-Broadway history, but none has remained the same theater except in name; adaptability was the price of survival. In order to last, a theater needed complementary talents, artistic and business. For success, the artistic leader was the more important; for survival, the business manager. The Circle, in Jose Quintero and Theodore Mann, had two individuals very different in talent and temperament to divide the functions. The Phoenix had Norris Houghton and T. Edward Hambleton; the Living Theater, the husband-and-wife team of Julian Beck and Judith Malina. In a sense the Becks were both business managers and artistic leaders interchangeably, very good at the job in the early days, less dedicated to business matters later on when they began to act out their philosophical distrust of the Establishment on every level. Sometimes both functions were united in one person, as they often are in the case of the Broadway producer. This was especially true of Joseph Papp in managing the increasingly complex affairs of the Shakespeare Festival although he, too, had a strong right hand and business head in Bernard Gersten. The accomplishments of each of these groups, especially of the Circle, are worth examining as lessons in artistic tenacity and cultural survival.

At the Circle, the relationship between Quintero and Mann at the outset was relatively simple and natural, based on a clear and necessary division of responsibility. Later it was to become more complex and strained as the theater gained stability and success, and finally the relationship was to disintegrate in mutual mistrust. For many young people, going into the theater involves defying parental wishes or violating some expectation that is part of their background. Only in the expression of this spirit of young revolt did the two founders of the Circle come together and share anything in common. Born in Panama City in 1924, Quintero broke with his family to come to California in the mid-1940's at first to study medicine. One of his professors at the University of Southern California suggested drama courses to improve his English accent. The first play he ever saw was *Life with Father* in Los Angeles, and one wonders what he must have made of this sudden exposure to domestic Americana. His association with student actors introduced him to Goodman in Chicago for more work in drama (and his chance meeting there with Geraldine Page). In the summer of 1949 when an actress friend at Goodman went east to Woodstock, New York, he climbed aboard a Greyhound bus literally without dinner money and followed. Quintero spent the year in Woodstock giving Spanish lessons. The summer theater, the Maverick, was housed in a substantial building of Stanford White design. Quintero was picked to be treasurer, a case of serious miscasting, and when the following season came around, he began agitating for a chance to direct.

If anything, Mann had rather less background in theater, and family tradition, left to itself, pointed to the law. Educated at Erasmus High School and New York University, where he excelled in basketball and tennis to the neglect of some scholastic attainments, Mann suffered an abrupt and influential change of environment during the war by being stationed in Carmel, California, whose soft, ocean-regulated climate and pleasing orchards drove out the memory of Manhattan. But upon discharge he enrolled in the Brooklyn Law School in keeping with parental expectations, stopping short, however, of going into law. In a vague search for a community of artists to live among, in the summer of 1948, at the suggestion of his father, he made his way to Woodstock ninety miles up the Hudson River. He took the next year out entirely, following a girl he had met at Woodstock back to Carmel, nearly crossing paths with the eastward-bound Quintero on the way. In an oblique attempt at turning himself into an artist he took up photography among the clusters of artists and writers in that sunny Pacific coastal town. Mostly he read, and thought his way out of becoming a lawyer. Once again, in the summer of 1950, he returned to Woodstock.

Quintero was getting his chance to direct. How preposterous it seemed, putting this dark-haired, inexperienced Central American with his shaky command of English in charge of a group of actors, for *Alice in Wonderland!* But it was a fateful choice. Never again would Quintero be thought of as anything but a director. As his replacement in the treasurer role Quintero recruited Mann, who had had a small non-speaking part in the *Alice* production. Now Mann's family business background came to the fore. He felt instantly at home behind a desk, armed with a telephone, and confronted with such matters of finance to work out as soft drinks concessions in the lobby.

As the Loft Players, the Woodstock group maintained an informal identity in New York in the winter. The summer of 1950 was a good one. At first they thought of staying on in Woodstock. But the summer residents melted away more rapidly than they had foreseen, and they turned toward the city once again, this time, however, with the intention of establishing a real theater with a full playing schedule. Besides Quintero and Mann, the founding group consisted of Emilie Stevens, Jason Wingreen, Aileen Cramer, and Ed Mann, who was not related to Ted. All were to be members of the original board of directors of Circle in the Square.

In a vacant nightclub once known as the Greenwich Village Inn at the bottom of two joined brownstones at 5 Sheridan Square, Ted Mann found their first home. On the initial inspection trip Quintero stood on the rectangular night-club floor with its low ceiling and supporting columns and began to see how actors could use this space as a stage. On the walls hung faded pictures of sailors and Hawaiian dancers. With an arm around one of the support poles, Quintero stood there while Mann talked business to the real estate agent. Yes, he thought, these supports could be used as part of the set—as trees, as umbrellas, as anything at all. He began to imagine patterns of stage movement flowing in and around the three-sided rectangular stage. Theoreticians are tempted to give Quintero and the Circle credit for the concept of three-quarter arena staging, for finding the way to break out of the dimensionality of the proscenium box. But the shape of the stage and the style of the playing derived less from theory than from necessity; given a nightclub, Quintero created a theater. He saw how actors would enter and leave and how they would play to a nearly surrounding audience. The proscenium stage dictated the horizontal movement of the actors from left to right. This space called for a curved, looping line of movement, one that more nearly fitted the contours of the human body. Quintero could feel the motion in his own body, how to fill the space and make it live, the actors not as paintings to be studied from one perspective but as sculpture to be viewed from all angles. It was this dance-derived sense of sculptured movement that was to give a distinctive shape to future Circle in the Square productions. With blinding Archimedean intuition, it all came to Quintero on that first day as he stood holding one of the support poles while Mann discussed a contract with the agent.

A specialist in real estate law, Mann's father helped work out the details of the ten-year lease and advanced the first month's rent of $1,000. In the fall of 1950, with total capital of $7,000, a new theater began functioning. They called the theater Circle in the Square, a conscious echo of the then-popular expression "chicken in the basket" and exactly descriptive of the arena-shaped stage and its location in Sheridan Square. The plays each were to run five weeks. The opening production was *Dark of the Moon* in February, 1951. Plays by Anouilh, Giraudoux, and Lorca, among others, followed —a total of seven before the Circle was to make its first big splash with *Summer and Smoke*. The openness of the Circle stage—the absence of the picture frame proscenium—made for extreme simplicity in the physical production. The budget for each of these early shows was as little as $100. The investment in scenery was no more than a rug or two, a few chairs, a table, some greenery wound around a column to suggest a garden, an armful of props to help set off the individuality of the characters. Most of the material was reusable. Overhead was kept low, and the theater was spared the accumulation of an inventory of lumber.

Life moved in communal patterns in the new theater. The actors and actresses, Quintero and Mann, and other members of the staff lived in rooms above the theater, intermingled, and cooked their meals side by side on the huge range of the nightclub kitchen, each squirreling away his limited supply of food in a secret cupboard or drawer. Their whole lives were bound up in the creation of the new theater. They were able to do the work for its own sake; the work repaid their concentration. The actors performed with the intensity and self-absorption that had intrigued Geraldine Page. To Quintero, this unity, the newness, the excitement of starting up, the concentration, and the singleness of purpose made for a freedom he had never known, comparable to nothing in his strict Catholic upbringing. Quintero was to remember this period as one of openness and liberation, never to repeat itself, as a time without admonishment or blame. "It was the first time in my life I could eat a fried egg exactly the way I wanted to. I suppose there is something in being able to eat a fried egg the way you choose that enables you to do the kind of theater you want."

The only structure was the work itself. Once the play was chosen it went forward unhindered. Quintero was able to shake off the Catholic guilt and sense of duty that lay like a hand on his past and in freeing himself to free the actors to do their best work. Those who worked with him, his close associates of those early days, still recall with astonishment the instant love affair, the deeply caring relationship he established with an actor. Director and cast worked as closely as dance partners. His own openness made this possible—his vulnerability, his willingness to draw freely on his life experience and tell stories about his family, arising intimately out of his religious training, stories that were performances in themselves, illustrative playlets within the play being rehearsed.

Once, in rehearsal for a play dealing with rape, he tried to convey to the actors the emotional horror of the act. He recalled how country priests in his native Panama would seek out the prettiest fourteen-year-old girl and cut her hair to the scalp. Telling the story, Quintero moved about restlessly, as springily as a boxer. Tall, lean, broad-shouldered, he would gesture with his arms and hands, jutting and dipping his shoulders, feinting like a prizefighter. The cast listened enthralled to this story of symbolic violation as he described the unctuousness of the priests and the supposedly sanctified purpose of their act. Out of the shorn hair of the young girl the priests would fashion a wig to lay on the head of an effigy of Jesus.

His early associate Isabel Halliburton once went on a trip to Italy with Quintero. Through the Panamanian representative to the Holy See they were invited to one of the larger papal audiences. The scene of pageantry was profoundly moving to Quintero—the Pope on his great gilt throne with his scarlet skullcap and his ermine cape, the Swiss Guards in uniforms designed by Michelangelo. Looking down on the scene, Quintero noticed a group of Spanish women in their black mantillas weeping and beating their breasts. Tears came to Quintero's eyes. Asked what affected him so strongly, he said, "See those women. See them crying. They are my mother and my sisters and my aunts." Such vivid memories out of his past were shared with the actors to give them an emotional key to moments of their own performance.

The theatrical instinct came to him early, fresh and primitive. His native Panama, in his memory a small and provincial country, had really no theater to boast of. His first theatrical experience was visiting the circus with his father and mother and sisters and brothers. The memory of the occasion is as vivid today to Quintero as yesterday's play. When the tightrope walker started down his swinging wire, his father imperiously pointed upward and ordered each member of the family to pay attention and watch him closely.

"There!" he said, shaking his finger. "There is the real thing in life—a man who can perform such a feat. Watch him! Holding his parasol. It doesn't matter what color his parasol is."

"Funny, I can remember my father saying that," Quintero said. " 'It doesn't matter what color his parasol is.' So all of us children fixed our eyes on the tightrope walker. The circus in Panama was not like Barnum and Bailey in Madison Square Garden. It was very small, only one ring, and we were sitting in the first row, eyes on the wire. Just then a clown passed in front of us and saw my mother. He came over and kissed her on the cheek. Imagine! A sad-faced clown besotted with love. He kissed my mother on the cheek absolutely besotted with love, this clown!"

The image remained with Quintero always, somehow explaining to him the essence of actor—the pure emotion translated into direct action, acting as an expression of love of audience. "I learned that then," Quintero said, "for the rest of my life." All good actors, he believed were really clowns at heart. Willingness was all—to make the open gesture to the audience, to act the clown by kissing a stranger. Geraldine Page copying the mannerisms of some other actress, trying to be another personality: that was false. But Geraldine Page as herself, and at her most clownlike, Quintero believed: that was greatness.

Possibly Quintero himself was prevented from becoming an actor only by his uncorrectable accent. The nature of a performer and the talent of storytelling enabled him to identify strongly with the actor. That rapport, in part, explains why Jose Quintero became certainly the finest director in the history of off-Broadway and one of the two or three best American directors of the last twenty years. There were problems, certain flaws in his inspirational way of working, and they were to appear to his disadvantage later, sending him into an apparent decline, but in the early 1950's the great years all lay ahead.

In origin the Phoenix Theater owed less to personality, less to experimentation, less to untested talent than Circle in the Square, and more to a fixed concept. Between the founders of the two theaters there were differences in motivation, experience, outlook, and age. Quintero and Mann were in their late twenties when they founded Circle in the Square in 1952. Houghton and Hambleton were in their early forties, more experienced, more theater worldly, when they established the Phoenix in the fall of 1953. In one sense, therefore, the Phoenix was a generation older than the Circle, and more historically determined, more institutionalized, even to having uptown sources of money the Circle was able to tap only after it had become famous.

Norris Houghton was a member of that richly endowed generation of theater people produced by Princeton in the 1930's. A 1931 Princeton graduate, he was a classmate of Joshua Logan. Bretaigne Windust, who was graduated two years earlier and was already established with the Theater Guild, with Logan and Charles Leatherbee, had formed the University Players at Falmouth on Cape Cod in 1928. Houghton joined the Players right after graduation at Logan's suggestion, and his first professional companions included Myron McCormick, Margaret Sullavan, Mildred Natwick, James Stewart, Kent Smith, and Henry Fonda. Houghton was to write about their work and summer adventures in *But Not Forgotten* in 1951.

Three years after Houghton left Princeton, Hambleton came out of Yale. He also gained his first professional experience managing the summer theater at Matunuck, Rhode

Island. He was a member of a well-known Baltimore family and the inheritor of a banking fortune established by his great-great-grandfather in 1860. His family had always maintained dual residences in Baltimore and New York, and Hambleton has continued the practice, although the demands of his theater have taken precedence over personal pleasures.

Both Houghton and Hambleton passed through layers of theater before they reached off-Broadway: college drama courses, summer theater, Broadway productions, Houghton as a designer for such shows as Michael Redgrave's *Macbeth* and *Billy Budd*, Hambleton, after an abbreviated career as an actor, as producer for, among others, *Ballet Ballads* in 1948. Both, separately, had become impatient with the artistic restrictions imposed by Broadway economics. In the summer of 1953 both were separately investigating alternatives to Broadway.

Visiting London, Houghton was impressed that summer by the Lyric Hammersmith, an off-West End theater where stars could appear for limited runs in classics or noncommercial plays. At lunch with the English actress Pamela Brown, he learned about the *Venice Preserv'd* she had done there with Sir John Gielgud with such success that it was transferred to the West End. This sort of theater, Houghton felt, was needed in New York—a theater where quality could be put ahead of economic expediency.

In August, 1953, after Houghton returned from England, Hambleton put in a telephone call to him in Stonington, Connecticut, where he was staying with friends. Hambleton offered to put up $50,000 if Houghton would raise the same amount toward the establishment of a theater. That telephone call marked the moment of conception. The total capital raised was $125,000, and as so often happened in large-scale theatrical deals in years to come, Roger L. Stevens was the financial catalyst, bringing in the decisive $25,000. The project was conceived much as a Broadway production is financed, with general and limited partners. Many well-known theater professionals were among the fifty or so limited partners—Jo Mielziner, Richard Rodgers, Elia Kazan, Tad Adoue, the late Russel Crouse, Mildred Dunnock, John Latouche, William Inge, the late Howard Lindsay, Edward F. Kook, Peggy Wood, and Clinton Wilder—and such prominent supporters of the theater as Howard Cullman, Mary Leatherbee, Barry Bingham, Mary K. Frank, the late Julius Fleischmann, Adele Levy, Mrs. John L. Loeb, J. S. Seidman, Alfred R. Stern, Mrs. Donald S. Stralem, and Donald B. Straus.

As in any marriage there were the inevitable doubts when the two prospective partners got together. Houghton told Hambleton two people couldn't run a theater. Hambleton replied, "You can't run it alone." Houghton took priority in artistic matters; Hambleton in business matters. Each would have a say in the other's sphere of interest, and no major step would be taken without joint approval. The partnership was to prove remarkably stable, trusting, and cheerful, in some respects without parallel in the modern theater, continuing in spite of the normal strains and appalling uncertainties of theater and notwithstanding Hambleton's own financial independence, which enabled him to continue through some of the darker days of the Phoenix after Houghton was forced for personal financial reasons to drop out.

The new partners spent the summer in Hambleton's station wagon scouting locations all over Manhattan. Their principal concern was that the theater should be well away from Broadway so as not to infect their new enterprise with any taint of show business or Times Square commercialism. When their friend, the theatrical lawyer John F. Wharton, who was to head the Phoenix board, suggested looking into the Avon Theater then on Forty-sixth Street next to the Imperial, they turned the idea down. The search eventually led to the 1,100-seat Stuyvesant Theater on the corner of Second Avenue and Twelfth Street. Built in 1925 for Yiddish theater, the Stuyvesant had switched to movies and was now vacant. In the beginning it seemed a little large for their plan and a little too far off the beaten track. They were counting on the support of upper East Side theatergoers who had probably never visited such exotic parts of the city and had certainly never ventured below Fourteenth Street to go to the theater. On the other hand, Second Avenue opened a direct route to the door. So they brought in designer Donald Oenslager to redesign the house and equip the stage with an all-purpose set. Taking a deep breath, they got ready to begin.

At lunch one day during the renovation period at Pete's Bar on Irving Place, a six-block walk uptown from their new location, Hambleton thought up a name more prophetic, more exactly descriptive of their eventual history than they could have then anticipated—the Phoenix. In the first ten years the Phoenix put on seventy productions—a record of energy and productivity such as the theater had rarely seen. But it was not always the same Phoenix. The statement of principle was broad: "To release actors, directors, playwrights, and designers from the pressures forced on them by the hit-or-flop patterns of Broadway" and, equally important, to give theatergoers "a playhouse where they can see top-flight productions of fine plays with professional casts within the limitation of their budgets." Yet in the pursuit of these goals the theater was forced through several metamorphoses. The theater would run through one cycle of growth and drop from sight, only to reappear again almost immediately and continue in a somewhat changed direction. This remarkable record of resiliency is due in part to the character of Hambleton, a man possessed of extraordinary recuperative powers in theater.

At the end of the summer of 1953, Houghton and Hambleton had the idea, the name, the partnership, the money, and the theater but no play for the opening. The fall was half over, and the season seemed to be slipping away when Hambleton was reminded by a newspaper friend in Baltimore of the 1939 out-of-town closing of Sidney Howard's *Madam, Will You Walk* when George M. Cohan had left the cast. It would be, in New York, a new work by an important American playwright and a good opening production provided the casting was right. Then Houghton and Hambleton were able to get Hume Cronyn and Jessica Tandy, Cronyn's wife. A number of years later the Cronyns were to devote a year to the start of the Tyrone Guthrie Theater in Minneapolis. Now, they became part of the beginning of the Phoenix. *Madam, Will You Walk* opened on December 1, 1953, in the midst of a strike of the New York daily newspapers. The first word of the new theater and its successful opening production filtered out on the radio. The papers returned a few days later, the critics caught up, and the Phoenix got all the proper set of birth notices. It was off to a good start.

Houghton and Hambleton followed up with Robert Ryan in *Coriolanus*, which hadn't been done in New York in seventy years, and then put on a musical, *The Golden Apple* by John Latouche and Jerome Moross, which had been turned down repeatedly for Broadway. The successful Phoenix run of six weeks helped springboard the show to Broadway and fourteen more weeks of life. It won the Drama Critics' Circle Award as the best musical of the season. Already the theater was working out the way they had hoped. They had wanted to do just this, to transfer their better work to Broadway and continue the run commercially, following the pattern of the Lyric Hammersmith in London. *The Golden Apple*, however, was not a success on Broadway. And except with *Once Upon a Mattress* some years later—which in any case was not really a Phoenix-conceived production—they were unable to jump up any more of their shows, at least not until the late 1960's, when Hambleton formed an alliance with Ellis Rabb's APA and the whole operation was shifted to the Lyceum Theater on West Forty-fifth Street.

For the final bill in May, 1954, the Phoenix mounted a

production of *The Sea Gull* inspired by Montgomery Clift, who was then the hottest film actor of his day and had just appeared in *From Here to Eternity*. Through Robert Whitehead, the producer, the Phoenix managers had learned of Clift's interest in doing a Chekhov play in New York. A major purpose of their theater was indeed to give established stars a chance to appear in work of their own choosing even if the commercial prospects seemed dim. In this case the adaptation had been the work of the stars—Mira Rostova, Kevin McCarthy, and Clift. Norris Houghton directed a cast that included Judith Evelyn, Maureen Stapleton, and George Voskovec. Throughout rehearsal Houghton had Arthur Miller, who was working with Clift, looking over his shoulder. Clift's presence, with Miller as his *éminence grise*, lent a certain mystique to the project, although the tepid reviews criticized the acting as mixed and unharmonious. But with Clift on the stage for the first time since becoming a film star, the Phoenix had a hit, and the lines formed down Second Avenue.

With one success after another, the Phoenix had an extraordinary first season, and the future seemed bright. A parade of stars had joined in the enterprise, all on the austerity salary of $100 a week. The budget for the first season had been $125,000, which allowed an average of $25,000 for each production. They had got back $85,000. The season was not without some vicissitudes and problems. The McCarthyites had harassed them for employing people whose names were on the lists of *Red Channels* and *Counterattack*, those McCarthy-era publications that were self-appointed watchdogs of the political morality of the entertainment industry. Norris Houghton was under suspicion for having visited Russia to study the theater. John Latouche was suspect for his questioning "Ballad for Americans." John Houseman, who had directed the *Coriolanus*, was suspect because of his association with Orson Welles in the Mercury Theater, which had put on a highly political *Julius Caesar* that had attacked

Fascism long before it had become fashionable to do so and a *Heartbreak House* that in a modern interpretation had questioned the ability of the British upper class to withstand the threat of Hitlerism. In the face of extreme pressure the Phoenix stood firmly behind its people. While never pretending to any political orientation as a theater, the Phoenix has remained steadfast through the years on the issue of free expression. It was not afraid of strong political themes when it offered Robert Ardrey's *Sing Me No Lullaby* as the first play of its second season, a strong contemporary political satire set in the American Midwest containing a line that in retrospect seems a little ahead of its time: "The United States is going down like a magnificent ship, but no one can find the leak." The second season continued with an original musical, *Sandhog*, about tunneling under the river and immigrant life in the early 1900's. The theater revived *The Doctor's Dilemma* in January, 1955, directed by television's Sidney Lumet, and the acting was criticized, then Ibsen's *The Master Builder*. The season closed with a hit revue with Nancy Walker. *Phoenix '55* became the first Phoenix show to exceed the standard six-week run and extend into the summer. Midway in this season the theater began to fill some of its dark Monday nights with so-called Side Shows—concert readings, musicals, dance events, and so forth. The most spectacular was the revival of John Webster's Gothic tale of blood *The White Devil*, directed by the late Jack Landau.

In spite of all this effort, the second season was a disappointment and economically a serious loss—five times worse than the first year. The Phoenix, financially, was never really to do so well again. In the nonprofit theater, success is actually penalizing, for long runs can turn into financial disasters by multiplying built-in losses. When the season's sole hit, the Nancy Walker revue, was extended into the summer, the Phoenix was obliged to put in air conditioning, and the bill came to an unforeseen $30,000. When the next season came around, after so promising a beginning, already the Phoenix was forced to cast about for a new policy.

No theater has shown greater adaptability than Joseph Papp's New York Shakespeare Festival, which had the traditional modest off-Broadway genesis in an hospitable church basement, soon ventured outdoors into the public parks for summer performances, much later established all-year-round multiple theater facilities in the magnificent Astor Library on Lafayette Street, and always, consistently, has held to a policy of complete openness—to ideas, to actors, to the public, to the notion of cultural diversity, to the commitment to free theater for the people. Fed by Papp's zeal, the Festival grew in quantum leaps. Today, an aura of invincibility surrounds it, and a respected permanence. Behind this institution lay a simple idea. Organizing a workshop in 1953 in the basement of a Presbyterian church on Manhattan's Lower East Side, near some of the first big low-income housing projects along the East River, Papp wanted to examine the techniques American actors could use to handle the poetics of Shakespearean drama. In a word, Papp sought an American style for Shakespeare, a way of playing that would not simply ape the posturing and proper accent of the English but would fit naturally into the pluralistic society of America. Papp in those days was a stage manager for CBS Television, and his theater work was a sideline. His earliest stage experience came at the end of the 1940's, when he directed a Sean O'Casey one-act play in the Yugoslav National Hall. Perhaps it is symbolic of Papp's persistence that he was able to survive the first critical onslaught at the hands of the respected Brooks Atkinson, who was later to become one of his staunchest supporters. Tartly Atkinson suggested in his review that Papp ought to retire from directing.

It was in 1954, shortly after the Phoenix Theater began and in the third season of Circle in the Square, that Papp's workshop secured a provisional charter from the New York

State Board of Regents and formulated its future policy, the establishment of an annual summer Shakespeare festival. Its first indoor production for an invited audience was *An Evening with Shakespeare and Marlowe,* and in 1955, one season before moving outside for its first park performances, the workshop put on a series of modern-dress Shakespeare productions, and then it was ready for the amphitheater and the shirt-sleeved audience and the swordplay of Shakespeare on summer nights. No group better illustrates the interplay of complex forces at work in the theater—economic restrictions, the availability of talent, interfering political interests, the needs of the public, the spectrum of current social concern and cultural thinking. The way Joseph Papp personally and his New York Shakespeare Festival absorbed and reflected the range of pressures of urban life will be described later. Possibly the Papp theater has had more to do with creating a protective cultural environment around the off-Broadway theater than any other.

If the Papp theater developed institutional strength, the Living Theater projected an intellectual viewpoint. Julian Beck and his wife, Judith Malina, were attracted to a poetic theater, to the work of modern poets with whom they felt a cultural affinity. It was much later, as if by a gradual but relentless conversion, that they became politicized. The initial impulse was intellectual radicalism, a restlessness and a curiosity about art, a desire for experimentation for its own sake. The spirit of inquiry derived from Beck's primary interest as an artist. Circulating in the art world, he was exposed to the daring and innovations of the modern painters. He developed an impatience with the stodginess and cultural conservatism of the stage. The Living Theater had its beginnings in 1948, when the Becks rented a cellar on Wooster Street to put on a series of Japanese Noh plays translated by Ezra Pound. Prophetically for the Living Theater, the plays were closed down by the police, ostensibly because the place was a front for a brothel. When Pound heard about this, he is reported to have said how else could a serious theater be expected to support itself in New York.

The Becks withdrew to their living room on West End Avenue and in the summer of 1951 gave a series of avant-garde one-act plays by Gertrude Stein, Paul Goodman, Lorca, and Brecht in order to raise money for a season on a proper stage at the Cherry Lane. The first play there, Gertrude Stein's *Doctor Faustus Lights the Lights*, was directed by Judith Malina and designed by Julian Beck, a division of responsibility that became a pattern; both participated in the business management. They did plays by Kenneth Rexroth, T. S. Eliot (*Sweeney Agonistes*), Stein, Goodman, and Picasso, but the summer of 1952 also ended badly. After three performances in August of Alfred Jarry's *Ubu Roi* the Fire Department closed them down, this time, they suspected, because the clinical references in the script of homosexual practices disturbed some high city official. The Becks were forced to halt production, and two years were to pass before they next opened in a loft on West 100th Street with W. H. Auden's *Age of Anxiety* in which James Agee was a member of the cast. Passing the hat in the intermission (an early off-Broadway and later off off-Broadway business practice), they performed Pirandello, Strindberg, Cocteau, and Goodman until still a third city agency, this time the Buildings Department, closed them down in 1955. The Living Theater was not really to make its mark before opening its Fourteenth Street theater in January, 1959, with *Many Loves* and, two productions later, *The Connection*, which was to give the theater immense notoriety, critical acclaim, and international fame and, eventually, lead to the most dramatic official theater closing in the twenty years of off-Broadway.

In the early days of off-Broadway, Circle in the Square, no more than the Living Theater, was immune to civic benightedness. Puritanical city administrators predictably looked askance at the weedy undergrowth of subterranean little stages with their squatter's meanness and taint of radical thought. The obvious "guilt" of off-Broadway was compounded by economic instability, disregard of convention, and the uncomfortably frank discussion of sex that seemed to commence the moment the curtain went up.

Ineligible for a theater license, Circle in the Square was forced to rely on a cabaret license and seat the audience at small serving tables. Serving the drama seemed more important, and the Circle managers were always taking out tables to make the place appear more theaterlike. They were removed on February 9, 1954, when *Summer and Smoke* was followed by *The Girl on the Via Flaminia*, dramatized by Alfred Hayes from his postwar novel. Another hit for Jose Quintero and Theodore Mann, it dealt without sentimentality with the uncertain bargain struck between a lonely American soldier in occupied Rome and a young Italian girl seeking a way to survive, an enforced personal submission played against a wider background of national subjugation. Leo Penn and Betty Miller in the principal roles of the uneasy lovers made an instant impression on the critics, and there was talk at once of transferring the production to Broadway, although such a move would entail changes in Quintero's arena staging.

At first resisted, this transfer, as it happened, became obligatory. With all its vulnerabilities, off-Broadway has found newly appointed city officials to be particularly dangerous. Shortly after Mayor Wagner made Edward F. Cavanagh, Jr., fire commissioner, the Circle found itself with padlocked doors. After receiving some audience complaints about fire exits, Cavanagh had the police pick up the cabaret license, effectively putting Quintero, Mann & Co. out of business. In April Mann pleaded guilty to four violations and was let off. *The Girl on the Via Flaminia* was moved to the then Forty-eighth Street Theater for none too successful a run. Circle in the Square was to suspend for more than a year. Quintero went off on the first of several Broadway misadventures (with the notable exception of *Long Day's Journey into Night* he was never really to have a great success outside the Circle). Quintero directed Jennifer Jones in an elaborate *Portrait of a Lady,* and Mann was hired by Roger L. Stevens as an assistant stage manager for *The Bad Seed.* But working on Broadway wasn't nearly so satisfying as working in their own theater in their own way. Determined to return, Mann joined the gubernatorial campaign of Franklin D. Roosevelt, Jr., in the hope of meeting someone of political influence to help him get his theater back. Eventually, through a law professor of his who knew the police commissioner, he was able to cut through the municipal red tape.

With fire violations corrected, Circle in the Square was reopened on June 1, 1955, with *The King and the Duke.* The play was a failure except in casting a young lyric soprano who carried the vocal line of the play. She was Patricia Brooks, shortly to be married to Theodore Mann and later to become one of the fine talents of the New York City Opera Company. Mann had picked her out at auditions of some children's shows and had told Quintero, before speaking a word to her privately, "There's the girl I'm going to marry."

Three successive failures were to take the Circle to the danger point once again before *The Iceman Cometh* brought into the house another smashing success comparable to *Summer and Smoke.* It is difficult now to trace exactly how the Circle first became interested in O'Neill. Allowing for Latin differences in temperament, Quintero out of his Catholic past and conformist upbringing felt an affinity for O'Neill. Both the young director and the famous playwright were burdened and haunted by relentless feelings of personal guilt: the limitless expectations, the littleness of their own possibilities, and the dark figure of the tyrannical father imposing his mature and boundless ego on the small and helpless boy. Some years later, Quintero was to say, "I know my own bond with O'Neill may be partially explained by his not presuming to judge me or laden me with guilt and by his positive attempt to make me understand my plight in living." In his own poetic imagination Quintero could make the leap across ethnic and cultural boundaries into the wintry New England world of Eugene O'Neill. Alien, he felt at home.

From a literary standpoint, part of the interest in O'Neill may have come from Leigh Connell, a bright, educated Southerner who was a friend of Quintero's and by this time had joined the Circle management to form a triumvirate with Quintero and Mann. To the Circle he brought play reading talent and a background in literature that the other two lacked. Certainly Connell had some hand in the choice of O'Neill. Routinely, from time to time, the Circle would apply for permission to Jane Rubin, agent for the O'Neill estate, only to be routinely refused. Control of the O'Neill properties, finally, rested with the playwright's widow, Carlotta O'Neill, who was waiting for a propitious time when the signs in the theatrical heavens would be right to start an O'Neill revival. One day a call came through from Jane Rubin that Mrs. O'Neill would like to see Jose Quintero. She was then living in the Lowell, an apartment hotel in the East Sixties, and when Quintero, then twenty-seven years old and less than ten years in the United States, arrived at the door, he was shaking with fear at the prospect of facing the wife of the famous playwright, who at this moment literally held the artistic destiny of the young director in her hands. When the maid opened the door, Quintero could hardly remember what name to say. He was shown into the presence of Carlotta O'Neill, dressed all in black, a woman more serenely beautiful than any Quintero had seen. She began talking, and still the fear Quintero felt, and his excitement, would not subside. There were pictures of O'Neill everywhere in the room. O'Neill the man or playwright was implicit in almost everything that was said. Quintero recited to himself the brief facts of his own life, the reality that ac-

counted for his insubstantial presence in that room suffused
with the presence of O'Neill. His Panamanian birth, he told
himself, made his embarrassing accent unavoidable. He could
not help his age either. He recalled that it was she, not
himself, who had sought this interview. But nothing helped
him conquer his fear. They talked for some time, mostly
about O'Neill and his work, until finally Carlotta O'Neill
asked him directly if the Circle wanted to do *The Iceman
Cometh*. In some mysterious way that he would never know,
Quintero had passed the test, and for the rest of his life in
the theater he would remember the anxiety of this moment
and be beholden to Carlotta O'Neill.

Iceman was the O'Neill work that Quintero especially
wanted to do. The play was one of the most massive works in
American dramatic literature, long, philosophical, difficult,
multicharactered, rich in American ethnic accents and drink-
ing lore, and climaxed by a monologue filling almost the
whole of the final act. Yet at its heart was a simple understanding of the frailties of man and a tolerance of man's need
for the comfort of his own illusions. The theme struck some
chord in Quintero's own being. Commercially, it was among
O'Neill's least successful plays, but it was not in Quintero to
be dismayed by the problems, only to welcome the opportunities. He left the Lowell light-headed and elated.

The decision to go ahead with *The Iceman Cometh* committed the Circle to a major production at a time when the
strength of the theater had been sapped by a succession of
failures. But if the Circle were to go under, the final failure
might as well be a big one. The ubiquitous Roger Stevens
lent Mann $2,000 to help get the production under way, and
casting began. There were many rich and difficult roles to fill,
from that of Harry Hope, the bluff but generous-spirited
saloonkeeper, to Jimmy Tomorrow, the slight, dapper newspaper correspondent. The key decision for Quintero was the
casting of Jason Robards, Jr., in the part of Hickey, the
flashy, reform-minded traveling salesman who disrupts the

lives of all the regulars of Hope's saloon and commands the stage throughout the final act delivering the spellbinding confessional monologue that lasts nearly forty minutes. Like O'Neill himself, Robards was the son of an actor but then a shy, if determined, beginner. He had appeared in an earlier Circle production, *The American Gothic*, and Quintero had made a mental note to cast him in the role of the correspondent, Jimmy Tomorrow, whose physical description he answered. At auditions Robards announced his preference for the role of Hickey, which he had studied overnight, rather than the lesser role. Physically, Robards did not in the least resemble Hickey. O'Neill described him as a short, roly-poly figure with a round, smooth face, and Robards was slight and gaunt-looking. But Quintero waved him ahead, and he began reading Hickey's long monologue. In the midst of the reading he paused and snapped his fingers, the fingers of both hands in unison, and then in the same cocky rhythm cross-slapped his wrists and snapped his fingers again. That decided Quintero. It was just the sort of gesture O'Neill's salesman would make. The casting choice was crucial to the eventual success of the production—one of those ostensibly inspired casting decisions that are more accidental than preconceived but seem fitting to the point of obviousness in the final outcome. Quintero remembers Mann's being so upset at the decision that he wouldn't speak to him for a week.

Because of its unusual length—the play ran more than four hours—the Circle opened *The Iceman Cometh* in the afternoon on May 8, 1956. When the play ended in early evening, the audience rose to its feet to applaud the nineteen actors in the cast as they filed out the aisles. The advance sale for an off-Broadway production had been sizable owing to interest in an O'Neill work. The critical praise was extravagant and nearly universal. In the New York *Herald Tribune* Walter Kerr referred to a "spiraling oratorio" and predicted "O'Neill is surely due now for thorough re-examination." O'Neill had been reborn on Bleecker Street nearly forty years after he was first heard at the Provincetown, only a few Greenwich Village blocks away.

Quintero was to find an artistic home in O'Neill. *The Iceman Cometh* ran nearly two years, from May, 1956, to February, 1958. Carlotta O'Neill gave Quinetro, Mann, and Connell permission next to produce O'Neill's masterwork, *Long Day's Journey into Night*, and seven months into the run of *Iceman*, on November 7, 1956, with Fredric March, Florence Eldridge, Jason Robards, Jr. (who was replaced in *Iceman* by Leo Penn) and Bradford Dillman, the play opened on Broadway at the Helen Hayes Theater. The Circle was started on a new cycle of success.

The Circle's production of *The Iceman Cometh*, like that of *Summer and Smoke* before it, expressed two aspects of the role off-Broadway was best able to fill. One was the rediscovery of the less successful work—in a commercial sense—of a famous playwright. The other, perhaps equally important, was the discovery of new performing talent. The history of the Circle is rich in the names of actors, besides Geraldine Page in the Williams play and Jason Robards, Jr., in the O'Neill, who have gone on to wider fame: George C. Scott, Colleen Dewhurst, Salome Jens, George Segal, Dustin Hoffman. The theater gained vitality from bringing young actors along, nurturing rawly talented but inexperienced actors who would mature as the theater itself grew in artistic power and sureness. The emphasis was on the work rather than on the return, on the process of dramatic creation rather than on measurable box-office result. While Broadway stood for the exploitation of talent that already existed and had proved itself, off-Broadway gambled on the unknown. The returns were sometimes enormous. The career of Geraldine Page—perhaps the finest actress of her generation—dates from her debut as a leading player in *Summer and Smoke* just as Robards' fame is traceable to *The Iceman Cometh*. The real chances were taken off-Broadway, many by Circle in the Square. It might have happened elsewhere, but it would have happened differently, and it did happen here.

Quintero personally felt an obligation to young, untried talent. In 1959 he told Joseph Wershba on the New York *Post,* "I have a strong resistance to Broadway stars coming down. I feel a responsibility to the new people in the theater. One of the joys of off-Broadway is that everyone is subjugated to the play and its values. You don't have to be preoccupied with Star X or Star Y as a commodity." Out of the Circle and its sister theaters downtown a new postwar generation of actors was to rise—and leave its imprint on American theater and films for two decades. Ted Mann first saw George C. Scott lying down on a couch in the dressing room backstage at Circle in the Square waiting to audition for Quintero. Mann was struck immediately by the concentration in the face, the unforgettable intensity in the eyes. In his first work on Sheridan Square, displaying even then the distinguishing mark of his stage presence, the brooding Scott contained an anger always on the verge of going out of control. In performance he held the play taut with the moment-by-moment intensity of his attention. In the same fashion, onstage, Colleen Dewhurst, big-boned and darkly handsome, breathed a sensuality into her playing that challenged and attracted cast and audience. Scott and Dewhurst separately got their first notice performing Shakespeare, cast by Joseph Papp, in the earliest days of the New York Shakespeare Festival. Colleen Dewhurst appeared in *The Taming of the Shrew* in the summer of 1956, when the Festival first played outdoors in the East River Park Amphitheater, and the following season, in Central Park, she was in *Macbeth.* That year, starting a winter season in the Heckscher Theater on upper Fifth Avenue, Papp cast Scott in *Richard III* and as Jacques in *As You Like It.* The critics took notice of the totally new reading given to the "Seven Ages of Man" speech. The two actors appeared together at the Circle in *Children of Darkness* in February, 1958, Scott playing against Dewhurst. The casting was rather more lucky than contrived or inspired, perhaps, but the Circle never produced a more volatile pairing. The revival of the Edwin Justus Mayer play, first produced in the Depression year 1930 to good notices but poor business, cast Scott as a villain and Dewhurst as the sensual daughter of a tailor. No play would have had an easy time following *The Iceman Cometh*, but *Children of Darkness* won the season's principal off-Broadway awards.

In Page, Dewhurst, and later Salome Jens in *The Balcony*, Circle in the Square set a new standard in what constituted good looks in a woman. In comedy and family drama Broadway was still busy perpetuating in its starting actresses the stereotype of the small, neatly made girl who looks well in a tennis dress and is adept at social small talk. Off-Broadway ignored this tradition from the start. Its starting actresses went immediately into big lead roles. The three standout leading women in Circle productions of the 1950's and early 1960's were all tall, and none was conventionally pretty. Page, whose features seemed ordinary enough offstage, had a sad luminosity that was transformed into remarkable stage beauty; Dewhurst and Jens each had a rawboned elegance that was overtly sensual.

Under Quintero's highly charged style of direction the Circle did not settle for secondary or simulated feeling; it went directly for the actor's own strongest, most primitive, and most closely held emotions. What was inside the actor counted for more than physical exterior. Robards was not always "right" in appearance for the parts in which he was cast. When in 1955 he read for the play (*The King and the Duke*) that reopened the Circle when the fire violations were satisfied, Mann said, "We didn't think he was right for the part, but we were impressed. Things were happening, waves were coming off the stage." It was that work which earned him his reading as Hickey for *The Iceman Cometh*. Off-Broadway's deemphasis of casting to type eventually was to influence the rest of the theater. Customarily theater ideas filter upward, and the revolution in casting that was going on in the little downtown theaters was to change the look of American films. Such beginning actors at Circle in the

Kerr Associates

Off-Broadway's first great success cast Lee Richardson as Dr. John and Geraldine Page as his next-door neighbor Alma Winemiller in Tennessee Williams' *Summer and Smoke*, a 1952 revival that celebrated a beginning and brought recognition to off-Broadway.

Jose Quintero, co-founder of Circle in
Square and director of some of off-Br
way's major successes, beginning
Summer and Smoke.

Ira Rosen

Theodore Mann, Quintero's partner,
who shared the producing decisions
and has managed the business affairs
of the Circle for over twenty years.
Ed Rooney

In the final scene of the Circle's *Summer and Smoke* Geraldine Page sits dejectedly by the fountain as another young man enters her half-destroyed life.

Roy Schatt

Behind the bar in the Circle's landmark production of Eugene O'Neill's *The Iceman Cometh* are Joseph Beruh (later to become an off-Broadway manager, theater owner, and producer) and Henderson Forsythe.

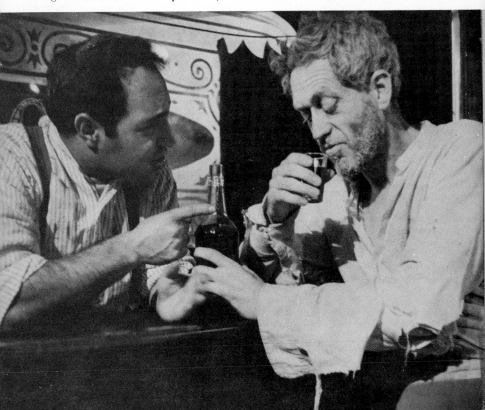

(*Left*) Three then-unknown young actors—Pat Hingle, Ben Gazzara, and Arthur Storch (in the brace)—in Calder Willingham's play about military school life, *End as a Man,* at the Theater de Lys in 1953. (*Right*) Lotte Lenya, who performed in her husband Kurt Weill's and Bertolt Brecht's *The Threepenny Opera* in Berlin in 1928, again was Pirate Jenny at the de Lys in 1954.

The Irish Players' great success was Synge's *The Playboy of the Western World* in 1958 with the co-founders of the Players in leading roles—Dermot McNamara, on the floor at left as Christy Mahon, and Helena Carroll, at right, as Pegeen Mike.

Bill Mitchell

Square in the 1950's and early 1960's as Geraldine Page, George C. Scott, Jason Robards, Peter Falk, George Segal, and Dustin Hoffman were to become the film actors of the 1970's. Falk had appeared in *The Iceman*, but Mann, who had his theories about how long actors should stick in an off-Broadway play, felt Falk had left too early to make even a minimal impression. Off-Broadway actors have always been tempted to grab their notices and run to more rewarding employment. Equity, traditionally justifying its relaxed rules for off-Broadway because of the showcase value to actors, permitted departures on short notice, and actors sometimes took advantage of this leniency not only to the detriment of the production but also, Mann felt, to the injury of their own careers. An actor in a lead generally should stay with a show, Mann felt, for six months to register his identity with the work. Notices were all very well. Of even greater importance to an actor was the chance to be seen, particularly by fellow members of the profession. The first weeks of the run, in Mann's judgment, are crucial: it is then that the critics, the writers, and the theater professionals—the "tastemakers" whose judgment really establishes the worth and popularity of a show—come to see it. It is their word of mouth that really determines audience acceptability. Theater always has had to find its first audience among its own. If its own likes it not, the chances of acceptance elsewhere are very slim indeed.

Actors and other theater artists of repute got started at the Circle in very different ways. James Ray, as a beginning actor in New York, had a bit part in the Circle's very first production, *Dark of the Moon*. Dustin Hoffman, already beginning to become known after two Ronald Ribman plays at the American Place Theater, was picked out of the Circle's production of *Eh?* for Mike Nichols' *The Graduate*. George Segal came to the Circle thanks to the intervention of his older brother, Fred, who knew Ted Mann and pleaded with him to find some spot in the theater, the more menial, the better, for his stagestruck brother. George Segal was hired as a porter (a theatrical euphemism for janitor or handyman), but he was able to understudy one of the roles in *The Iceman Cometh*. David Hays became a Circle set designer after creating Harry Hope's bar for the O'Neill work. Early recognition of Patricia Zipprodt's versatility as a costume designer came from her work on *The Balcony*, whose bizarre costume designs demonstrated how important the visual element was in setting the theatrical tone of the play. The continual outpouring of theater talent from the Circle has had an impact on the whole theater.

Success in a continuing theater such as Circle in the Square depends, as we have said, on the parallel strengths of the artistic and business sides, and beginning in the late 1950's the delicate balance of responsibility within the Circle began to suffer a subtle alteration.

Mann's skill and diligence in promoting the shows, in holding down costs, cultivating audience, and managing the staff freed Quintero, who had no business sense or interest whatever, to give himself utterly to the actors and to the play. He made his own hours; his schedule related only to the work; there were few points at which his life and the ordinary business routine touched. So long as the division was understood and trusted the relationship held. To Quintero it was like a love affair; like a love affair, it began to turn sour when each partner took to jockeying for power. The rupture between Quintero and Mann was not to come for several more years, but the turning point undoubtedly arrived in late 1959, and a direct cause arising out of their dissimilar habits of work can be found in the move from the original theater on Sheridan Square to the new location on Bleecker Street.

After *Children of Darkness* and *The Quare Fellow*—Brendan Behan's first play to be done in this country—there was one last production before 5 Sheridan Square was torn down for a modern apartment house: a superb and again apparently well-timed revival, Thornton Wilder's *Our Town*. For critics and audience there was more than a hint of longing and regret in the realization that Grover's Corners with its simple fervors and self-contained life had been run through as if by a high-speed expressway in the time since Wilder's classic had been first performed twenty-one years earlier. Restless time had heightened the poignancy and appeal in Quintero's honest revival, which became as big a hit as *Summer and Smoke* and *The Iceman Cometh*.

The play opened in March, 1959, went into the summer, and in August the Circle was notified of the demolition plans for the building. The Circle's own life had passed its Grover's Corners. As the search for a new location began, a call came into the office for Quintero from a man who said he admired Quintero's work very much and wanted to inform him of the availability of a possible new location, the Amato Opera House on Bleecker Street, where *The Respectful Prostitute* had played ten years before. Quintero was not in the office to receive this crucial call. Unless rehearsals were in progress he was not regularly in the theater. When work was under way, he put his whole being into it. No amount of time, no expenditure of emotion or energy were too much, but after the show opened, he rarely returned, like other directors, to recheck performances. There were no "brushup" rehearsals with Quintero. Mistaken for indifference, this habit was disquieting to actors. After so much loving attention during the endless rehearsal hours, they suddenly felt lost and forsaken. On the day after *Long Day's Journey into Night* opened on Broadway his friend and then assistant Isabel Halliburton went shopping with him on Fifth Avenue so he could buy presents for members of his family. All during the walk Quintero complained that directing was all he was capable of doing. He had no firm belief in the importance of something that came so naturally to him. It was as if driving a car, which he had never learned, were of a higher order of worldly value. For several weeks after a play opened he would be unreachable even by phone. Shortly after *Long Day's Journey* Kermit Bloomgarden, the Broadway producer, wanted him to direct *Look Homeward, Angel.* Quintero took the script home and studied it, but he neglected to answer Bloomgarden's calls, and the next thing anyone knew he was on a boat sailing to Spain. The emotional drain of one play was such, Isabel Halliburton thought, that he simply couldn't face another rehearsal.

Perhaps it was for some of these same reasons three years later that Quintero was not around when the call came through about the Amato Opera House. Mann instead answered the phone and went alone to inspect the building. Mann, alone, instead of Quintero and Mann together, signed the lease. Quintero was not around but he never really forgave Mann for acting without him. Work on the new theater went forward with his lessened interest and participation. David Hays designed the new theater to resemble the old, except that the stage was unencumbered by support poles, and real theater seats were introduced, arena fashion, at one end and along the two lateral arms of the stage. Upstairs Mann laid out a comfortable office for himself, but Quintero refused any special space. Theaters have a way of ending up in the hands of business managers who keep regular office hours, possess the files, and make sure their signatures appear on the key contracts.

The attitude toward real estate reflected a perhaps fundamental difference in viewpoint between Quintero and Mann on what exactly a theater was, and it was all summed up for Quintero in a remarkable benefit performance put on by the Circle actors to raise money for the new theater. The evening consisted of scenes from famous Circle productions performed by the original actors. Geraldine Page, then appearing in *Sweet Bird of Youth*, hurried downtown when the curtain fell at the Martin Beck to do a scene from *Summer and Smoke*. Onstage there were only a few prop chairs and a table. She put on the hat and long gloves she had worn in

the play and was Alma Winemiller again. The chairs were
rearranged, and George C. Scott and Colleen Dewhurst revived *Children of Darkness*. Betty Miller and James Greene
did a scene from *The Girl on the Via Flaminia*. In a felt hat,
Thornton Wilder assumed the stage manager role in *Our
Town*. Then Jason Robards walked on. He summoned actors one by one out of the audience. Each brought his own
chair onstage, and once again the Circle was transformed into
Harry Hope's bar in *The Iceman Cometh*. It was an exhila-
rating and altogether remarkable evening. The actors had
made it. To Quintero it conveyed the meaning of off-Broadway. Whatever name was on the lease, to the actors was due
at least a share of Circle in the Square. Quintero thought
the theater belonged to them. Mann felt it was his.

The changeover in theaters was accomplished in January,
1960, without skipping a beat, thanks to Mann's precise planning. *Our Town* played its 333d performance on January 8
at Sheridan Square and the following evening gave its 334th
performance in the new Circle on Bleecker Street, five
blocks away. Mann believed strongly in continuity and continuous performance. A string of interesting productions
would induce theatergoing habits ultimately stronger than
those conditioned by subscription. Mann once wrote in the
New York *Herald Tribune* (August 11, 1963): "To survive
off-Broadway, it is essential to produce plays fifty-two weeks a
year. We consider ourselves professionals at Circle in the
Square, and a basic professional obligation is to stay in business. To achieve continuity, we have found it necessary to
operate our own theater, keep it alive with plays, and at the
same time use the total facilities of the building for additional income." The "total" utilization of the building was to
involve a theater school. With Mann nothing was left to
chance. Given an artistically strong production, he knew how
to promote it, how to bring audience in, and how to keep it
going. No matter how promising the show, Mann looked for
ways to stimulate audience, organizing high school groups

and theater parties, planning special promotion, keeping the show running and the theater lit. Quintero never questioned the importance of this side of the theater operation. The artistic director gets the acclaim, and envy, humanly, could have been the source of some of the developing friction. Even then Mann aspired to try his own hand at directing. In another year he would be getting his feet wet with a touring company of *The Fantasticks*, and in the fall of 1961 Mann's ambition to go further, beyond what he may have felt was a secondary role at the Circle, led him into a brief producing partnership with George C. Scott in which they raised money largely in Detroit to mount two artistically interesting but commercially disastrous productions on Broadway (Alice Cannon's *Great Day in the Morning* with Colleen Dewhurst and Ira Levin's *General Seeger* in which Scott replaced William Bendix only a few days before the opening).

For his part Quintero also began to look outside the Circle. In 1961, after *The Balcony*, he was to take a sabbatical year abroad to direct Vivien Leigh in the film of the Tennessee Williams novel *The Roman Spring of Mrs. Stone*. He grew uneasy over some of Mann's business decisions, even such minor matters as the dilution of the orange juice served at intermission. The areas of friction widened, their separate roles became confused in their own minds, the creative innocence of their beginnings suffered the corrosion of success, and the remarkable partnership whose creative output had dominated the off-Broadway scene for a decade began to fall apart. But there was still good work ahead and one more stunning success in *The Balcony* before the final rupture.

Four

The early 1950's brought a resurgence of interest in Shaw, O'Casey, Synge, Strindberg, Chekhov, and Ibsen. Little theaters such as David Ross' Fourth Street dedicated themselves to the work of one or another great playwright. The reexamination of the classics produced a series of adaptations "from the works of" some revered master, Ethnic companies such as the Irish Players adopted production programs that grouped plays along national lines.

Not all this attention can be attributed to the high state of cultural enlightenment of off-Broadway producers. Doing the work of long-dead playwrights to whom no royalties are owed and putting new talent together with old plays were one way of meeting the economic stringencies. As for the actors, their long-standing complaint of themselves being the principal subsidy for off-Broadway was validated back in these years when rehearsal pay was a standard $5 a week and performance pay was $25. Shaving expenses had more to do with off-Broadway's preference for young talent and choice of material than some early managers would care to admit. The tradition fostered by Richard Barr and Edward Albee, was not to come until some years later. But the postwar European intellectual was brought to off-Broadway. There were, for example, Patricia Newhall's production of Sartre's *No Exit* at Theater East in the fall of 1956 and, two years later at the same theater, Leo Garen's production of Genet's *Deathwatch* affording an interior (and criminal) view of prison life. Sometimes, as was the case with a theater started by Terese Hayden, established actors came off-Broadway to perform in proven work, and occasionally in a new play such as Calder Willingham's *End as a Man* there would unexpectedly appear such an array of stunning new acting, writing, and directing talent as to astound the critics.

Both Miss Hayden's group and the Willingham play, as it happened, played at the Theater de Lys, shortly to be enshrined by *The Threepenny Opera* as one of the landmarks of early off-Broadway. For thousands of theatergoers, a visit to the de Lys was the authentic off-Broadway experience. Off-Broadway meant the discovery of new talent and fresh theatrical experiences in unfamiliar parts of the city. It meant the rediscovery of old plays and the reinterpretation of the classics in settings that did not overwhelm them or place them in unbalanced competition with the commercially slick and fashionable works of Broadway. Theater seemed more worthwhile the more risks one took. Finding the out-of-the-way theater added to the sense of overall discovery. The de Lys at the far end of Christopher Street, near the Hudson River docks, was situated in a borderline neighborhood between the known residential part of the city and the open seaport. The unknown world beyond, in imagination, merged with the pulsing underworld life of *The Threepenny Opera* and became sinister, exotic, and menacing.

To this day, in spite of changes of ownership, the theater bears the name of its founder, William de Lys, a shadowy, briefly important figure in early off-Broadway with no previous or subsequent connections in theater. Out of a circus and carnival showman's background de Lys formulated his rather grandiose plans for renovating and programming the old Hudson movie house on Christopher Street (whose suitability as a legitimate theater had been pointed out to him by Harold Stern, the critic). A small, energetic figure in his late thirties, de Lys set in motion an expensive refurbishing program to fix the theater up, lay gold cloth on the walls, design a "Kabuki" lounge with Oriental furnishings, and plan a series of shows. In December, 1951, he took out a lease with option to buy. His projected ten-play series opened on September 29, 1952, with *Frankie and Johnny* by John Huston. The cash outlay was between $100,000 and $125,000. Dance events, concerts, varieties, and jazz were promised. The Huston play was a disappointment, and the whole program quickly sank of its own weight. Some artificial respiration was effectively administered in early 1953 by Max Eisen, press agent and adviser to the de Lys. Silent movies such as *The Hunchback of Notre Dame* and *Dancing Mothers* with Clara Bow were rented from a camera store for weekend showing and drew good audiences. Invariably a cease-and-desist telegram would arrive on Monday morning from the producing company whose title it was, but by that time the damage had been done and the non-licensed films back in the store until the next weekend's program. The proceeds at least paid for the electricity. In the spring the construction company involved in the renovation took over the theater for nonpayment of bills. William de Lys disappeared from the scene, but Eisen remained as consultant to plan and book the needed shows.

It is at this point that Terese Hayden enters the history of off-Broadway. It was a case of the theater recognizing its own. She came to New York from Nashville, Tennessee, in 1941, at the age of seventeen and enrolled in the American Academy of Dramatic Arts. One of her first jobs was in the road company of *Angel Street* during the war years. Like anonymous charities, many of her later good works are unrecorded. For whatever personal needs, she has given her whole life to the theater for thirty years. Any outside work was only to sustain her theatrical activity. She revered talent and trusted theatrical experience. It was Terese Hayden who started Equity Library Theater, ever since a showcase for unknowns seeking their first hearing in front of the casting agents and directors in New York. With much the same aim, she put together the *Players' Guide,* a thick annual directory of actors carrying pictures, credits, and agent's phone numbers sectionalized under leading men, leading women, ingenues, character women, and so forth. Today it is an essential reference in every casting office.

Practical idealist, gifted, determined, Miss Hayden was never able to turn her ventures into commercial successes. Her first attempt to put together a theater came in 1950 with the help of the actors Sam Wanamaker and Anthony Quinn. But after three or four scheduled bills at the then Fulton Theater, the project, known as the Festival Theater, folded. The second attempt was made off-Broadway with Eisen's counsel and help at the Theater de Lys in June, 1953. Historically, its importance lies in inducing actors of solid reputation to appear off Broadway for the first time in any numbers. Within a repertory framework established actors were able to do plays and take parts they would not ordinarily have had a chance to perform in the context of their commercial careers. Broadway encouraged the actor to exploit his personality and repeat his previous successes. What he needed was a chance to grow, develop, and expand his craft. Many of the company came out of the Actors Studio as disciples of Lee Strasberg: Patricia Neal, Eli Wallach, Anne Jackson, Leo Penn, Rebecca Darke, Salem Ludwig, Bradford Dillman, Albert Salmi, David J. Stewart—at the then ridiculously low going rate. The four plays were a revival of *Maya* by Simon Gantillon about a Marseilles prostitute who is all things to all men and which Aline MacMahon had played on Broadway in 1928; *The Little Clay Cart,* a Hindu play translated by Arthur William Ryder, first done by the Neighborhood Playhouse in 1924; *The Scarecrow* by Percy Mackaye, first done in 1910 and directed in this production by Frank Corsaro, another Studio regular; and Sheridan's *School for Scandal,* last done on Broadway with Ethel Barrymore in 1931 and directed this time by Miss Hayden. The total budget of $5,000 was low by any standard. The plays were not a great success. The financial base was not sound enough to assure any continuity. Miss Hayden's project, however, cannot be counted a loss. New talent was given a start. Susan Strasberg made her acting debut in *Maya*. The scenic designers William and Jean Eckart did some of their first work for these productions. But the main accomplishment was to get name actors to work willingly off-Broadway. Off-Broadway was itself the beneficiary of the kind of recognition that could come only from the active participation of established actors at some sacrifice to their regular careers.

From the Actors Studio also came the next Theater de Lys production, Calder Willingham's *End as a Man*. It had one of the most talented casts of unknowns off-Broadway has ever seen and made a star of Ben Gazzara. The play was adapted by Willingham from his 1947 novel of Southern military school life with its martinet discipline, sadism, cruelty in hazing, brutality, and overtones of schoolboy homosexuality. It began as a classroom exercise at the Studio in 1953. Jack Garfein, the director, then attending classes at the Studio, met Willingham at a party and asked to see the script. Garfein showed it to Strasberg, who approved it as an experimental project. A professional production off-Broadway was the next order of business. The cast was set: besides Gazzara, William Smithers, Arthur Storch, Pat Hingle, George Peppard, Anthony Franciosa, Paul Richards, Mark Richman, and Albert Salmi. At the de Lys, Max Eisen suggested to Garfein and producer Claire Heller that at least one known actor of sufficient drawing power to attract the critics should be added. They gave the cadet commander part to Frank M. Thomas, who had appeared in dozens of cowboy films and television shows. When the play opened on September 15, 1953, Thomas was the only actor anyone had ever heard of. Today, he is the only obscure name in the cast. Out of the company came a generation of leading male actors. After the usual four-week de Lys run *End as a Man* was moved to Broadway in October, first to the Vanderbilt Theater and later to the Lyceum for 148 performances. Willingham, Garfein, and Gazzara were also involved in the film, *The Strange One*, in July, 1956, an early instance of an off-Broadway play being made into a movie. Six of the nine other members of the off-Broadway cast were also used in the film—a record perhaps never equaled. Out of the off-Broadway success also came immediate Broadway careers for Gazzara and Salmi in *Cat on a Hot Tin Roof* and *Bus Stop*, respectively. After *End as a Man* the Merce Cunningham dancers worked at the theater. In January, 1954, Leslie Stevens' *Bullfight* brought Joseph Anthony his first notice as a director. Then, in March, the four-week booking policy brought in *The Threepenny Opera*, the play with which this theater was to be associated in the minds of nearly a decade of theatergoers.

Not before or since has Brecht succeeded in New York on any large scale. Broadway theaters such as the Martin Beck and the Lunt-Fontanne, where a *Mother Courage* and an *Arturo Ui* later played, seemed inappropriately commodious and elegant, as if a Gothic cathedral were sheltering a congregation of revivalists. Brecht in New York has been more successful in miniature. The two young producers, Carmen Capalbo and Stanley Chase, still in their twenties, had rightly gauged time, place, and dimension. Their choice and handling of the Brecht-Weill show reflected their own uneasiness with the realistic theater and anticipated the audience's. The open Brechtian epic form carried its own commentary on the narrow, realistic, Ibsenesque psychological drama of the 1940's and 1950's. The sets were nonrealistic. Entrances were made down the aisle. Actors occasionally addressed the audience directly from the thrust stage. Songs were sung straight out. The coming cult of the antihero was celebrated in the character of Macheath, the thief. The show's menacing first song, "Mack the Knife," was the perfect opening num-

ber, setting the tone of the show and summing it up all at the
same time. In its various recordings this number, together
with the torch song "Surabaya Johnny" and "Pirate Jenny,"
were superb promotion and helped sell more cast albums
than any other show then playing was able to sell with the
sole exception of *My Fair Lady*.

The Kurt Weill-Bertolt Brecht work in its Marc Blitzstein
adaptation had been done in concert version at Brandeis
University in June, 1952. The producers turned down several chances to take it to Broadway, favoring a small theater
off the beaten track. Perhaps more than any one single decision, this choice may have determined its eventual success.
Director as well as producer, Capalbo assembled a strong cast
headed by the nearly legendary Lotte Lenya, Weill's widow,
whose husky vocal style was as distinctive as Dietrich's, to
re-create the role of Jenny she first performed in the original
Berlin production in 1928. Scott Merrill was cast as Macheath (Mack the Knife), Gerrianne Raphael as Polly Peachum, Beatrice Arthur as Lucy Brown. Joseph Beruh, the
theater owner, producer, and dean of off-Broadway theater
managers, played a bareknuckled Crookfinger Jake in Macheath's gang of thieves. The mostly brass and percussion
band numbered eight. In the last days of rehearsal half an
hour was cut out of the show, and the opening was delayed
twenty-four hours. Two new Weill songs had been added
since Brandeis ("Ballad of Dependency" and "Solomon
Song"), and *The Threepenny Opera* opened on March 10,
1954. In this first run the show played twelve weeks before
being forced out by a prior booking obligation. No succeeding show equaled *Threepenny*, and Brooks Atkinson took to
adding a line at the end of his reviews of de Lys openings
—"Bring back *The Threepenny Opera*." It was to be fifteen
months before Capalbo was able to do so.

Between the two productions interest in *The Threepenny
Opera* remained alive. Lotte Lenya was in Germany recording Weill songs but was to return in time to appear as Jenny.

In January, 1955, Capalbo and Chase moved briefly into one of Broadway's smallest theaters, the Bijou, to put on *Purple Dust* and *A Moon for the Misbegotten*, both of which plays were to fare better in off-Broadway productions. After a bitter lawsuit, the de Lys fell into the hands of Lucille Lortel. The sale to her was contested through three courts by Max Eisen, who had become a 50 percent owner of the theater after de Lys' untidy departure and who maintained that the offer and sale to Miss Lortel were made without his consent. After more than four years of litigation, Eisen lost in the court of appeals in a split vote. It is some small consolation to Eisen that the minority decision in the case is studied today in the law schools. For many years Miss Lortel has run the ANTA Matinee Series out of her theater, and summers she managed her private White Barn Theater in Westport to test promising dramatic material for possible further production in New York. But her most enduring connection with the off-Broadway theater came when she joined Capalbo and Chase for the renewed *Threepenny* run which they had been reluctant to undertake on their own. The initial engagement, for all Atkinson thought about it, was by no means a sellout. For the second go-round, *Threepenny* opened on September 20, 1955. Jo Sullivan, who most recently had been playing Julie in a City Center revival of *Carousel*, came in as Polly, and Charlotte Rae as Mrs. Peachum. This time *The Threepenny Opera* was there to stay. Atkinson had been heard. On opening night Lotte Lenya predicted it would run for five years. She was short by fifteen months. The show, with its driving, quirky music, became a fixture off-Broadway. Indeed, it came to stand for off-Broadway.

Late in the run Capalbo estimated that he had witnessed some or all of at least 500 performances. At any point he walked in on the evening he could recite the next lines said or sung. He himself had played some of the roles. In the last two years he couldn't bear to look at it. Cast replacements were a constant problem. Some 709 actors in all rotated in and out of the twenty-two roles. The show itself never seemed to grow tired or sloppy. The structure of the play, the power of its music were so strong, so sure that no amount of acting ineptitude could twist it out of shape entirely.

Capalbo and Chase first put up the "last weeks" sign in May, 1961. Two road companies, including one led by Gypsy Rose Lee, were unsuccessful. But the show continued. The closing was not to come until December 17, 1961. The cost of production had been kept under $9,000. At closing gross receipts came to nearly $3,000,000 with a top ticket price of $4.90. Stefan Brecht, the playwright's son, went through Harvard on the royalties. *Threepenny* had played 2,611 performances—the longest run for a musical in the history of the American theater up to that time.

The long, self-sustaining run of *The Threepenny Opera,* whose professional production would not have been attempted anywhere else in the American theater, justified off-Broadway. Norris Houghton, of the Phoenix Theater, wrote in the New York *Times* (November 27, 1953) that the enriching variety of dramatic literature was made available through off-Broadway theaters. He spoke of Broadway, by contrast, as "like a bookshop from whose shelves every title has been cleaned except the handful that make up the 'best-seller' list. How frugal would be our intellectual diet, how empty the shelves, if publishers withdrew from the public all those books that didn't get the nod from the Book-of-the-Month Club, the Literary Guild or their cousin outfits."

If off-Broadway was a library, David Ross was the curator of the Chekhov and Ibsen wings. In eight years he produced and directed more than a dozen of their plays in his own theater, a one-man classical revival unparalleled in off-Broadway history and some of the finest Chekhov and Ibsen New York has seen, regardless of size or expense of production. In his Fourth Street Theater just west of Second Avenue, Ross operated from a small thrust stage that was placed oddly in the middle of the side wall, dividing the 143-seat theater into two equal sections so that the audience faced its other half across the stage. His first production was Ansky's *The Dybbuk*. It was a significant choice in terms of his personal development, tying together his Jewish heritage and his ambition to break into the theater and expressing his own wish to become an actor, for he had saved a part in the play for himself. In furtherance of some parental ambition, Ross, who had come from St. Paul, Minnesota, had studied to become a rabbi. Other abortive career attempts followed. He took up the violin in the hope of becoming a concert violinist. He went into his father's electroplating business and gave that up. He participated in some theatrical activities at the University of Minnesota and decided on an acting career. One summer he served as an apprentice at Richard Aldrich's Cape Playhouse. In New York he took a course with Lee Strasberg. Black-haired and big-chested, Ross was a good-natured bear of a man who suggested the working-class intellectual. But there was no great call on his acting talents. No one is more theatrically addicted than the failed actor. To make a place for himself, Ross decided to start a company of his own. When he was unable to find a director for *The Dybbuk*, he assumed the staging also and cast himself in a part calling for rabbinical robes. With Ludwig Donath as the star, the play opened on October 26, 1954, and won respectful reviews, although nothing that would put the new company quite in a class with the Habimah, the famous Israeli national theater. Ross' opening helped shift the center of gravity of off-Broadway eastward toward Second Avenue, in the orbit of the Phoenix farther uptown at Twelfth Street.

Ross had, as it developed, a huge appetite for classical theater. He was able to infect the actors with his own robust tastes. In recognition of his lead the theater community followed, and then the audience. Quickly he moved into what became his abiding interest. The series of Chekhov revivals began with *The Three Sisters* in 1955 and continued with

The Cherry Orchard in October, 1955, *Uncle Vanya* in January, 1956, and *The Sea Gull* in October, 1956, the last being the least successful. The *Uncle Vanya*, with a cast Broadway could envy, consisting of Franchot Tone, Signe Hasso, Clarence Derwent, and George Voskovec, was perhaps the finest Chekhov New York had seen in years. For his part, Tone got some of the best notices of his life. The success of the production, the public notice it got, the prestige of doing Chekhov well, the excellence of the supporting cast quickly erased all possible stigma attached to going off-Broadway, to lowering oneself by appearing in a tiny theater for little money at some risk to career and reputation. Ross practiced the most eloquent persuasion to get his actors to come downtown; success reinforced his arguments and helped him recoup money lost on earlier productions. His *Uncle Vanya* solidified his own position as a director and the Fourth Street Theater as an off-Broadway institution worthy of comparison with Circle in the Square, the Theater de Lys, and the Phoenix.

The *Vanya* success so buoyed up Ross that in the spring of 1956 he was off to Moscow to study the Russian theater. He was feted there, where they had not seen the size of his theater, as an American genius. Returning, he assembled another surprisingly distinguished cast for *The Sea Gull* in October: Betty Field, Jacob Ben-Ami, Shepperd Strudwick, Barbara O'Neil, William Smithers, Ludwig Donath, Bryarly Lee, Lou Polan, and Gerald Hiken. The production, however, was a twenty-five-performance disappointment, and Ross switched to Strindberg briefly with *Easter* in the beginning of 1957 and then tried a couple of diversions hoping for an easy commercial popularity, *The Italian Straw Hat* and Wedekind's *Lulu*, for which he persuaded the exuberant Eva Gabor to come down to Fourth Street in September, 1958, an event that caused Gene Gleason to write in the New York *Herald Tribune*, "A grim Germanic sex tragedy collided head on last night with the corset-bursting Magyar ebullience of Eva Gabor and was knocked into a cockeyed comedy." As a curious footnote to these productions, Lore Noto played minor roles in both. Later he was to emerge as the fortunate producer of *The Fantasticks*.

In the main, Ross was uncannily right in his casting, mixing tested talent with new talent, working in relative newcomers with some of the theater's major stars. Actors with big reputations such as Franchot Tone, Morris Carnovsky, Betty Field, and Signe Hasso were supported by players whose reputations, many of them, were to begin with their work on Fourth Street—Gerald Hiken, George Voskovec, Anne Meacham, Nancy Wickwire, Sandra Churchill. The more productions he mounted, the wider the pool of actors Ross had to work with. Ross scarcely hit upon a more fortunate cast than that assembled for his second production of *The Three Sisters* in September, 1959, re-creating once again on the tiny thrust stage the drawing room of the Prozoroff home in provincial Russia. As Olga there was Carol Gustafson, a tall, severely handsome actress who had played the same role in the earlier production; as Masha, the dark-haired, more softly handsome Barbara Ames; and as Irina, the delicate Kathleen Widdoes with her wide, innocent eyes and slim vulnerability. The Hungarian actor Sandor Szabo made his American debut as Vershinin, and Gerald Hiken, by now a veteran of Ross revivals who had won awards for his work in *Uncle Vanya*, played Andrey, the pathetic, half-destroyed brother. Boris Tumarin, a fine classical actor, was cast as the captain, and Peter Donat as Tusenbach, the baron. The production, in honor of the 100th anniversary of Chekhov's birth, ran successfully for 257 performances.

By the spring of 1960 Ross undoubtedly felt he had exhausted the possibilities of Chekhov both for himself and for his audience. He began to plan an Ibsen cycle of similar scope and ambition. Ibsen would serve as Ross' own commentary on the quality of contemporary drama which, he was quoted in the *Times* as saying, "has drifted into a sort of limbo of pessimism, nihilism, and weird fantasy, without discernible purpose and without any particular moral or social objective." Ibsen's robust morality could be relied upon even if the admiration of a critic such as Walter Kerr were tempered. As the master builder of plays, Ibsen was sometimes too transparent in his methods; one saw the workmanship along with the work as he slipped the bricks into place in the structure of his play.

Ross was fortunate in developing support for his Ibsen cycle from such members of the theater community as Joshua Logan, Arthur Laurents, William Inge, Rod Steiger, and Eli Wallach. The series he proposed included *When We Dead Awaken, John Gabriel Borkman, Ghosts, A Doll's House,* and *Hedda Gabler.* Such a schedule, had it been followed, might have carried him into the mid-1960's. As it was, serious casting difficulties caused a change of plan. A few weeks before the scheduled October, 1960, opening of *When We Dead Awaken,* Franchot Tone withdrew abruptly, differing with Ross in his interpretation of the play. The touchy Tone was to become involved in a similar incident later, when he walked out of the Circle in the Square production of *Desire Under the Elms.* Ross responded to the crisis by switching plays and summoning Mai Zetterling from England to play Hedda. The substitute play was rehearsed, an opening was announced, and preview performances were under way when Miss Zetterling fell ill and on doctor's orders was not allowed to return. Miss Zetterling was not used to the doubling up of performances off-Broadway on Saturdays and Sundays to take advantage of the heavy weekend trade. She played the first Saturday performance, which ended at 9 P.M., and rested between shows for an hour. She returned to the stage at 10:15. Forty-five minutes into the first act of the second show she collapsed.

Gambling desperately, Ross early Sunday morning put in a telephone call to Anne Meacham and thereby set in motion one of the most remarkable last-minute relief actions in off-

Broadway history. Miss Meacham was a spirited, intense actress of high temperament, not so much underrated as typically underworked. She had been the unlucky victim of one or two recent Broadway flops. Time was short; there were only four days of rehearsal left for Ross to keep to his scheduled opening. Not having read Ibsen since college, Miss Meacham went to work at once. That first night she got only two hours' sleep. For twelve hours straight on Sunday with the cast she felt her way into the long, difficult role, trying to master her acting points before fully memorizing her lines. As director, Ross reblocked the entire play, readjusting the moves of the other actors—Lois Holmes, Lester Rawlins, Lori March, Mark Lenard—to suit her playing, her timing. "Rely on your instincts," Ross advised her. It was all she could do in the time left.

After two and a half hours' sleep she was back at work Monday. She gave her first performance at Tuesday's preview. With Ross' wife, Carmel, cueing her, she missed lines in only twelve places. Tuesday she had three hours of sleep and five more on the eve of the opening—a total of twelve and a half hours since Ross' call early Sunday morning. "Even if I had stayed up twenty-four hours," she said, "there wouldn't have been enough hours." On the final day the fourth act was blocked from five fifteen to six fifteen. On first night she was like a racehorse at the gate trained to the last nerve. Wednesday evening *Hedda Gabler* opened on schedule. Between acts she continued to rehearse her lines back and forth. The performance went off faultlessly. She missed no line, no cue, no planned move. Whatever effort in self-control it cost her, the performance was brilliant, Meacham as self-absorbed on stage as if she had forever been Ibsen's Hedda. At the end of the season she won the Obie Award as best actress. Some people said she was the best Hedda of all time. Pay television bought the production, which ran at a $3,000 weekly profit. Miss Meacham went on to a longer run in *Hedda* (340 performances) than Mrs. Fiske, Nazimova, or Eva Le Gallienne.

Ghosts came the following September with Leueen Mac-Grath, Staats Cotsworth, Carrie Nye, and John McQuade for a record-breaking run lasting through the spring. Next came *Rosmersholm*, translated by Carmel Ross, with Donald Woods and Nancy Wickwire, but this time, with the profits of *Hedda*, Ross was beginning to think in terms of the new theater and the larger operation that would prove to be his undoing. In all he had mounted thirteen revivals on Fourth Street. His work had earned critical respect and, more important, the admiration and support of the theater community. Certainly the little Fourth Street Theater seemed small for the kind of success he had achieved.

Ross located an empty turn-of-the-century church on West Fifty-fifth Street, off Ninth Avenue, in what he identified hopefully as "the Lincoln Center area," a district of future expansion and theatrical growth. The Fourth Street Theater was taken over by a new group, the Writers Stage Company. In a very short period, Ross spent between $130,000 and $150,000, mostly accumulated from profits, renovating the building, taking out the pews of the First Evangelical and United Brethren Church and putting in real theater seats, a box office, a stage, lighting equipment, dressing rooms, and, out front, awnings and radiant heat. It was named Theater Four more in the interests of continuity than geographical identification. The new stage was three times as large as the old platform on Fourth Street. Ross opened the new theater on November 14, 1962, with *The Cherry Orchard*. Again there had been a cast change at the last moment, Marian Winters coming in for Signe Hasso. The play lasted sixty-one performances. Hurriedly, for Ross now had to cope with a sizable overhead, the new Theater Four booked in a promising musical, *The Boys from Syracuse,* which had the blessing and support of the Richard Rodgers office. It was an immediate hit, but Ross' own producing career was nearing an end. He was to do one more play, *A Month in the Country,* for the first time using a rented theater not under his

own control. For the same reasons William de Lys lost his
theater, Ross lost Theater Four. Disillusioned and disheart-
ened, he left for England on an extended trip and died in
1966 at his mother's home in St. Paul after a long illness.
Theater Four was to have its own hits, first *The Boys from
Syracuse*, then *The Boys in the Band*, but nothing of Chekhov, nothing of Ibsen. It is often argued that there are no
good locations or bad locations for a theater, only good plays
and bad plays, and all it takes is a hit to get people there, no
matter how out of the way or unpromising the location.
Such statements smack of the syllogistic; there is always refu-
tory evidence to support the other side. One might say, for
instance, theater that flourishes in one place will not neces-
sarily do well in another and that transplantation is generally
harmful. A more possible theory, I think, is that Ross, having
run his Chekhov cycle, may also have run his own cycle.
Off-Broadway was moving into new work and taking on
young playwrights. One lesson to draw from the history of
off-Broadway groups, projects, and schools is the principle of
cyclical change—a turnover every five or so years. Ross had
survived nearly nine years. He had made the low-budget
revival respectable for actors and audience. He had given
almost a decade of theatergoers the living experience of two
of the masters of modern drama. Perhaps that was enough.

Besides the classics, off-Broadway was also successful with
more recent revivals on the order of *Summer and Smoke*.
Louis Peterson's *Take a Giant Step*, which was produced on
Broadway in 1953, was revived by the New Theater Company
headed by Ira Cirker in September, 1956, with Bill Gunn, a
playwright and novelist as well as an actor, playing the lonely
grandson in a New England town. With some rewriting, Arthur Miller's *The Crucible*, that compelling play about character defamation which seems to be topical every decade or so
in American life, was redone by Paul Libin and Word Baker
at the Martinique in 1958 with the seductive Ann Wedgeworth as the thwarted Abigail Williams and Michael Higgins

as the unjustly accused John Proctor. Jack Ragotzy, the director who came to off-Broadway from summer theater work in Michigan, put on Arthur Laurents' *A Clearing in the Woods* with Nancy Wickwire for a second showing that the critics all considered superior to its Broadway first run.

The lesser work of established playwrights such as Tennessee Williams also got a favorable hearing off-Broadway. No production was more memorable than *Garden District* with Anne Meacham, directed by Herbert Machiz at the York Playhouse in January, 1958, with its startling imagery and suppressed savageness. New plays were perhaps scarcer. Two exceptions were James Lee's *Career*, a biting documentary of theater life which showed the business' perennial self-absorption, and George Panetta's comedy *Comic Strip*. Panetta was an original writer, and the play had a good run at the Barbizon-Plaza in 1958.

The existence of off-Broadway made possible the revival of Irish drama in New York. The interpretation of Irish literature was attempted by a number of producers but by none more successfully than Paul Shyre in his O'Casey readings and the Irish Players, formed in the mid-1950's by Helena Carroll and Dermot McNamara. Ireland had produced some of the greatest playwrights of the century; the policy of the Irish Players was to do them faithfully in New York, a city strangely inhospitable to Irish work. Looking back through the record books, Carroll and McNamara found that no Irish play had run longer than six weeks in New York since *The White Steed* by Paul Vincent Carroll, Helena's father, in 1939.

The Irish Players got their start in a Jewish synagogue, the large Labor Temple on Fourteenth Street at Second Avenue, and to their own surprise became a success from the moment they opened the doors. They had picked Helena's father's *Shadow and Substance* partly for its familiarity and special meaning to them. There were parts for both of them

—Helena, with her dark hair and her husky Irish-Scottish brogue, making a wondering Brigid, the canon's maid in the play, and Dermot playing a rough neighborhood boy. Both had behind them considerable repertorial experience in Ireland, England, and Scotland. They had come to this country with the Dublin Players and stayed. Naturally a good deal of Irish sentiment was going for them, especially in the East Side Irish pubs that were kept fully informed of their plans. To raise front money to open in the temple, McNamara and Carroll prepared a souvenir program. In search of ads one afternoon they set out on foot starting at Forty-second Street. Helena took Third Avenue, and Dermot took Lexington, and they stopped in every Irish pub along the way. Not only did bartenders and proprietors buy ads, but unasked customers contributed also, ordering rounds of drinks to speed the actor-salesmen on their way. The two met finally at a prearranged point on Eighty-sixth Street and saluted each other unsteadily. The campaign was so pleasantly productive they later repeated it in Queens and the Bronx.

Shadow and Substance dealt with contrasting manifestations of religious spirit—on the one hand, the ascetic and scholarly canon living in a small town among clods and fools and, on the other, his young servant, Brigid, seized with the spirit and subject to beatific visions. Procuring props and costumes was an inconsequential matter to them, for they were able to call upon a neighboring Catholic church for cassocks and the needed monsignor's purple robe and crimson hat. For auditions and rehearsals they used an Irish ballroom, a commodity plenteously available. One of the actors auditioned for the canon was an intense, insistent young man not really old enough for the part. Everyone but McNamara wanted him, and McNamara was adamant. The young rejected actor was George C. Scott.

The play concerns the legend of St. Brigid. To discourage the men who were attracted to her, she "disfigures her loveliness" at Fanghart, her birthplace in Ireland. They opened

the play on St. Brigid's Day, February 2, 1955, and the
people poured in filling the 500 seats in the temple. Technically, no admission could be charged. They set up a table and
chair at the door manned by Helena's sister Kathleen who
cheerfully collected $3 "donations." Sometimes even $10
bills went into the box. "You might have thought we were
running guns for the IRA," Helena said. The venture became so unexpectedly successful the young managers felt they
ought to take the play off and give it a proper professional
mounting. This was not to come until four years later.

Answering a call for an Ibsen play on Second Avenue,
McNamara ran across a potential backer. He was a wholesale
meat dealer named Abraham Woursell, who, under the persuasion of McNamara and Carroll, was to forsake his love of
Ibsen and make possible their first professional venture, three
one-act plays by John Millington Synge for the small Theater East on Sixtieth Street just off Third Avenue. The subterranean little theater seated 128 under an oppressively low
ceiling. For an oddball theater, they reasoned, oddball plays.
On an investment of $5,000, they grossed $65,000 for the
305-performance run, which lasted until Christmas, 1957.
Helena was co-manager but was not in it because she was
playing on Broadway as the eccentric maid Doreen in *Separate Tables*. Besides McNamara, those in the cast included
Elspeth March, Gerry Jedd, Stephen Joyce, Rex O'Malley,
and Grania O'Malley. At the end of the run they toured the
plays to Toronto, where they did *The White Steed* as well.
Their next project was to be *The Playboy of the Western
World*.

Paul Shyre's skillful adaptations of O'Casey's autobiographical books were begun really as actors' vehicles. Shyre
was trained as an actor but was later to subordinate acting to
writing, directing, and producing. At the American Academy
of Dramatic Arts he was in the same class with Rae Allen,
with whom he was to work on many projects, Jason Robards,
and Colleen Dewhurst. (Shyre, Robards, and Dewhurst once

appeared in a play while they were still going to school—
Shaw's *Buoyant Billions* at the Twenty-third Street YMCA.
Their director was Harding Lemay, the playwright and author of the autobiographical *Inside, Looking Out*, who had
come out of the Neighborhood Playhouse school. Lemay was
strict with his charges and told them sternly they would
never amount to anything. "You don't work hard enough,"
he said. Their show, for all their promise, never pulled very
much of an audience.)

A couple of years after graduation Shyre, Rae Allen, and
Stuart Vaughan, the director, found themselves together in
an acting class with Harold Clurman. Shyre proposed that
they do something about O'Casey's autobiographical books
—Shyre adapting them, Rae acting in them, and Vaughan
directing them. Shyre went to work and produced a script
culled from O'Casey's writings which they rehearsed in Miss
Allen's apartment. In March, 1956, *I Knock at the Door*
opened on a snowy evening at the Ninety-second Street
YMHA on Lexington Avenue. Aline MacMahon and Staats
Cotsworth were both members of that initial cast. Luckily for
the project Brooks Atkinson was in the audience for the
Times. To his initial response, in part, Shyre owes his career
in the field of dramatic adaptation. In May at the Y they did
Pictures in the Hallway. This became the most popular of all
the adaptations and has been revived five times in fifteen
years, including a Broadway production in September, 1956,
at the old Playhouse, and most recently at the Forum in
Lincoln Center in 1971.

I Knock at the Door was also done once on Broadway, at
the Belasco with Aline MacMahon, and revived once in 1964.
The third of the O'Casey adaptations was *Drums Under the
Window*. More political, more intellectual, it had more action and less sentiment, less of the youthful poignancy of the
others. It was given a reading full of martial excitement and
Dublin street politics at the Cherry Lane in 1960 but was
never as popular as the others. O'Casey died at his home in

Torquay, England, on September 18, 1964, at the age of eighty-four. One month later, on October 11, Shyre combined sections of two of his adaptations for a special memorial evening at the Imperial Theater sponsored by the New York Shakespeare Festival. A larger than usual cast was assembled for the occasion. It consisted of Rae Allen, Eric Berry, Morris Carnovsky, Fred Clark, Staats Cotsworth, Mildred Dunnock, Lillian Gish, Julie Harris, Kevin McCarthy, Mildred Natwick, William Prince, Martin Sheen, and David Wayne.

Adaptations were by no means new to the theater, but Shyre discovered for himself the dynamics of the form and perfected it for O'Casey. With his actor's ear he sensed what would work on the stage and what was better left on the printed page. And very often material that read poorly could be made to play well. To preserve the form of a reading, the actors in all of Shyre's productions sat on stools in a row at the edge of the stage with lecterns before them holding the open script. The script purposely was always there to refer to. Even though an actor knew the lines by heart, the printed page kept in view held him to the reading format. restraining him from the temptation to overphysicalize, to veer into actual performance. Once the form was broken Shyre sensed he would be in trouble. The narrator set the scene, and the actors painted the pictures in their reading of O'Casey's vivid lines. In one adaptation Shyre takes a whip to the young O'Casey. Sitting three stools away from Shyre, the actor playing the boy flinches each time Shyre cracks his imaginary whip. The audience "see" an actual whipping even though the two separated actors are six feet apart. Had Shyre got up from his stool and acted out the scene in front of the boy, the illusion would have been destroyed.

Of the O'Casey plays proper, Shyre to date has done only two—*Purple Dust* at the Cherry Lane in 1956 and *Cock-A-Doodle Dandy* at the Carnegie Hall Playhouse in the season of 1958–59. Shyre picked *Purple Dust* as among the funniest of O'Casey's plays and one he thought American actors could do well. He co-produced it with Noel Behn, who operated the Cherry Lane, and it ran 430 performances—longer than any O'Casey play has run anywhere. In the cast were Kathleen Murray, Peter Falk, and Alvin Epstein. Shyre himself left the company four months into the run to visit O'Casey at his home in England. Shyre has many photographic mementos of that visit showing O'Casey in his various caps—he was addicted to hats—and puffing unsmiling on his pipe. O'Casey was grateful to Shyre for his success with his work and, suddenly, concerned about the actors who had to do it eight times a week. "Don't you think we should close it for a while and give the actors a rest?" he asked. He had no experience with off-Broadway managers.

For the Irish Players the most ambitious undertaking of all was *Playboy*. By this time financial backing came more readily to the successful actor-manager team of Helena Carroll and Dermot McNamara, and a new theater was quickly made available to them. The substantial red brick Stanford White building at 120 Madison Avenue which is now the American Academy of Dramatic Arts and was formerly a Catholic women's club had been taken over by a wealthy real estate man and made into a luxury arts complex called the Seven Arts Center. The Irish Players moved into the upstairs theater— there were two in the building—and named it the Tara. Helena Carroll took the role of Pegeen Mike Flaherty, the daughter of the pubkeeper on the wild west coast of Mayo, and Dermot was Christopher Mahon, the "last playboy" who has murdered his father. They opened the Synge masterpiece on May 8, 1958, to unanimous rave notices. The play ran nearly a year. A dozen years later the Lincoln Center Repertory Theater was to put on a respectable, well-acted, but plodding *Playboy*. Carroll and McNamara played it for all its malice and savagery. They brought out the off-center craziness in the play which made it work. The play was in their blood. Almost any other cast in the country, no matter how talented, would be falsely assembled, and even by 1971, long after the Irish Players had dissolved, enough of them were around to dare anyone else to do the *Playboy* as well.

The Irish Players followed up their stunning success of *Playboy* with the quieter, poetic *Shadow and Substance*, also at the Tara Theater. Paul Vincent Carroll had turned the play over to his acting daughter. Again the notices were excellent, and a run was assured. Among the backers were a Madison Avenue bus driver named John Horan and his wife, a Commodore Hotel waitress. During the afternoon run he would stop his bus at the theater's door, making his passengers wait, and step out to check the box office. At off hours he was content simply to call out the name of the theater and praise the play to the passengers as the bus went past the Seven Arts Center.

During the *Shadow* run they got a hurried call from David Susskind one day to do the play on television's *Play of the Week* when there was a sudden cancellation. Because of a rights problem, they offered instead to do *The White Steed*, beginning casting one morning at nine, moving into rehearsals by five the same day, hurrying down to the Tara in time for the evening curtain of *Shadow*. They finished the taping in six days.

One month after the opening of *Playboy*, Marjorie Barkentin, Padraic Colum, and Burgess Meredith triumphantly brought Joyce to the stage in their brilliant, phantasmagoric *Ulysses in Nighttown*. The dramatic version was taken from the heavily dialogued "Nighttown" section of the novel in which Stephen Dedalus, a son without a mother, and Leopold Bloom, a father without a son, wander through the whorehouse district of Dublin encountering each other and confronting the wildest images of their guilts and hallucinatory fears. *Ulysses* indeed had something in common with *Threepenny Opera* in its haunting evocation of the nightmarish underside of city life. *Ulysses* opened across town from *Threepenny* in the Rooftop Theater south of Houston

Street on the Lower East Side. The events of *Ulysses* all took place on the same day, June 16, 1904, which to Joyceans is kept hallow as Bloomsday.

Going alone to *Ulysses in Nighttown* on Bloomsday, 1958, when the very spirit of Joyce was in the air, I cannot recall so strong a feeling of immersion in a strange and compelling new milieu as on that night, or such a sense of dislocation, fleeing the late light of June which made still bright the broad East Side streets, taking the elevator up to the theater, and entering upon the hectic gloom of Joyce's swirling world. One had a sense of being seized, sucked up, by the poetic flow of Joyce's language. The balletic movement devised by Valerie Bettis made concrete images of Bloom's unconscious. The music, alternately dirgelike and gay, set the pace for the bewildering parade of Dubliners. Zero Mostel played Bloom in one of the great characterizations of his career. The dark, liquidly handsome Pauline Flanagan was his errant wife, Molly. Beatrice Arthur played the fleshy whoremistress, Bella Cohen, and Robert Brown was the young Stephen Dedalus. Beside the narrators, sixteen actors played sixty-six roles. Mostel played Bloom for all his sad vulnerability, his humiliations, his pathetic temptations, and his exultant dreams. It was an hypnotic and unforgettable production—the most fully realized attempt in off-Broadway history to put a great novel onstage, true to its essential spirit, showing its chief characters in the flesh.

As for the Irish Players, they were not again to match the excellence of *Playboy* and *Shadow*, and they were foreclosed from even attempting O'Casey. In the late 1950's O'Casey refused to give his plays to anyone Irish. A bitter fight with the Dublin Festival had ensued after *Bishop's Bonfire* and *Drums of Father Ned*, and O'Casey wrote Carroll and McNamara caustically that he would not allow his plays to be done "by anyone who had the green name of the Irish Players." They were forced to turn to other work. The first was Donagh MacDonagh's *Happy as Larry*, for which Lucille

Lortel put up most of the money after giving the play a tryout at her White Barn Theater in Westport. But a series of disasters struck. In Westport one Friday, Felix Munso, a key member of the cast, got into a bitter argument with Miss Lortel, his hostess. Plates of lunch were being served around the swimming pool to all the actors—tuna fish sandwiches for the Catholic members of the cast, hot dogs for the others. By the time the platter reached Munso, who was Jewish, all the hot dogs were gone. Furious, he crushed the last remaining tuna fish sandwich in his fist and threw it into the pool where it spread out cloudily like the contents of a burst garbage bag. To appease the upset Miss Lortel, Munso was let out of the play, although he had been perfect in the role and somehow had caused the play's crazy humor to work. Just before opening, Miss Lortel relented, and they got Munso back for a few previews. He still held to his own grievance, however, and two days before the opening he telephoned to say he was out of it. Grudgingly his replacement consented to return in time for the opening, but, practically speaking, it was too late, and the play was a one-week disaster at the Martinique Theater. Their next play, *Sharon's Grave*, in November, 1961, was also a fiasco, and the Irish Players broke up nearly seven years after they began on St. Brigid's Day in the synagogue building on Fourteenth Street. In Carroll and Mc-Namara, off-Broadway lost that rare and rather old-fashioned combination, the actor-manager. They had optioned the scripts, raised the money, and produced the plays while at the same time acting in them and sometimes directing them themselves. In their own subsequent careers both kept alive the traditions of Irish drama, but in the late 1960's, like the pubs on Third Avenue, off-Broadway had moved somewhere else.

Five

The Period of Expansion 1959–1963

Significant changes came to off-Broadway at the end of the 1950's and in the beginning years of the 1960's. Off-Broadway developed its own sort of musical and produced long-running shows of surprising durability. One need only mention *The Fantasticks*. Off-Broadway turned to the topical revue and hard-hitting polemical plays. For the first time off-Broadway became the spawning ground for young new writers such as Edward Albee, Jack Richardson, Jack Gelber, Arthur L. Kopit, and Murray Schisgal, and the American platform for the European intellectuals Beckett, Ionesco, and Genet. Most significantly, off-Broadway gave voice to the earliest expression of black self-identity long before it erupted in militancy in the streets.

In the revues, in the concerns of the new writers, in the modes of thought of the foreign intellectuals, and in the emergence of a black theater, off-Broadway served as an advance post, a kind of intellectual lookout. In the terms of the sociologist, off-Broadway was prefigurative, anticipating the shape of things to come, heralding change rather than merely reacting to it, some years after the fact, in the manner of postfigurative Broadway. *The Connection* probed the scabrous surface of dope addiction with pitiless intensity long before the problem became a matter of national alarm. In its earlier days off-Broadway had been most successful in re-

(*Left*) Before Zero Mostel became a musical performer on Broadway he starred off-Broadway as Leopold Bloom in Padraic Colum's reconstruction of Joyce, *Ulysses in Nighttown,* in 1958.

(*Below*) One of off-Broadway's most remarkable actresses, Colleen Dewhurst, rehearsing as Lady Macbeth with Roy Poole as Macbeth for the New York Shakespeare Festival in August, 1957.

Terence McCarten

Morris Warman

Joseph Papp (at the right, with his arm upraised in a directorial gesture) surrounded by the company of *Henry V* on the temporary stage below Central Park's Belvedere Tower in 1960.

George C. Scott playing Shylock in *The Merchant of Venice,* the production that christened the New York Shakespeare Festival's 2,300-seat Delacorte Theater in Central Park in June, 1962.

George E. Joseph

Anne Meacham as Hedda Gabler in the David Ross revival of the Ibsen play at the Fourth Street Theater in November, 1960, when Miss Meacham rehearsed and opened in the part in just three days.

Irene Worth in the title role of Schiller's *Mary Stuart* in 1957, one of the earliest and greatest successes of the Phoenix Theater.

Friedman-Abeles

Kathleen Murray in a demure pose in the 1959 off-Broadway revival of *Leave It to Jane* by Jerome Kern, Guy Bolton, and P. G. Wodehouse.

June Havoc (at right) in the Phoenix production of Farquhar's *The Beaux' Stratagem* in 1959 with Patricia Falkenhain and David Kingwood.

Friedman-Abeles

claiming Broadway's mistakes and in reviving classics that
were anathema to commercial producers. Now, in some areas,
it began to move significantly out in front of Broadway.

Some of the first musicals were imitative. The revival of
On the Town in January, 1959, for example, was an attempt
to re-create within the limitations of off-Broadway a musical
success in the Broadway mold. The show, with its exuberant
view of New York, was the firstborn show of four remarkable
talents—Betty Comden and Adolph Green, Leonard Bernstein and Jerome Robbins, contemporaries, friends, and on-
and-off collaborators for many years. Bernstein's driving score
was the chief motive power for the show about three sailors
on a twenty-four-hour pass sampling the promising pleasures
of the big city. It had such lovely Comden and Green songs
as "Lonely Town" and "Lucky to Be Me." In its initial
Broadway production in 1944, it had the style of Robbins'
movement. If their show was to be revived, especially off-
Broadway, the authors wanted to make sure it would be
good. So they kept a close watch on the young producers,
Douglas S. Crawford and Nancy Nugent, a couple in their
late twenties from the Midwest. As director they picked Gerald Freedman, who had been assistant to Jerome Robbins for
Bells Are Ringing and for the just-opened London production of *West Side Story*. As choreographer they took a
chance on a young dancer named Joe Layton.

The talent was young and untried; the press agent at least
was an old hand—Richard Maney, the irascible dean of the
business who avoided all off-Broadway assignments because of
his disdain for lofts and cellars. But he was a friend of Nancy
Nugent's father, Elliott Nugent, and wanted to lend a hand to
the third generation of this theater family.

For the cast of *On the Town*, the producers and director
picked Harold Lang, Pat Carroll, and a pert dancer named
Wisa D'Orso. The theater they booked was far from Greenwich Village, on elegant Fifty-seventh Street, the Carnegie
Hall Playhouse, and the budget was an unheard-of $29,000.

Opening night was stylishly un-off-Broadway. The illustrious authors and their wives and husbands were all seated together in a front row, confident, but a little self-conscious. Once again the show proved to be a maker of talent. *On the Town* gave as big a boost to Joe Layton's career as it had done to those of Robbins and Comden and Green. Layton went on to work under George Abbott as choreographer for *Once Upon a Mattress.* That success led to *The Sound of Music,* after which, in surprisingly short order, he served in the double capacity of director and choreographer for Noel Coward's *Sail Away,* for Richard Rodgers' *No Strings* and *Two by Two,* and for *George M.* Later he was mastermind for the Barbra Streisand specials on television.

A week after *On the Town, Fashion* opened in an antique little theater, the Royal Playhouse on shabby East Fourth Street. Again New York in theme, this was a revival of Anna Cora Mowatt's 1845 satire on the elegance of New York society. Rated the first good American play in the textbooks, it is taught in college drama courses. Harp music accompanied the between-scenes singing of twelve songs of the period by Enid Markey, Will Geer (as an upstate farmer bumptiously out of place in New York drawing rooms), and others in the cast to give the show a perhaps dubious musical standing. As a nineteenth-century critic, Edgar Allan Poe had visited the play five nights in a row before pronouncing a favorable judgment. Off-Broadway, of course, was the only place where one could risk an old work such as *Fashion,* and the little upstairs playhouse with its decorated corrugated tin ceiling had precisely the right period feeling, an old-fashioned tin candy box holding a faded flower memento.

The first big off-Broadway musical success, aside from *The Threepenny Opera,* was *Leave It to Jane* in the late spring of 1959. It was an example not so much of artistic selection as improvised theater management. Uptown, on Broadway, management and production functions were wholly unrelated, but off-Broadway the separation was seldom practiced, and theater managers were accustomed to finding "the product" themselves. Joe Beruh and his partner, Philip Minor, had a ten-year lease on the Sheridan Square Playhouse, a prize off-Broadway property around the corner from Jack Delaney's Restaurant and the old Circle in the Square and directly across Seventh Avenue South from the Actors Playhouse, where *An Enemy of the People* was then playing. They leased the building with its square three-quarter stage from an Italian businesswoman in the Village who had refused repeated offers to buy. Their first show on the lease, *Bonds of Interest,* lasted only three weeks. The projected cycle of Arthur Laurents plays followed but was limited to the 105-performance run of *The Time of the Cuckoo* and the 102-performance run of *A Clearing in the Woods,* and Beruh and his partner were forced to hunt. Beruh, who had studied at Carnegie Tech in the late 1940's, remembered that George Ade's *The College Widow* had been surefire in school. Perhaps it could be turned into a musical. Searching the rights, he discovered to his surprise that it was already a musical. He had never heard of Jerome Kern's 1917 show *Leave It to Jane* with book by Guy Bolton and P. G. Wodehouse. Beruh now moved quickly. On Friday he got the score out of the library of Tams-Witmark, the music publishers, played it on Saturday, and on Monday decided to move into production. Kathleen Murray, who was married to Beruh, would play the title role of the campus queen. There was a brief delay when Kern's widow balked at granting permission. Bolton and Wodehouse, on the contrary, were all for it. Checking legalities with a Yale law professor, the hopeful producers discovered that one of the joint owners of copyrighted material could not hold out on the others so long as his financial interest was not jeopardized. While admiring Kern's score—it had such numbers as "Cleopatterer," "The Siren's Song," and the title song—Beruh and his colleagues were less enchanted with the Bolton-Wodehouse book, reread in the context of 1959, and Beruh and Larry Carra, the director, set about rewriting it, going back to the Ade original Beruh remembered so happily from schooldays. There were twenty-seven roles to be filled. Out of the company were to come some famous graduates. Patricia Brooks was in the chorus, as were George Segal and Lainie Kazan, who was later to understudy Barbra Streisand in *Funny Girl* and go on to become a supper club star. The show opened on May 25, normally a red-line time off-Broadway since slow hot-weather business closed most shows for the summer. It was not until a few years later, after *Leave It to Jane*, like *Summer and Smoke*, had proved its staying power through the hot months, that summer became a boom period off-Broadway. The show, capitalized for $14,000, was brought in $3,000 below budget. In the first struggling summer, owing to a large cast and high break-even, it went $81,000 into debt. Among the original backers was J. I. Rodale, the organic gardening enthusiast who made a lot of money publishing health periodicals and subsequently earned a perhaps unjust reputation as an eccentric, self-proclaimed playwright by attempting to advance his health theories in propagandistic plays such as *The Goose* (1960), which was essentially an antisugar tract. Rodale, years later, was to come into his own. Just at the time of his death, which came while taping a Dick Cavett show, he won respected recognition for his contribution to organic gardening theories in a lead piece in the Sunday New York *Times Magazine*. Now, however, Rodale earned the gratitude of his theatrical business partners by guaranteeing the summer's losses to keep *Leave It to Jane* going. The show survived, and by November Rodale was paid back. Mrs. Kern came to a performance and gave her blessing, allowing the producers to waive her royalties on slow weeks. Thanks to the faith that kept *Jane* open in its first perilous summer, the musical revival ran three years. The pattern of success followed by Beruh may have had a decisive influence on the future of *The Fantasticks*, which opened a year later, also in May, and faced similar difficulties getting through the first summer. Lore Noto, the producer of *The Fantasticks* came to Beruh for advice. Beruh told him to hang in for the losing months if he had faith in his show. At this distance it is staggering to contemplate how great a run was made possible by a small supportive investment to cover a few weeks of operating losses.

Now less than ever before did off-Broadway seem like a showcase theater for beginners or for actors who hadn't yet "made it" uptown, and more like a separate theater with its own identity. In the season of 1958–59 *Variety* estimated the total amount of investor money that had gone into the making of the period's seventy-six productions and came up for the first time with a total that exceeded $1,000,000. There were now some thirty off-Broadway theaters where only a handful existed a few years before, and off-Broadway was beginning regularly to send out its hardiest and most newsworthy productions on tours, usually limited to a few key cities or college towns having aware theater audiences. By this time *The New Yorker* had designated a special critic for off-Broadway. In 1961 Edith Oliver took over the post full time, an outspoken, perceptive, and fair critic and, best of all for off-Broadway, one of unflagging enthusiasm.

Off-Broadway had grown big enough both to draw fire and to sustain serious attack, as when the composer and sometime Broadway producer Jule Styne wrote in the Sunday drama section of the New York *Herald Tribune* (August 2, 1959) that while off-Broadway was to be congratulated for the talent it brought into the theater the quality of the productions was "deplorable" and the theaters didn't look like theaters. Joseph Beruh answered by citing such evidence of the increased professionalism of off-Broadway as the improvement in actors' wages (to a range of $40–$70 depending on how much a show grossed) and the availability of established stars to off-Broadway managements. Styne drew immediate answering fire. Off-Broadway was the alternative to the hollowness of Broadway's professionalism, which Styne celebrated

unquestioningly. Off-Broadway put a higher value on what
went into a theater than on the luxury of its appointments
and the comfort of its seats. Styne, to the off-Broadway es-
thete, with his belligerent contempt for amateurism, was the
epitome of the Broadway philistine.

Off-Broadway's first successful original musical was Rick
Besoyan's *Little Mary Sunshine*, which opened in November
at the Orpheum on Second Avenue, just below St. Marks
Place, and began a tradition of musical parody that runs like
an unending stream through the entire history of off-Broadway. Besoyan's heroine, the adopted daughter of Chief
Brown Bear, was faced with the government foreclosure of
the mortgage on her Colorado Inn. Besoyan, a singing coach
by profession, had forest rangers flanking finishing school
girls to chorus such songs as "Colorado Love Call" and
"Look for a Sky of Blue." It was a parody of the old operet-
tas of Strauss, Rudolf Friml, and Victor Herbert. He wrote
the book, the lyrics, and the music, and directed the show—
doing everything but tearing the tickets on the way in. Eileen
Brennan, an actress of rather ungainly charm, played the lead
with such knowing humor that she was next cast in a supporting role to Carol Channing in *Hello, Dolly!* Besoyan
made an attempt in 1963 to capitalize his off-Broadway success into a show for Broadway, *The Student Gypsy* or *The
Prince of Liederkranz*. Again he attempted everything but
producing, this time with disastrously opposite results.

Joseph Beruh had predicted that a lot of people would
lose money as a result of his success with *Leave It to Jane*. In
April, 1960, an off-Broadway producing office opened ex-
pressly to reclaim another Bolton-Wodehouse show, the 1926
Oh, Kay!, with its George Gershwin score and Ira Gershwin
lyrics, and proved Beruh right. Then, the next month, came
The Fantasticks, which made its own rules and continues to
break its own records.

To many people in the first-night audience, *The Fantasticks* seemed too slight and fragmentary a work, almost in-

complete, charming but not memorable. The idea, which was developed from *Romanesques* by Rostand, seemed simple and ingenuous: parents, secretly approving the match, purposely make difficulties, hoping that their favored children will fall in love. At the end of the show, so light in feeling was the evening, one was tempted to ask, "Is that it? Is that all?" But the appearance of sketchiness was altogether deceptive. The underlying structure, a play on the Romeo and Juliet theme, was as strong as steel. The elements of the show—boy and girl, opposing parents, interfering outsider, garden wall—were used in ritualistic relationship. *The Fantasticks* was the acting out of a deeply embedded fantasy.

The play actually was written in Texas. Tom Jones, Harvey Schmidt, and Word Baker, the librettist-lyricist, the composer, and the director, respectively, were students at the University of Texas in the late 1940's. Together they were responsible for one campus hit, *Mipsy Boo*. Success encouraged them to write a second, which became *The Fantasticks*. With this score in their suitcase, they came to New York in 1955 and began writing revue sketches for Julius Monk's Upstairs at the Downstairs, a nightclub that featured New York self-parody and satire. Harvey Schmidt, son of a Methodist minister and a talented artist, was a high-paid commercial illustrator until stage success deflected him. All the admired graphics for the show are his. He is also the author, with Robert Benton, of *The In and Out Book*, which came out in 1959.

In the summer of 1959, in a program of one-act plays put on at Barnard College in a theater program then presided over by Mildred Dunnock, they presented a short musical named *The Fantasticks*. In the audience was a would-be actor, sometime producer, and artist's agent named Lore Noto. Charmed by what he saw, he commissioned the authors to make their slight sketch into a full-length play. By the following spring the expanded show was ready and the money was raised—a total capitalization of $16,500. When opening night came, only $14,000 had been used. The cast consisted of Rita Gardner as the Girl, Kenneth Nelson as the Boy, Jerry Orbach as the Narrator (he had spent several years in *The Threepenny Opera* as the Streetsinger and Mack the Knife). Tom Jones appeared in the cast in disguise under the assumed name of Thomas Bruce.

Opening night, May 3, 1960, at the little theater on Sullivan Street passed pleasantly and smoothly, but no one present really suspected that a hit was in the making and that this quiet residential street just south of the roiling mainstream of Village life in Bleecker Street would soon become hallowed theatrical ground almost on a level with O'Neill's birthplace at the Provincetown or *Threepenny*'s home at the de Lys. The cast party was held afterward at the home of Ed Wittstein, who had designed the simple, serviceable platform set, and it was there that tears came to the eyes of Word Baker, the director, as he read out the first less than ecstatic notices. Thus, Walter Kerr in the *Tribune*: ". . . the business of stretching it out to cover two acts and twelve tunes means that here are not only sleepy passages but passages that cannot be too thoroughly anticipated. *The Fantasticks* does not hold its mannered head aloft for the full run of the book, or the somewhat better score. It attracts you, settles back a bit limply, wakes you up again and averages out a little less than satisfactory." Other notices were not especially good either, and the pros were soon advising Lore Noto to take into consideration the lateness of the season, the imminence of summer, and close at once, thereby saving his backers at least some of their money. "You know you can't make it," they said. Stubbornly Noto refused. The weeklies rewarded him with brighter notices. He began his own personal fight to keep the show open, taking to the streets like a sandwich-board man, carrying the lettered window card, with the title inked in Harvey Schmidt's angular script, wherever he went. The confidence of one or two old theater hands around the show, such as David Powers, the press agent, never faltered.

Theater people, such as producers Cheryl Crawford and Robert Fryer, were among the show's first supporters. The word of mouth was good. Joe Beruh's advice steeled Noto to see the dry summer out, although at one point he was forced to back his faith with almost all his savings. He sold part of his producer's share to keep going. Even on the slowest days Noto refused to "paper" the house: every customer a paying one. On principle he never passed out free tickets unless they would help the show.

Emerging from a curiously obscure background, Noto began, like so many producers, off-Broadway and Broadway, to operate as a loner. His upbringing conditioned him early in life not to accept a dependency role but to fend for himself, always consulting his own judgment, never placing too much reliance on the evaluations of others not so deeply interested as himself. Born in New York of Italian-American parents and motherless at three, Noto and two brothers, one older, one younger, were brought up in the Brooklyn Home for Children. Their father owned and ran a poolroom, which wholly absorbed his time. Sent home at sixteen, they discovered their father's business occupation for the first time. Noto was a moody, talented boy. He sang soprano in an Episcopal choir and went to the High School of Industrial Arts. In his spare time he visited the movies. His father was ambitious for Lore, his favorite and most promising son. He wanted him to become a lawyer. Noto himself aspired to the actor's life. Differences between father and son led to clashes and arguments, and Lore always carried, in the words of one of the songs from the show, "the hurt that saves the heart from hollow." He found work in commercial art, joined the Merchant Marine in the Second World War, and was seriously wounded in Antwerp by a V-2 rocket explosion. After the war he moved into the hazardous world of off-Broadway.

Noto, of course, has been amply repaid for his faith in *The Fantasticks*. In the good years he was earning $75,000 to $80,000 from the show, counting subsidiary income derived from album sales, touring companies, and foreign rights in more than fifty countries. In nearly twelve years the show had grossed more than $3,000,000 on Sullivan Street and played to more than half a million in New York alone. In 1965 Noto's dream was to put Marjorie Kinnan Rawlings' *The Yearling* on stage as a Broadway musical. A lot of his Sullivan Street profits went into the project—a three-performance failure. Today Noto is virtually retired. He lives with his family in Forest Hills, spends his afternoons at the West Side Tennis Club, and comes into Manhattan in the evening to do the bookkeeping on the show in his Times Square office and, usually alone, take in the new plays. At the end of the evening he has supper at Downey's and then goes next door into McGirr's basement to play pool among some of the city's roughest characters often until the 4 A.M. closing time. Then he heads home for Forest Hills on the E train.

Tom Jones was thirty-two at the time *The Fantasticks* opened, Harvey Schmidt two years his junior. They, too, have had their aborted projects. Projecting a second show directly after *The Fantasticks*, they hoped to do a musical version of *Roadside* by Lynn Riggs, whose *Green Grow the Lilacs* had become *Oklahoma!* Riggs heard the score before he died and liked it, but rights problems developed after his death. Jones and Schmidt went on to write *110 in the Shade*, based on *The Rainmaker; I Do! I Do!*, based on *The Fourposter*; and *Celebration*, an original story. In their own studio-theater west of Times Square they experimented with new material before small invited audiences. Meanwhile, *The Fantasticks* went on and on.

The season brought in retrospect to a triumphant close by *The Fantasticks* had been one of intense activity but also one of extensive failure. The ratio of off-Broadway to Broadway shows had now widened to two to one, with 100 plays being put on in theaters of under 300 in capacity as opposed to 55 on Broadway, most of them, of course, financial failures. Revivals were still the greater part of the product. Although off-Broadway, in the words of Molly Kazan, was still "a set of economic conditions which made sense," all costs had gone up—set construction, costumes, salaries—and now production budgets for relatively simple shows required an outlay of between $12,500 and $15,000. By and large the backing came from close to home. Off-Broadway investors belonged to three main categories: friends of the producer, friends of the author, and friends of the director.

To the older off-Broadway hand, the influx of new "one-shot" producers imitative of Broadway's commercialism was disquieting, especially to one so immersed in the little theater mystique as Jose Quintero, who saw off-Broadway in terms of continuity, commitment, and the interconnectedness of artists bound together in permanent companies. The upstart producers, the opportunists, the vanity producers were flooding in at an alarming rate to undermine the foundations of off-Broadway and to threaten with further diffusion an audience perhaps already spread tenuously thin.

In late 1961 Walter Kerr would write: "There is an enormous danger, now that off-Broadway activity has mushroomed so, of drowning what is good in the tidal wave of the preposterously bad. Off-Broadway is far too valuable to be overrun by the amateurs who want to get into the act. If the *bête noir* of Broadway is its openness to commercialism, the specter that now threatens off-Broadway is its openness to sheer opportunism."

Complaints of vanity productions multiplied, but the amateur spirit of off-Broadway and its countercommercialism, which derived from George Cram Cook, Susan Glaspell, and the Provincetown Players, had its eloquent defenders. The late actress Gerry Jedd argued the uses of vanity: "The line between vanity and resourcefulness or initiative is such a slight one. The same motives can only be judged by success or failure. The early efforts of Carmen Capalbo and Judith

Malina and Julian Beck at the Cherry Lane were judged by some at the time to be vanity productions. It's only in perspective that they become the first step in careers of merit. The gall to perform or produce seems to me to be compounded of vanity, until somebody says that the performers or producers are not just empty conceits."

It was not by accident that in the early 1960's off-Broadway took to revues. Psychological, sociological, and increasingly political in content, they were a straw in the wind of our coming discontent. In the later years of the decade an unaccustomed mood of self-examination and self-criticism was to develop into a severe anxiety neurosis. An early sign of disenchantment, the satirical revue attacked our self-satisfaction and self-esteem while the expanding civil rights movement uncovered the repressed prejudices of Americans and exposed injustice and inhumanity, while violence surfaced in riots, in the assassinations, and in police efforts to suppress a rising discontent, while the deepening involvement in Vietnam began to undermine confidence in the military and in the official conduct of a hated war. Small stages were the creeks and inlets into which, at first silently, the tide of disenchantment came flooding in.

The revue form permitted a directness of comment and expression the early 1960's seemed to demand. The Kennedys brought an unexpected contemporaneity into national politics. A new generation "born in this century" had assumed power. Small children the age of one's own were running about the White House. Losing their remoteness, state affairs for once seemed almost accessible to the present writing and acting generation and therefore material for stage comment. What chiefly distinguished the new intimate off-Broadway revue from the brashness of the comedy sketches put on uptown was the growing fearlessness of its political comment.

Chicago, the "second city," had the odd function of supplying New York with the preponderance of its revue talent—Nichols and May, Barbara Harris, Paul Sills, Theodore J.

Flicker, and many others. Perhaps, geographically, this phenomenon was not so curious. The new kind of revue depended very largely on the personal expression and individual
viewpoint of the performer, both as a self-watcher and as a
nation-watcher, and Chicago, in the middle of the country, in
its own cultural wasteland, stimulated this new kind of personal satirical outcry. Nichols and May, who were the Adam
and Eve of the new revue, met in Chicago and first worked
together in 1955 at David Shepherd's Compass Theater, a
nightclub featuring clever young performers who improvised
scenes, where the first signs of an irritated frustration with
the Establishment erupted in the impatience of a man in a
telephone booth trying to get his dime back. Two non-Chi-
cago revues that made an impression were the *Billy Barnes
Revue* (from Los Angeles) at the York Playhouse in June,
1959, and Jerry Herman's *Parade* at the Players Theater in
January, 1960. Both were more in the mold of the old
Broadway revue. More typical of this period of off-Broadway
history was *The Premise,* which opened in a remodeled hof-
brau just off Washington Square, a blood relative of the
Compass in Chicago and the Crystal Palace in St. Louis
(where the Compass moved in 1957 after its operations in
Chicago shut down) and a more distant derivative of German coffeehouse theater of the 1930's between the wars. The
title stated one of the ground rules—the audience would
suggest some premise for a scene which the actors would
thereupon act out, without premeditation or rehearsal. Dramatically, this sort of revue arose out of a generalized interest
in improvisational acting that was highly developed in this
period. It expressed the need of the improvisationally trained
actor to make his own comment in his own way. Any present-day social or moral situation of topical interest that
seemed susceptible to satirical comment was material for the
revue, even if it was as marginal a concern as Joan Darling's
complaint of having caught measles from a mechanical doll.
Considering the tolerance threshold for humor of succeeding

administrations, one marvels at the audacity of revue skits of that period, including the one that advanced the monstrous suggestion that Caroline Kennedy, surprised by a photographer in her mother's shoes in the President's office, was the Kennedy who was actually running the country. The First Family, accustomed to dealing in the currency of the joke, were perfectly capable of taking such barbs from the Second City people in stride.

The Second City was an on-Broadway revue first, but later editions came more naturally to off-Broadway, and thus *Alarums and Excursions* in 1962. Talent of a high order could be discovered in the smallest sketches—Alan Arkin bent into the shape of a New York pretzel vendor, for example. Arkin was a talent of great flexibility, with an aptitude for expressing self-bafflement and a whining distrust of life. He was one of the "discoveries" to come out of the revues.

The uneasiness over Vietnam infiltrated the script, and in *Alarums*, while American involvement was still in the form of "technical assistants," a hapless American Army colonel declared, "I have on my hands an Army of pacifists." To the cabaret performer—and such names as Anthony Holland, Eugene Troobnick, and Howard Alk belong to this period—Vietnam was never the right war. The Kennedys, Castro, Khrushchev, Red China, and the UN were all comment-worthy, along with the population explosion, a worrisome phenomenon as yet in those days to be invested with the sinister ecological implications to come.

When one revue ran out of steam, performers and titles would change, although the essential spirit and method of attack would remain the same, whether it was *To the Water Tower, New Show at the Premise, Put It in Writing, The Living Premise,* or *When the Owl Screams,* all of them coming in 1963. In June of that year a black coloration pervaded *The Living Premise,* staged by Theodore J. Flicker as the *Premise* idea became three years old. Blacks outnumbered whites in the cast three to two. The new racial sophistication was such that a Negro couple was shown being nice to their Jewish maid and the romance of a black girl and a white boy cooled, in a kind of interracial *Fantasticks* in reverse, when their parents beamed approval. Players in the darker *Premise* were Godfrey Cambridge, Al Freeman, Jr., and Diana Sands, who earlier figured in the cast of the short-lived revue *Another Evening with Harry Stoones* in October, 1961, along with a then little-known performer, Barbra Streisand.

The English counterparts of this sort of social satire were the Broadway revues *At the Drop of a Hat* and *Beyond the Fringe,* imported by Alexander H. Cohen. Off-Broadway, they found a more pointed political expression in *The Establishment,* written by Peter Cook, one of *Beyond the Fringe's* original four, and put on by the Strollers Theater Club in the remodeled El Morocco nightclub on East Fifty-fourth Street. Here mockery of British politicians and officialdom went to lengths of irreverence not yet attempted by any American group. *MacBird!* was yet to come.

The revue was a collective enterprise, although the individual performer's special personality or viewpoint often stood out. As Comden and Green had discovered in 1958 in putting together their team revue at the Cherry Lane, *A Party with Betty Comden and Adolph Green,* which was later moved to the Golden Theater on Broadway under the auspices of the Theater Guild, off-Broadway, with its more informal, unpressurized atmosphere and its somewhat higher threshold of pain where the critics were concerned, was the ideal break-in place for the solo performer or the team testing new material. Although Hal Holbrook had played colleges and libraries and special engagements, he made his first appearance in New York as Mark Twain at the Forty-first Street Theater on April 6, 1959. Earlier that year John Gielgud had held a Broadway audience spellbound for two hours from the stage of the Forty-sixth Street Theater, normally reserved for musicals, with his flawless recitation of Shakespeare in *Ages of Man*. Audiences had been and were to be treated in seasons to come to all sorts of readings, staged biographies, and skillful impersonations. Emlyn Williams as Dickens, Martin Gabel as Douglas in the Lincoln-Douglas debates, Michael McLiammoir as Oscar Wilde, Bramwell Fletcher and Max Adrian as Shaw, Dorothy Stickney reading Edna St. Vincent Millay, James Whitmore as Walt Whitman and Will Rogers. None of them was more comfortably or convincingly suited to his part than Holbrook as Twain. He was thirty-four at the time, an actor with no great roles to his credit and no name, but he had mastered this one part to the finest detail of dress, accent, gesture, posture, pause, and lecture hall timing. In three hours of preperformance preparation at the makeup mirror—on a matinee day Holbrook spent eleven hours in the theater—the youthful-looking Holbrook wrote into his own features the lifelines of Twain's advanced age and mischievous humor. Secure in the white wig and drooping mustache, in Twain's summery white linen suit, with his gold watch chain spangled across his vest, Holbrook moved laboriously in Twain's lecture platform shuffle, pausing in mid-joke to strike a safety match to his cigar, allowing for one or two misfires while the joke advanced to its punch line, taking his first puffs as the laughter subsided. The timing was uncanny, the control of audience reaction absolutely sure. The material—the stories, anecdotes, jokes, personal idiosyncrasy, homespun philosophy, and homily— was endlessly rich, permitting Holbrook to vary his program from night to night, allowing for variety in his own routine, and assuring a very high level of moment-to-moment entertainment that was timeless in its appeal. Holbrook's living biography of Twain was a masterful personal achievement.

In its choice of material off-Broadway revealed a political awareness and sensitivity far more developed than Broadway's. In February, 1959, Gene Frankel directed a production of Arthur Miller's adaptation of Ibsen's *An Enemy of the*

People that raised moral questions of individual responsibility for actions that affect the general well-being—questions that are at the root of every citizen effort today to make giant corporations accountable for the daily environmental erosion they cause. In Ibsen's play the town's prosperity and the mayor's political power depended on the commercial use of baths which were discovered by Dr. Stockmann, the mayor's brother, to be polluted. Ibsen examines the web of commitments that inevitably defeat the good intentions of one man standing alone on principle. The play, ten years ahead of modern events, defined a dilemma that predictably will extend into the 1970's as far as we can see.

In the fall serious examination of the American political and social tradition was proposed in a production of Robert Penn Warren's *All the King's Men* at the East Seventy-fourth Street Theater and in Paul Shyre's adaptation of Dos Passos' *U.S.A.* at the Martinique. *All the King's Men* with Clifton James giving a powerful reading of the corrupt and earthy Willie Stark was Penn Warren's telling of the Huey Long story (read George Wallace for today). Warren put out of his mind a previous dramatic adaptation, also based on his novel, and the film and wrote this play without reference to the earlier texts, as if starting from scratch with only the characterizations lodged firmly in his head. From Dos Passos' massive documentary novel, Shyre took pieces that would stand by themselves but would have some bearing on recent events, and he liked to think of the strung-together vignettes as a dramatic vaudeville show. Six performers, including Sada Thompson (giving an arresting account of Isadora Duncan's auto accident), Rae Allen, and Salome Jens, played the parts of thirty. Based on the "living newspaper" dramatic form, the show, with songs of the period on tape integrated into the newsreels, moved at the quickstep pace of a topical revue.

But it was *The Connection*, which had opened in June at the Living Theater, with its mercilessly realistic examination of the drug culture, that brought the theater of social and political meaning joltingly into the present. Jack Gelber's disquieting piece has to be examined in the context of the continuing work and involvement of the Living Theater, which will come later.

Early 1960 brought Edward Albee into the American theater (he was already somewhat known in Germany) with *The Zoo Story,* and another new playwright of promise, Jack Richardson, showed up at the Downtown with a play entitled *The Prodigal.* Fond as the theater is of claiming young new American writers, of greater historical significance in 1960 was the appearance here of Genet, first with *The Balcony* at the Circle in the Square and second, a year later, with *The Blacks* at the St. Marks Playhouse, two of the most significant productions in the twenty years of off-Broadway. Both were immensely complex plays, poetic in language, filled with imagery, ritualistic in construction and concerned with Genet's mirror view of reality, subject and reflection being interchangeable and indistinguishable from each other. Thus, the authority figures in Madame Irma's House of Illusions in *The Balcony* discover for themselves a heightened sense of identity in the deferential hands of whores. The Negroes in *The Blacks* find their self-definition in the eyes of other Negroes playing whites sitting in judgment over them. Discarding the linear plotting of conventional drama, Genet's two plays moved in circular paths, like a ball on a tether pole first being wound in one direction, then unwound, and rewound in the other. *The Balcony* opens with the figure of a bishop in miter and cope closeted with a young girl penitent whose sins invoke the forgiveness which sanctifies him; a judge in robes and an executioner with a girl thief whose crimes define the power of judicial office; and a general with a girl acting as his prancing horse to assure him of a splendid heroic immortality. Through the walls of this grand brothel the sounds of gunfire penetrate. A revolution is under way outside; the real world intrudes on the illusory. The grandly attired clients are revealed to be quite ordinary townfolk—a gasman, a plumber, a waiter. Outside, the revolution succeeds. The queen is dethroned and the revolutionaries invade the brothel itself; Madame Irma is installed as queen; the clients become state functionaries. Their fantasy roles having become real, they find they must return to their brothel world. At the end the queen reverts to the role of Madame Irma and begins to prepare the ritual rooms where her visitors are entertained once again, each to his own taste and necessity, as in the beginning. The play has come full circle.

It has been suggested by Kenneth Tynan and other critics that Genet may have had an easier time setting up the hypotheses of his play than in working them out. Jose Quintero considered *The Balcony* his most difficult directorial task at Circle in the Square. It is no derogation of his work to suggest, as have some critics, that he may not have understood the play fully or grasped all the multiple meanings Genet apparently intended. Certainly Quintero was notably more successful directing the opening expository scenes, invoking the reality of a symbolic brothel, than in directing the scenes of resolution at the end. The dizzying alternations of realities in the last half of the play teased the audience to accept now the painted backdrop of the play as the living foreground, now the solid foreground as the insubstantial backdrop.

The brilliance of the physical production heightened the peculiar sense of dislocation that is part of Genet's genius as a dramatist. Physically, David Hays' set, whose main elements were movable crystal chandeliers, was hung from a network of wires above the Circle's rectangular arena stage. In Patricia Zipprodt's costumes the authority figures were clothed in padded robes and wore ten-inch lifts that emphasized not so much their grandeur as their pathetic littleness on resuming their normal identities and leaving the House of Illusions. The women were all figures of remarkable and mysterious sensuality—Nancy Marchand playing a tall, severe Irma; Betty Miller as her pretty, trusted favorite, Carmen; Grayson Hall as an abject penitent; Sylvia Miles as a voluptuous thief; the long-legged Salome Jens as a provocative mount with leather haunches and a nylon spray tail that shook the air as her "nervous legs and well-shod hooves" went into a spirited gallop around the general's favorite battlefield. (Quite possibly the whole "leather look" in fashions in recent years may have derived from the use of the leather corselets and boots designed by Miss Zipprodt.)

Genet was concerned not so much with the lusts of the flesh as with the insane longings of the mind. He had invented a brilliant sexual metaphor to express the craving for power, the desire for conquest or spiritual dominance, and the need for self-deception that govern each person's existence. As the Circle's tenth anniversary production, *The Balcony* opened on March 3, 1960, the night, as it happened, of a major snowstorm which had begun gently as the opening-night audience assembled on Bleecker Street and gathered momentum, unknown to the audience, during the performance. When the strange play was over, the audience, released from the nightmare of Genet's unholy imagination, reentered a city transformed by the storm. The streets were deep in snow. Traffic moved only on the traveled avenues, and then only intermittently—a lone cab with clanking chains passing across one's blurred vision every five minutes or so. The temperature dropped below 20. It was the worst snowstorm in five years in New York. Thirteen inches were to fall before the night was over. But the unseasonable weather that ushered in *The Balcony* was no hindrance to its success. There was never a serious question of whether it would run, only how long it would run. Here, the business insight of Theodore Mann was decisive. To mount *The Balcony*, the Circle had accepted Lucille Lortel, of the de Lys, as a partner. At an early sign of slowing business she was in favor of closing. Mann, regarding the Genet play as the Circle's most important production to date, was convinced that if the show could get through its first Christmas season, when business, especially off-Broadway, traditionally was at a near standstill, then the show would gain enough momentum to get through the following summer and have another whole year's run. Mann's business judgment was confirmed. *The Balcony* run extended to 672 performances. A play's influence increases in relation to its longevity. *The Balcony* would not so prominently overhang the historical perspectives of off-Broadway had not Mann so adroitly laid the business and promotional foundations.

As the first Genet play to be produced in America, *The Balcony* prepared the way for *The Blacks*, which opened on May 4, 1961, at the St. Marks Playhouse on Second Avenue, which was reached either by climbing a steep flight of stairs off the street or by entering a small elevator. The theater physically assumed a special importance. It was to take its personality from this production and become a "black" theater off-Broadway. The narrow foyer hall led into a theater laid out in arena fashion with rows of seats rising sharply on the right and the open stage to the left. Against a backdrop of hanging lengths of rope, a curving ramp led to an upper platform where Negro actors in menacing-looking white masks arranged themselves in the formal attitudes of a court consisting of a queen, a judge, a governor, a missionary, and a valet. As the play unfolded, they appeared to be judging a group of Negroes below for the murder of a white woman, ritualistically represented by a black actor in a hideously smiling apple-cheeked chalk-white mask. By means of these devices Genet had set up the same sort of illusory world as he created in the opening scenes of *The Balcony*. Just as the distant revolution materialized in *The Balcony*, reality breaks through in *The Blacks* in the form of an execution which has taken place offstage while the play has been under way—not of a white person but of a black traitor to an unspecified movement. The event suddenly jars the action of the play into the present tense. The character Newport News announces the deed: "He has paid, we shall have to get used to the responsibility of executing our own traitors." As the news is brought in breathlessly through the unseen underbrush, the ritualistic whites remove their masks. Their black faces are revealed. Dropping their white identities, they abruptly discard their earlier playacting to consider the "actual" execution that has taken place offstage. But as the play draws to a close, they are made once again to resume their ritualistic white roles of the queen and her court. Whites and blacks exchange places on the spiral ramp. The judges become the judged. In a final series of ritualistic murders the white court pays with their lives and the blacks prevail. "One can't hold all of Africa responsible for the death of a white woman," the judge had said earlier in the play. In the closing scene, with the "whites" heaped into a funeral pyre, this thought returns like a mocking echo.

Genet himself described the origins of this play: "One evening an actor asked me to write a play for an all-black cast. But what exactly is a black? First of all, what's his color?" The mysterious, evanescent quality of personal identity was Genet's first concern. Removed to America, where this question in relation to color was just beginning to surface in the national consciousness, the play assumed quite a different importance. Coming in the spring of 1961, *The Blacks* opened a little more than a year after the first lunch-counter sit-ins in Greensboro, North Carolina, at the very beginning of the Movement. The year 1961 was the year of freedom rides, of desegregated bus stations, of voter registration drives in the South. And yet the play itself spoke in more revolutionary terms than anything yet contemplated within the Movement, and the black actors in their roles adopted an overt militancy.

The key figure in the American production of *The Blacks* was the director Gene Frankel, who in 1961 was no stranger to black theater, although it was not then thought of in such terms. Frankel had directed *They Shall Not Die* about the

Scottsboro case in 1949 and *Nat Turner*, about the early abortive slave rebellion, at the People's Drama Playhouse in 1950 with Frank Silvera and Lloyd Richards in the cast. Lorraine Hansberry, whose first play, *A Raisin in the Sun*, Richards was to direct on Broadway, came again and again to *Nat Turner*—sixteen times in all by Frankel's count. Later she was so affected by *The Blacks*, two seasons after *A Raisin*, that she wrote a six-page review of it for the *Village Voice* in which she called Genet "a white Negro," a term Ralph Ellison had applied to Norman Mailer. Mailer used the term as the take-off point for his famous essay on "the hipster," "The White Negro," reprinted in his *Advertisements For Myself* (1959), and he also wrote in the *Voice* welcoming Genet into the ranks. Hansberry's *Les Blancs*, produced posthumously in 1970, in its African setting was a conscious echo of *The Blacks*.

One of off-Broadway's most intellectually aware directors, Frankel was drawn to social themes while maintaining a home base in an acting studio on Macdougal Street. He learned about Genet on a trip to Europe and had not at that time seen the Circle's production of *The Balcony*. At the off-Broadway Rooftop Theater in the season of 1956–57 he had directed a stunning *Volpone* which won awards. When *The Balcony* opened, he was absorbed in a stylized revival of Sophie Treadwell's 1928 play *Machinal* about the Snyder-Gray murder trial. In this play, as later in *The Blacks*, Frankel demonstrated a talent for working a visual logic into his production with his designer, letting the space provided determine the form, and allowing the physical mechanism to operate as balance wheel for the action, as the circular ramp designed by Kim E. Swados did for *The Blacks*. For *Machinal*, which was played on a series of platforms on the very narrow stage of the Gate Theater, Frankel and the designer Ballou heightened the sense of menace by having black-garbed scene shifters in harlequin masks dart in from the wings.

Frankel was intrigued by improvisational acting techniques as a means of reestablishing actor-audience contact. After *Machinal* he was given an unsolicited Ford grant to go abroad. He used it to study the national theaters of London, Paris, and East Berlin. In East Berlin he saw Helene Weigel's Berliner Ensemble production of *Mother Courage*—in his opinion one of the finest productions of all time. Later in Paris when Frankel told Stefan Brecht he considered his father the greatest of modern playwrights, Stefan answered, "There's one better—Genet." It was then that Frankel looked into *The Blacks*.

Rights to *The Blacks* in the United States were held by Geraldine Lust. Roger Blin had directed a brilliant Paris production, and Miss Lust was determined to have him direct the play in New York. Frankel argued his one great advantage over the European: as an American he understood American Negro actors. No one off-Broadway had worked so closely with more black actors than Frankel. When Blin bowed out because of other commitments, Miss Lust turned to Frankel, and now the production began to coalesce around him. Frankel approached Sidney Bernstein as a producing partner. An accountant strongly attracted to social theater, Bernstein had co-produced *Nat Turner* with Frankel. He was married to a Negro actress, Brunette Bernstein, who had been Lorraine Hansberry's theater teacher in Chicago. There were some heavy initial expenses to be met—an advance of $3,000 required by the author and a reimbursement of $4,500 to Miss Lust. Two other co-producers came in—George Edgar, who put up $18,500 of the total $31,000 capitalization, and Andre Gregory, who was later to make his reputation as an independent producer-director. When they decided on the St. Marks Playhouse because of its arena stage and necessary height, the additional expense of moving a previously booked De Ghelderode play to another house had to be met. It took truckloads to provide all the lengths of hanging rope they specified for a backdrop. Despite all these extras, *The Blacks* was brought in $8,000 under budget.

Frankel knew all the working Negro actors in New York. A sense of Negritude, he felt, was essential to the play, and he ruled out an actor if there was a "trace of whiteness" in him. As a kind of litmus paper test of color awareness, auditioning actors were put through a series of special exercises and improvisations. But Frankel was not to remain in unchallenged control of the production, and his authority, despite his record, was to be tested many times in stormy rehearsals, interrupted as they were by angry cast meetings sometimes lasting until early morning. Always in these discussions the two primary concerns of the actors, aired again and again, were the whiteness of the author and the whiteness of the director. The play, with its explosively provocative attitude on color, had aroused the interest and concern of the Negro cultural community. James Baldwin and Ossie Davis were present at some of the cast meetings. Frankel himself sometimes attended and sometimes was excluded. The cast numbered such outspoken black actors as Charles Gordone, who was later to write the Pulitzer Prize drama *No Place to Be Somebody*, James Earl Jones, Cicely Tyson, Godfrey Cambridge, Louis Gossett, Roscoe Lee Browne, and Cynthia Belgrave. Frankel told them, "It's perfectly all right for you to have your own meetings, and I think you should, but when it becomes a question of the work and the future of the work, I think I should be there." Baldwin supported Frankel in this position.

The cast worried particularly about the ending of the play, although a Negro victory is celebrated. Was it right? Was it good for the cause? Genet's intellectual involutions baffled them, and they were never confident of having a sure grasp of his meaning. Frankel was less concerned about textual ambiguities. The mysteries of the play were its virtue.

Rehearsals were periods of sometimes bruising confrontations between the black cast and the white director. To Frankel, again, this was precisely the point of the American production—the materialization of his theories of actor interacting with audience, blacks for the first time on the stage facing whites in the audience and making nakedly plain the resentment and hatred they felt. In rehearsal he set himself up as the surrogate audience. He was a sounding board off which they could bounce their hatreds and resentments. He told the cast, "Everything you think about me and everything you think I think about you is right. No matter what you think, it's right." To Frankel, *The Blacks* was a "hate-therapy" play.

The rehearsal effort took its personal toll. Frankel's wife of six years worked at his side as his assistant, but personal differences flared up, and their divorce came as a direct outcome of Frankel's complete absorption in the project. "I never knew you could be so implacable," she told him, "and it scares me." In truth Frankel was the beleaguered minority, fighting two battles, his own and the play's, and his own victory was in the play's triumph.

Genet, perhaps after his experiences with the London production, which he attempted to stop, professed no interest in the American *Blacks*, although his personal representative, Bernard Frechtman, translator and brilliant interpreter of Genet and Sartre, was on hand as his representative and occasionally relayed Genet's request for a curtain to be drawn (not raised) which Frankel and his associates had ruled out. Even after its successful opening, even into the long run, Frankel had no indication of Genet's approval of the production. Genet never came to see it. Frankel subsequently spoke to him only once in Paris and was treated rudely. Genet's sole question was, "How come you have forty percent of the movie rights?" Nor was Genet satisfied with Frankel's explanation of the percentage as a standard contract provision.

In any case, almost from the moment of rehearsal, in an emotional sense the American production belonged more to the black actors, who were expressing their own cause through their roles and releasing genuine emotion in the guise of projecting a character's hidden feelings, than it belonged to the playwright or the director or the producers.

Richard N. Coe, the critic who edited *The Theater of Jean Genet: A Casebook* (Grove Press, 1970), wrote, "In 1959, a 'political play' was a play which *discussed* politics; it was not (save in the marginal sense of Brecht) a political act in itself." For the black intellectual, *The Blacks* served a predictive political function, even to the use of its title as the name preferred by Negroes to describe their difference. In a larger sense the bloody retributive justice preached by the play foreshadowed the future thrust of the movement. A speech uttered by Roscoe Lee Browne as Archibald, whose continual disclaimers that the audience is witnessing only actors and playacting become suspicious, bespeaks a belligerence and pride that blacks were not then even admitting to themselves and were only able to articulate much later: "I order you to be black to your very veins. Pump black blood through them. Let Africa circulate in them. Let Negroes negrify themselves. Let them persist to the point of madness in what they're condemned to be, in their ebony, in their odor, in their yellow eyes, in their cannibal tastes. Let them not be content with eating Whites, but let them cook each other as well."

The Blacks ran for 1,408 performances. Genet's play was the real beginning of the black theater. It is hardly a coincidence that the Negro Ensemble Company, formed by Robert Hooks and Douglas Turner Ward, located itself in the same St. Marks Playhouse and that many of the members of the NEC came out of *The Blacks*. In its three years of life a generation of black actors rotated through the play, and the experience changed them for life. White audiences, whose presence Genet insisted upon even if only a symbolic white was seated, had their first experience of being challenged from the stage, face to face, as it were, black to white, to admit to their unspoken prejudices. Such confrontations were to become quite usual later, but it was *The Blacks* that broke the ground, and it was those first actors to perform Genet's ritualistic drama who did so much to rally their colleagues to use their voice on the stage.

An earlier Genet work, *The Maids*, was performed off-Broadway in November, 1963, and established a precedent for the kind of role reversal that became his dramatic trademark. Like a magic realist painter, the playwright played vanishing games with his three characters, Madame, and her two maids, Claire and Solange, who, as the curtain is raised, are found one in the role of Madame before her dressing table mirror and one impersonating the other maid. With Kathleen Widdoes as Claire, Lee Grant as Solange, and Eunice Anderson as Madame, the play was performed at One Sheridan Square under the direction of the Italian Aldo Bruzzichelli whose plans also to present an American production of Genet's *The Screens* unfortunately never materialized.

After *The Blacks*, Martin B. Duberman's *In White America* was off-Broadway's next important examination of race, undertaken from a historical rather than a psychological viewpoint and presented by one of off-Broadway's then most venturesome young producers, Judith Rutherford Marechal, at Joe Beruh's Sheridan Square Playhouse on October 31, 1963. The cast consisted of Gloria Foster, Moses Gunn, Fred Pinkard, Claudette Nevins, James Greene, and Michael O'Sullivan. Duberman documented the black man's experiences on this continent from the slave ships through Little Rock, with passages culled from historical records and with the actors voicing selections from the lives or writings of Nat Turner; Sojourner Truth, the illiterate ex-slave who spoke up at a women's rights convention; John Brown; Frederick Douglass; and Marcus Garvey, the early black nationalist leader.

A year before *The Blacks* a stage attempt to illuminate an aspect of the Negro condition had been made by Lionel Abel in *The Pretender*, which was produced at the Cherry Lane by Frank Perry in his apprentice days at the Theater Guild before he went on to make a name in films. *The Pretender*, with James Earl Jones in the cast, suggested that Negroes may have to make quite preposterous demands in order to achieve quite ordinary goals. It would be interesting to have seen the play at some later, post-*Blacks* stage, for at the time the audiences, and the critics, were simply baffled or antagonized by the sight of a Negro aping the manners of an aristocratic Southern gentleman who dressed for dinner and took pride in the elegance of his leather-lined library. If the playwright was to anticipate the public mood, as possibly Abel had done, subtlety, at least on so sensitive an issue as color, was probably a detriment.

In the early 1960's Brecht was successful off-Broadway, and not just through *The Threepenny Opera*, as Brecht was never to be successful on Broadway. The Living Theater put on *In the Jungle of Cities*, Brecht's Chicago drama, in late 1960, and in January, 1962, George Tabori, a student of Brecht, pieced together the playwright's diverse writings—poems, scenes of plays, comments on theater, instructions to actors—in an autobiographical reading which he entitled *Brecht on Brecht*. It was first done as part of the ANTA Matinee series and then taken over by Cheryl Crawford for a regular production at the Theater de Lys, following in the track of *Threepenny*, with Gene Frankel as the director and a cast that included Tabori's wife, Viveca Lindfors, Lotte Lenya, Anne Jackson, Dane Clark, George Voskovec, and Michael Wager.

Later that year there were rival productions of *Man Is Man*, the play about an Irish day laborer transformed into a human fighting machine: one by the Living Theater in a translation by Gerhard Nellhaus which was directed and designed by Julian Beck; the other, *A Man's a Man*, adapted by Eric Bentley, staged by John Hancock, who had studied with the Berliner Ensemble, and produced by Konrad Matthaei. The rehearsal schedule of the two productions collided dangerously. The openings looked as if they would coincide to the day. The Living Theater cast Joseph Chaikin as Galy Gay, the would-be soldier, and its production opened one day ahead of the Bentley version. Walter Kerr, conscious of the impending opening of the second production, wrote, "At this precarious moment in time the one that hasn't opened is ahead." John Heffernan was Galy Gay in the second production, done in chalk-white clown face—this was the one Kerr eventually favored—and Olympia Dukakis played the Widow Begbick. The second production outran the first by ten performances, 175 to 165. While the Living Theater went on tour in the summer of 1961, its theater was taken over by Arnold Weinstein's *Red Eye of Love*, the first play of an original talent but one which for inexplicable reasons off-Broadway stubbornly failed to recognize.

Paul Shyre in the fall of 1961 was to do two of the shorter works of Eugene O'Neill—*Diff'rent* and *The Long Voyage Home* at the Mermaid Theater. The production of the two plays led to a close friendship with Carlotta Monterey O'Neill which was cemented over regular Saturday luncheons. The standing appointment was unquestioned and unbreakable, as if Carlotta O'Neill were a royal presence of unassailable prerogatives. Shyre would call for her punctually at eleven forty-five at the aristocratic Carlton House on Madison Avenue at Sixty-second Street to take her to the Quo Vadis. She was always early, waiting in the lobby, with her cane, dressed all in black. She never made a reservation, but her table always awaited her, and her special "Monterey" cocktail, and like royalty, she never paid her bill in the restaurant. Shyre found Mrs. O'Neill a loyal but exacting friend, with a fully developed sense of the social formalities all the stricter for the demimondaine nature of her San Francisco origins and her Gigi-like upbringing. To those like Shyre capable of demonstrating the unqualified loyalty she demanded, her generosity with the possessions of O'Neill was unfailing, and Shyre's own library has been enriched with O'Neill memorabilia and books, each item self-consciously inscribed in the flourishing hand of Carlotta O'Neill. If she liked a man, she generally disliked his wife, and her friends were usually men.

There was one notable exception: she disliked O'Casey but got on well with his wife. Although refusing to have anything to do with the Irish Players, O'Casey had partisans besides Shyre off-Broadway, one being the gifted blind producer Stella Holt, who operated out of the low-ceilinged Greenwich Mews Theater in the basement of a Village church and put on *Red Roses for Me* there in November, 1961.

Circle in the Square began 1962 with a sprightly Thornton Wilder behaving with effusive generosity almost like a playwright-in-residence proposing to write a cycle of plays or short sketches, as they were referred to, on the seven deadly sins and the seven ages of man just for the Circle. *Plays for Bleecker Street*, however, began and ended with three short works directed by Quintero, and indifferently reviewed, on Infancy, Childhood, and Lust.

Kermit Bloomgarden became one of the first of the major Broadway producers to take a script off-Broadway, and much was made of his apostasy, although the nature of the play, Errol John's *Moon on a Rainbow Shawl*, called for an off-Broadway setting and it seemed to fit perfectly into the converted church on East Eleventh Street that Bloomgarden found for it. George Roy Hill, who had directed Bloomgarden's *Look Homeward, Angel* on Broadway and had gone on to big-time moviemaking, returned to New York to direct a cast that included James Earl Jones and his father, Robert Earl Jones, Ellen Holly, Vinnette Carroll, and Bill Gunn—practically a Who's Who of the Negro acting community. The play, coming out of Trinidad, expressed the promise of immigration, the way Brian Friel's *Philadelphia, Here I Come!* later would for a young Irish boy, except that John's frustrated hero, trying to escape the back alley life of the island, longed for the fuller freedom of London but was doomed miserably never to escape his backyard. The play was performed like a long, shrill cry of anguished confinement. At the Phoenix, in February, Arthur L. Kopit's *Oh Dad, Poor Dad, Mamma's Hung You in the Closet and I'm Feelin' So*

Sad opened to great éclat, forcing the transfer of Frank D. Gilroy's play about the war and postwar, *Who'll Save the Plowboy?* In March Arnold Weinstein, Elaine May, and Kenneth Koch combined talents to present three short works: Weinstein's *The Twenty-five-Cent Cap*, Elaine May's *Not Enough Rope*, a macabre piece about a desperately lonely girl trying to commit suicide in a city tenement; Koch's irreverent *George Washington Crossing the Delaware* caricaturing the founder of the Republic in a way that anticipated by six to eight years the whole counterpatriotic trend. The plays *3 x 3* lasted only five performances at the Maidman Theater.

By this time the old Phoenix Theater on Second Avenue was renamed Casino East and had reverted to earlier days by showing Ann Corio's *This Was Burlesque*. Once again there were baggy-pants comedians and lovely strippers following the old formulas. The show looked forward and backward simultaneously, anticipating the coming theatrical fixation on stage nudity but clothing it nostalgically in the acceptable garments of burlesque. Into this same theater, in natural sequence, came Kenneth Tynan's *Oh! Calcutta!* whose whole point was that it could be done, not just nude women onstage but nude men, and not separately but together, and together, furthermore, in positions of simulated copulation. But *Oh! Calcutta!* belongs to a later period.

In the spring of 1962 Ellis Rabb's Association of Producing Artists came to New York. Acting out the recurring dream of performers to be their own producers, Rabb, in 1959, had put together a group of actors, directors, and designers of similar training to work out ways of doing selected plays from stage literature without being beholden to any commercial management but their own. Purposely, during this break-in period, they avoided New York while sorting out company problems in eleven engagements and building a repertory of sixteen plays. They had met with success in various places, and they enjoyed a continuing connection

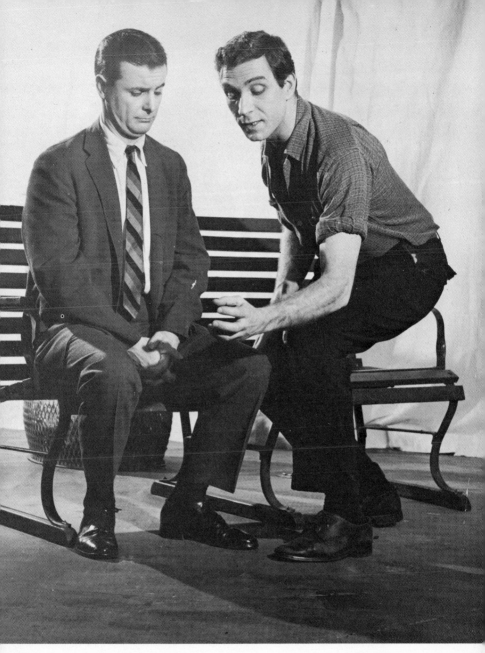

On a park bench in Central Park William Daniels and Mark Richman enact the two roles in Edward Albee's argumentative first play *The Zoo Story*, which opened in January, 1960.

Jerry Orbach, Rita Gardner, and Kenneth Nelson of the original cast of Tom Jones and Harvey Schmidt's *The Fantasticks,* which opened on May 3, 1960 and is the longest running musical in the history of the American theater.

...akespeare provided the ...oenix Theater with some of ... greatest successes, among ...em *Henry IV, Part II* in ...60. From the left, Edwin ...erin as Prince Hal, J. D. ...nnon as Poins, Eric Berry as ...lstaff, and Patricia Falken-...in as Doll Tearsheet.

Henry Grossman

The Phoenix's *Hamlet* with Donald Madden holding Yorick's skull, Jared Reed as the first gravedigger, and Ray Reinhardt as Horatio, in 1961.

Henry Grossman

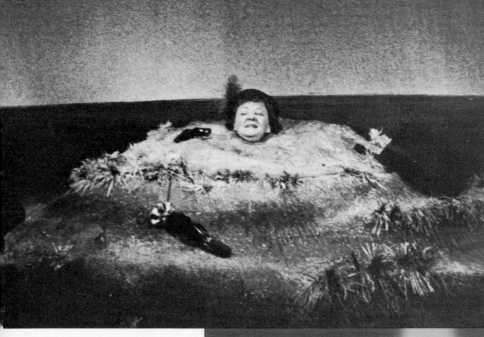

Alix Jeffry

(*Above*) Buried to her neck in a mound of earth, Ruth White barely appeared in Beckett's *Happy Days* at the Cherry Lane in 1961.

(*Right*) *The Blacks,* in Gene Frankel's superb production of the Jean Genet drama, introduced a new, black theater to off-Broadway at the St. Marks Playhouse in May, 1961.

with the University of Michigan's theater program, headed
by Robert C. Schnitzer and his wife, Marcella Cisney, which
gave them a part-year base in Ann Arbor.

Rabb had developed a repertory company with no special
point of view, no ax to grind. His group had no social or
political positions to propagandize, no "with-it" topicality, no
impulse to be experimental—nothing but a respect for dramatic literature and a devotion to theatrical arts. The company came to the out-of-the-way Folksbiene Theater in the
Jewish Daily Forward building on East Broadway and pro-
ceeded to amaze and delight New York critics prepared by
the improbability of the location if not for something ethni-
cally obscure at least for something collegiately effete. They
discovered in a superlative *School for Scandal* a company
already well developed, capable of high style, and made up of
players of superior ability. Possibly this was the most skillful
and exuberant production of the play ever seen in New York.
The rustic solemnity of Will Geer as Sir Peter Teazle was
the perfect foil for the rippling gaiety of Rosemary Harris,
who was the acting jewel of the company. Nancy Marchand,
George Grizzard, and Clayton Corzatte were among the other
members. In the same engagement the APA also performed
The Sea Gull with Miss Harris as Nina and, for farce, George
M. Cohan's primitive melodrama *The Tavern*. The ideal of
ensemble acting, about which theater people talked inces-
santly, here was on view in the work of a tightly knit and
homogeneous company that trained together, traveled together, and shared the same artistic ideals. Artistic decisions
were a matter of group determination under the overall
direction of Ellis Rabb, whose reedy slightness and careful air
of languor as an actor belied a tenacity and sense of purpose
that were the real cause of the company's cohesiveness. A new
sort of off-Broadway enterprise seemed to be in the making,
yet Rabb sensed that the company's strength lay in its broad
national appeal and that it was not yet ready to commit itself
to New York as a main base. APA's entrance into New York,

however tentative at the time and particularly in retrospect, was the biggest theater news of the spring.

In the fall, some of the regular producers were back. Judith Rutherford Marechal, the young Vassar graduate who apprenticed briefly with Quintero and Mann at Circle in the Square and who on her own had put on *In White America*, touring it after its off-Broadway run in the increasingly significant college market, produced a new play with Ulu Grosbard—William Snyder's *The Days and Nights of Beebee Fenstermaker* with Rose Gregorio and Robert Duvall playing major parts. In October William Hanley's two one-acts *Whisper in My Good Ear* and the moving *Mrs. Dally Has a Lover*, in which Estelle Parsons' fine performance earned her some early attention, were done at the Cherry Lane. In November they were followed by Pinter's *The Dumbwaiter* and *The Collection*. New groups of rather small life expectancy were always forming off-Broadway, and the Writers' Stage, as one example, began with a bright board of managers and a ringing declaration of intentions that seemed a blueprint at the time for the kind of theater off-Broadway was already turning into. The principals of the Writers' Stage were Andre Gregory; Doris Belack, the actress wife of producer Philip Rose (*A Raisin in the Sun* and subsequently *Purlie*); Michael Kahn, who later was to become chief director of the American Shakespeare Festival at Stratford, Connecticut; Judith Peabody, one of the mainstay board members of the New York Shakespeare Festival; the critic Gordon Rogoff; and Ed Wittstein, the designer. They took over David Ross' old home on Fourth Street and, in a statement of purpose written by Gregory, began to ask the right questions: "In an age in which mankind has developed the means to annihilate itself, the problems of the individual are only important in their relationship to and reflection of the major problems of our day, moral, political, social, atomic. We would like our theater and our audience to ask themselves collectively what our theater has to do with Survival, Peace, Sobel, Chessman, or the movement to the far right." As a theatrical manifesto, this statement was almost more significant than the work that followed. It constituted at least a preamble to the death sentence pronounced by the new movements and writers of off-Broadway on the individualistic psychological drama of the 1940's and 1950's that brought Miller and Williams and Inge and Anderson and Chayefsky to fame. It heralded the distrust of individualism, Freudian analysis, Horatio Alger success stories, the glamorization of wars of national purpose, and unthinking patriotism that were to distinguish the generation coming into maturity. For one reason or another the plays—David Rayfiel's *P.S. 196* and Deric Washburn's *The Love Nest* in January, 1963, and Lewis John Carlino's *Telemachus Clay* the following November—although in themselves of considerable interest, were not able to position themselves securely within the terms of this broad scheme. Individually in their subsequent careers the founders have perhaps realized a portion of their purpose, but the theater itself failed one of the major tests it set for itself—survival for at least five years. It lasted less than two.

Into an increasingly vital theatrical atmosphere, more and more Broadway actors came for their own intellectual refreshment and perhaps also out of recognition of the added luster that the newer writers could bring to their own careers. Eli Wallach and Anne Jackson did no harm to their professional careers and at the same time helped Murray Schisgal realize his potential as a dramatist in this country (he was already recognized in England) by appearing in his one-acts *The Tiger* and *The Typists,* breaking ground at the same time for Schisgal's enormously successful *Luv* on Broadway in which the Wallachs also appeared. Another new playwright of the season was Oliver Hailey, whose *Hey, You, Light Man* was put on at the off-Times Square Mayfair in March. Also in March, William Ball, a contemporary of Ellis Rabb with similar theatrical aspirations as an actor-manager, directed a fine *Six Characters in Search of an Author* at the

Martinique. Ball had directed a first-rate *Ivanov* in 1958 and *Under Milk Wood* in 1961 at the Circle—both with Sada Thompson. For the Pirandello work Ball this year won the Lola D'Annunzio Award for "the most outstanding contribution to the off-Broadway theater."

The Establishment Theater was to make its first showing with *The Ginger Man*. This was one of off-Broadway's more successful dramatizations of a novel, with Patrick O'Neal playing the Rabelaisian Sebastian Dangerfield, Margaret Phillips his wife, and Marian Seldes Miss Frost, the prim, awakened boarder. It was done at the Orpheum Theater while Ivor David Balding and his colleagues, who included some of the English *Beyond the Fringe* people, got ready their permanent headquarters in the old El Morocco on East Fifty-fourth Street. Here, *The Establishment*, with all its modern English irreverence, was already set up in the Strollers Theater Club on the old nightclub floor where a very non-off-Broadway clientele used to cavort. Downtown at Circle in the Square the Greek director Michael Cacoyannis—no less an interpreter of Euripides in Europe than Quintero was of O'Neill in the United States—put on his production of *The Trojan Women* (which he was not to repeat until his film with Katharine Hepburn until 1971), and a new era had opened for Circle in the Square. Jose Quintero was no longer with it. Theodore Mann was alone in charge.

Six

The Phoenix Rises

Heading into its third season in the fall of 1955, the Phoenix Theater was still casting about for a self-identifying policy. There was small philosophy simply in declaring oneself to be different from Broadway and in putting on plays Broadway wouldn't touch. Norris Houghton, perhaps more than T. Edward Hambleton—for Houghton was the theorist, the idea man, and publicist of the new theater—yearned for some distinctive tag line to go below the brand name. He was impatient to institutionalize the Phoenix, to see it develop a personality, even while intellectually he understood that theatrical seedlings, however zealously tended, don't sprout into sturdy oaks overnight. The history of the Phoenix teaches us that economics, far more than theories and good intentions, determines the shape of the institution. Time and again the realist in Hambleton prevailed over the theorist in Houghton.

In the early years the Phoenix was a theater in search of the Old Vic. The two Phoenix founders were extravagantly admiring of the forerunner of the British National Theater —and Sadler's Wells, the Moscow Art Theater, the Abbey in Dublin, the Comédie Française in Paris, theaters that had stood the test of time, as models for their own. They drew inspiration from the great institutional theaters of Europe, and the Old Vic so dominated early thinking that Tyrone

Guthrie, responsible for the success of the modern Old Vic, was invited to New York to put the Phoenix on course. The third season opened poorly with an original work, *The Carefree Tree*, which brought the unkindest criticism to date. In common with many other then-developing theaters around the country the Phoenix found the critical honeymoon ending. Critics wax enthusiastic when everything is new and full of promise. They grow testy and more exacting, and their judgments become harsher, when maturity sets in.

Guthrie came to the rescue with a production of *Six Characters in Search of an Author* which he adapted with Michael Wager. Guthrie was an exuberant director of immense verve, but his virtuosity and inventiveness often got him into critical trouble with the textual purists. With *Six Characters*, as with subsequent productions, the Guthrie overlay of style was blamed for blurring the author's meaning. Despite the few reservations, the Pirandello production was popular, the run was extended, and Guthrie became the patron saint of the Phoenix. As a theater, the Phoenix was to pass through five distinct, identifiable phases, and Tyrone Guthrie was instrumental in seeing the Phoenix from its second phase into its third, or repertory company, phase in the latter years of the 1950's.

The Phoenix generally was to look to Europe not only for material and brains, but also for acting talent. After *Six Characters* came Strindberg's *Miss Julie* and *The Stronger*, directed by George Tabori and starring his Swedish wife, Viveca Lindfors, and then Chekhov's *A Month in the Country*, directed by Michael Redgrave with Uta Hagen and Alexander Scourby. In concept and casting both productions were really international.

The Phoenix maintained certain peripheral activities in line with its aspirations to become an important institution. One was the director's series sponsored by Roger L. Stevens on "dark" Monday nights, which was responsible for Virgil Thomson and Gertrude Stein's opera *Mother of Us All* and a production of Elmer Rice's *The Adding Machine* with which the irascible Rice was said to have been well satisfied. The Phoenix showed an eye for foreign talent fully as canny as that of any import-minded Broadway producer by introducing the great French mimist Marcel Marceau to the United States in a two-week preseason Phoenix engagement in early September which was extended for two more weeks on Broadway at the Ethel Barrymore Theater. Over Christmas, Bil and Cora Baird's Marionette Theater gave ten matinees. No theater survives entirely without error; the Phoenix managers turned down an early chance to put on *The Fantasticks.*

Still searching for a style, the Phoenix next projected a season of "theatrical masterpieces" chosen from among the great plays of the last hundred years: from the works, specifically, of Brecht, Shaw, O'Casey, and Ostrovski. The season following it was to be drama in and around the Elizabethans: "We plan to move on—or back—to the Seventeenth and Eighteenth Centuries: to Shakespeare, the Restoration, Molière, perhaps even back to the Greeks." Another year it was to be plays by Nobel Prize winners exclusively. In these programs was an exemplary regard for unplayed dramatic literature but no overall design really, no plan other than a somewhat naïve belief in the theatrical efficacy of categorization. Here were certain superficial file-card affinities—plays nesting together under *N* for Nobel Prize—but no necessary thematic cohesiveness. There was no relationship between the liberalism of Shaw's nineteenth-century Socialism and the twentieth-century Communism of Brecht, and neither bears very much on the individualism of O'Casey. It was the Phoenix's fourth season (1956–57), and it did not get around to O'Casey, but Brecht's *The Good Woman of Setzuan* was put on in an entirely new version adapted and directed by Eric Bentley, the outstanding scholar and spokesman of Brecht in America. Even with Uta Hagen, Albert Salmi, and Zero Mostel, it was not a success. As Henry Hewes put it in *Saturday*

Review, "The results are not good Brecht, good Bentley, or good theater." Ostrovski (*Diary of a Scoundrel*) earlier had fared no better, but the lead-off attraction with Siobhan McKenna—it was her first appearance in New York since *The Chalk Garden*—in the Cambridge Drama Festival production of *Saint Joan* was such a hit that it was brought back after *Scoundrel* for a return engagement and then transferred uptown to the then Coronet Theater. Once again the Phoenix was beholden to foreign talent.

Also in this season the Phoenix tapped the resources of the American Shakespeare Festival in Stratford, Connecticut, bringing in at midseason its *Measure for Measure* and *The Taming of the Shrew* and beginning a continuing relationship with John Houseman as an adviser and occasional director. In March, 1957, the Phoenix offered *The Duchess of Malfi*, co-produced by Houseman and his assistant, Jack Landau.

After four seasons the Phoenix was ready for the reorganization that led into Phase Two—its changeover to a nonprofit organization. The annual balance sheets since the opening had shown deficits, and for the first time, in the fourth year, the net loss had climbed above $100,000. Their ambitions for the theater were greater than ever; Houghton and Hambleton had been holding serious discussions with Guthrie, and a regular acting company was deemed essential to further growth. Only a permanent company working under a permanent artistic director could develop the unified style required for a repertoire of classics. Ahead, they envisioned national touring companies to extend the life of their productions and truly nationalize their theater. A bit of the rhetoric of the time went as follows: "Alone among the great countries of the Western world, the United States has no institutional theater to perform classics at home and represent it on the world stage." These were the Eisenhower years, years of self-improvement and optimism, of world competitiveness as yet uninhibited by inner anxieties. It was wholly in keeping with the national mood for the Phoenix to judge itself against world standards. The scope of its ambition inevitably meant larger deficits which could no longer be supported by the old structure—essentially the financing of productions on the Broadway model of the limited partnership form of agreement. The Phoenix needed nonprofit status to attract the big tax-deductible personal donations that would be necessary in the future. A framework for the reorganization existed in the form of the largely inactive Theater Incorporated, of which Norris Houghton was a founding director. Formed in 1946, it had brought the Old Vic over and had produced a *Pygmalion* with Gertrude Lawrence and Raymond Massey. Dormant in recent years, it provided the perfect nonprofit shell for the Phoenix. Theater Incorporated "acquired" the Phoenix Theater. Roger Stevens became president and Houghton and Hambleton managing directors answerable to the board. A drive was begun to raise a quarter of a million dollars.

On October 8, 1957, Guthrie opened the new season with a production of Schiller's *Mary Stuart* which, with Irene Worth as Mary and Eva Le Gallienne as Queen Elizabeth, became one of the greatest single accomplishments of the Phoenix and advanced the theater toward the national standing it aspired to. Two years later a recast production with Signe Hasso in the Irene Worth role was to begin a hugely successful national tour in San Francisco. Guthrie also directed the season's second show, Karel Capek's *The Makropolis Secret* with Eileen Herlie in a production designed by Houghton. Another British director, Tony Richardson, was invited in to put the next bill together, Ionesco's *The Chairs* and *The Lesson* with Eli Wallach, Joan Plowright (later to join Laurence Olivier on Broadway in *The Entertainer*) , and Max Adrian. Then, with Ming Cho Lee's sets, Cocteau's *The Infernal Machine* became the Phoenix's outstanding visual production up to that time.

The Phoenix's admiration of the company idea, and its eye

for foreign attractions, led to an invitation to the Stratford, Ontario, Shakespeare Festival to bring in two productions directed by Michael Langham—*Two Gentlemen of Verona* and *The Broken Jug* by Heinrich von Kleist—and Jean Gascon's Le Théâtre du Nouveau Monde, also from Canada, to perform *Le Malade Imaginaire.* Each was a move closer to the company policy, and in the sixth season—the crucial season of 1958–59, when the theater for the first time was unable to complete its subscription season and was forced to make refunds—Stuart Vaughan appeared as the chief candidate for the job of artistic director. Indiana-born and -educated, Vaughan had studied the English repertory system on a Fulbright and had been notably successful directing Shakespeare for Joseph Papp in Central Park. For the Phoenix he was the right man at the right time. This season the unifying thread was to be the Nobel Prize winner playwright—T. S. Eliot, Shaw, Pirandello, Albert Camus, Eugene O'Neill, Maeterlinck, Gerhart Hauptmann, William Butler Yeats. Still the search for consistency, for continuity, and for a recognizable style. Houghton was quoted as saying, "The most important thing is that we know that the Phoenix, if it is to have any future, must acquire a definite personality, a personality that we hope may become as strong in its way as the personality of the Moscow Art Theater or the Abbey Theater."

Actually, perhaps unrealized by Houghton or Hambleton, the Phoenix had already developed a personality of its own —a fusion, really, of the distinctive and complementary personalities of the two founders. For all their compulsion to emulate the Europeans they were on their way to developing a style of their own. Of the two, Houghton was the more articulate. Academically inclined, he was the theorist; Hambleton was the doer. With people, Houghton was witty and enthusiastic and had a never-failing fund of good spirits. In contrast Hambleton was taciturn, noncommittal, enigmatic —the ideal negotiator with a mind that could never be read perfectly. About half his time was spent fund raising. "It's always nagging at you," he said. Personally wealthy, Hambleton moved in a society that had money and power and appreciated the arts. With his connections he had easier access to money than almost any other producer in New York. But he was forced to go back to his sources again and again and again. He was a man of tremendous physical vitality. In the end it was his dogged determination that was to hold the Phoenix together.

Maneuvering their European-style theater in waters where only commercial theater had right-of-way was immensely difficult and often discouraging. The Broadway managers belittled the Phoenix as the plaything of amateurs and dilettantes, yet Hambleton had to move partly in their world, incurring the penalties without the advantages, as a member of the League of New York Theaters, as an increasingly important employer in the eyes of Actors' Equity, the stagehands, the scenic designers, and the other unions. Hambleton's record speaks for itself; he has confounded many a preening professional by lasting as long and accomplishing much more than most.

T. S. Eliot was the first Nobel Prize author, and his play, *The Family Reunion*, was the first Vaughan directed for the Phoenix, but the idea of carrying through a season of Nobel laureates was promptly shelved. In place of the previously scheduled Shaw, *Arms and the Man*, Graham Greene's *The Power and the Glory* was hurried into the lineup. Fritz Weaver, Eric Berry, Patricia Falkenhain, and Robert Gerringer became the nucleus of the acting company to come. June Havoc, giving a delicious performance in *The Beaux' Stratagem*, earned delighted reviews from most of the critics, except Brooks Atkinson, but very little audience interest developed for a Restoration comedy, and the Phoenix slid into its worst position in six seasons. Losses of $148,000 for just three productions forced a suspension of operations.

The theater abounds in small ironies. At this low point the Phoenix was about to open the show that became the greatest financial success in its history, the musical *Once Upon a Mattress*. And it came out of the blue, or rather, out of Tamiment, the vacation resort in the Poconos, where a number of serious young professionals had used Hans Christian Andersen's "The Princess and the Pea" as the basis for a show. The composer was Mary Rodgers, for whom her father once predicted success in his own field because, as he said, "She has the necessary drive, the talent, and the ability to talk to people." (In this estimate Rodgers gave interesting priorities to what he felt were the ingredients of a show business career.) Three friends together wrote the book, Jay Thompson, Marshall Barer, and Dean Fuller, and Barer wrote lyrics to Mary Rodgers' songs.

The Poconos' results encouraged them to hope for a New York showing, and two eager but novice producers, the set designers William and Jean Eckart, offered to take on the project cooperatively. The Phoenix was just the size theater they needed, and the Phoenix needed a show. But the key to the project turned out to be George Abbott. Unused to off-Broadway, Abbott was made for this situation. On the one hand, an overabundance of exuberant young talent, and on the other, the disciplined hand of experience. Carol Burnett was the great talent "discovery" of the show, playing Princess Winnifred ("Fred," for short) and with her tomboy clumsiness singing the song "Shy" in unexpected notes too bold for her theme. Joe Bova played Prince Dauntless, and there was just the right disparity in height between him and Miss Burnett to make his courtship an uphill fight. Jane White played the tyrannical queen—an early instance off-Broadway of the casting of a black actor in a nonspecified role solely on ability and suitability, without reference to color.

Abbott had two young assistants on the project. Joe Layton, another Tamiment veteran, came from *On the Town* to stage the dances and musical numbers, and Jack Sydow, the Tamiment director of *Mattress* (for short), to help handle the staging of scenes. But the major plus for the project was

simply the presence of unchallenged authority amid so many
evenly matched and contemporary talents. Nothing is more
crucial to the success of so complex and delicately balanced
an undertaking than one voice that can say "No" without
question or argument. That was Abbott's formidable hidden
asset.

Hambleton and Houghton joined with the Eckarts as producers of record, and *Mattress* opened at the Phoenix on May
11, 1959. It was a success from the beginning. Nothing like it,
of course, had ever been seen off-Broadway. "Our attitude,"
said the authors, "is that it is a Broadway show that happens
to be playing on Second Avenue." The show was later transferred to Broadway, and from theater to theater on Broadway, when the Phoenix wanted its own theater back to resume its schedule the following fall.

To organize for the new season, the theater now launched
a major subscription drive to support the repertory company
idea and enter the third phase of its development. As Emory
Lewis had written in *Cue* in February, "Everybody has hoped
that somehow, miraculously, a repertory company might
grow out of the off-Broadway stimulus. It has not happened
—yet. Most of us have pinned our greatest hopes on the
Phoenix." To support such an ideal, a sizable subscription
was necessary. Hambleton felt the security of a large advance,
although not the complete answer, was an important prereq-
uisite. "The only way we can provide protection is to sell
ahead," he said. "The only way to sell ahead is to know what
we're going to do." But the Phoenix subscribers would be
buying the past record, the capabilities of Houghton and
Hambleton, and the promise of Stuart Vaughan's success
with a permanent company. Putting together a large committee mostly of women, the theater began a concentrated two-
week telephone subscription drive, utilizing a carefully com-
piled list of 100,000 names. The goal was a better than 10
percent return—12,500 subscriptions. For the permanent
theater, ideally, the permanent audience.

Foundation money began to come in for the first time in any sizable amounts. The two Mellon family foundations, the Old Dominion and Avalon, put up $75,000 each, contingent upon the success of the theater in enrolling 9,000 subscribers. By late June the Phoenix's extended drive was declared a success with 9,030 subscriptions, the grants were validated, and a new season was assured.

Then, just as the damage of the most disappointing season to date was being repaired so satisfactorily and the goal for which it had been working all along at last appeared attainable, the Phoenix suffered an unavoidable but serious loss from another direction. Norris Houghton was forced to resign his managing directorship. The reasons were financial. He was offered a post at Vassar leading into an academic career. In the business office of the Phoenix the question had become whom to pay first—their creditors or themselves. Hambleton, who was not dependent upon the theater for support, offered to carry Houghton for a time. Houghton thought not: no longer would they share the equality of partnership enjoyed from the beginning. He would continue as a director of Theater Incorporated. He would be available on weekends, and always his personal concern and interest would remain. Houghton's connection with the theater he helped found was never really broken, but the burden of carrying on fell to Hambleton.

In the next two seasons, along with some mistakes, the Phoenix was to enjoy its greatest success especially as Stuart Vaughan and the company he recruited moved onto the familiar ground of Shakespeare. The *Henry IV, Part I* and *Henry IV, Part II*, with Eric Berry playing Falstaff, and the Donald Madden *Hamlet* "for the young in heart" are some of the finest achievements of this period of off-Broadway history. With *Once Upon a Mattress* still running strong downtown, the Phoenix was forced to open its seventh season in a Broadway house, the Coronet, later named the Eugene

O'Neill. It had hoped for a change of name in time to coincide with the opening play, O'Neill's *The Great God Brown*, but had encountered some initial resistance from the playwright's widow, who protested her husband's utter disinterest in the Broadway theater. The renaming was nevertheless accomplished subsequently, and the old Coronet became the only theater on Broadway named for a playwright. *The Great God Brown* is performed with masks to distinguish between each character's public person and his hidden psychological self. The play expresses O'Neill's awareness of Freudian formulations. It also deals with the duality and private war within a person that results from the clash of the business mores of American society with an artistic nature. O'Neill sets up the values and the conflicts quite transparently in his characters and emphasizes the sexual awards that are to be found symbolically at the center of the conflict. Fritz Weaver, the Phoenix's leading actor, played the esthetic but foolish Dion Anthony, Nan Martin the handsome Margaret whom he wins and marries, Gerry Jedd the complaisant tart Cybel, and Robert Lansing his rival, the materialistic and plodding Brown. As Kenneth Tynan has pointed out, in its interweaving of dissimilar and competing personalities, the play is also a sketch for the family relationships later explored so deeply in *Long Day's Journey Into Night*.

Proudly advertising a company of twenty, the Phoenix, perhaps anxious to affirm its versatility at once, turned to *Lysistrata*, using Jean Gascon as a guest director from Canada, but it was a disastrous choice. The critics pounced on it for "vulgarity" and "tastelessness," and the Phoenix was forced into disorderly retreat, withdrawing the production in three weeks, and hurrying into the breach Paul Shyre's *Pictures in the Hallway* with Mildred Dunnock in the hope that O'Casey's musical reminiscences would erase the stigma of their tastelessness.

Next came a very ambitious attempt to put on Ibsen's massive *Peer Gynt* with a score by David Amram. In the choice of play there seemed to be no natural progression from the earlier classics, and the assault on Ibsen, one suspected, was attempted for no greater reason than that Ibsen was there, a mountain to be conquered. Shakespeare made for an easier because more familiar ascent, and the theater immediately recovered its stride putting on historical Shakespeare, which was suited to Vaughan, to the trained actors of the company, to the theater itself, first *Henry IV, Part I* and then *Part II*, when the first *Henry* showed an energizing strength at the box office. With this production off-Broadway for the first time made contact with the city's vast student audience. The offering of special 50 percent student discount tickets brought in 14,300 in the first six weeks, and the Phoenix realized it was onto something. The play gave the company a chance to show their abilities—Weaver in the title role, Albert Quinton, Rex Everhart, Nicholas Kepros, Nan Martin, J. D. Cannon, John Heffernan, and the others—a first-rate company. In *Part II* Eric Berry's rich, roisterous Falstaff was one of the most enjoyable impersonations of the season, aided and abetted as it was by Gerry Jedd as Mistress Quickly and Patricia Falkenhain as Doll Tearsheet. By May, 1960, the Phoenix had a whole new lease on life. Subscriptions were up to the 12,000 level, and the Ford Foundation came through handsomely with a grant of $120,000 over three years to subsidize actors' salaries to the level of $200 a week. Through this largesse Ford wished to prove a point— that good actors could be induced to stay with repertory theaters in New York and other key cities and not be lured away by temporarily higher paying but perhaps impermanent jobs in the commercial theater. The grant stipulated a ceiling of $200 for all members of the company, resulting in the loss of such higher-paid performers as Fritz Weaver and Nan Martin. Hambleton questioned whether this form of subsidy was good for the Phoenix. "What we really needed," he said, "was money to adequately publicize and attract an audience."

To capitalize on the success with Shakespeare, a new subscription drive was mounted. The two parts of *Henry* were
played in alternate repertory, so that now the theater could
legitimately boast of attaining its long-term goal. Eric Berry,
who had scored an enormous personal triumph as Falstaff,
was quoted as saying, "I fled from England to get away from
rep and here I find it in New York. Wherever I am it grows
like a weed." Nevertheless the Phoenix in repertory had
achieved the highest level of attendance since its first year.
The losses were also the highest ever—now more than
$200,000.

In the future at least one Shakespeare play was to be
included in the schedule each season. For the following season the plan was to do either *King Lear* or *Richard III* and
to counterbalance the classics with one new play, preferably
by a playwright working directly with and for the Phoenix
company. Once more Tyrone Guthrie swept into the city
from Canada, exuding the kind of confidence that never
failed to encourage more cautious colleagues. His bright,
spanking Stratford production of *H.M.S. Pinafore*, with
Douglas Campbell, in a seven-week early season engagement,
served to boost subscriptions to 11,000. The regular season
opened with Gerry Jedd taking over some of the major acting chores, Kate Hardcastle in *She Stoops to Conquer* and
Nora in O'Casey's difficult and, for the Phoenix, not altogether successful masterpiece, *The Plough and the Stars*.
(Gerry Jedd was to die shockingly on November 28, 1962, in
the midst of a performance of *Brecht on Brecht* at the Theater
de Lys. She was singing the Pirate Jenny song from *The
Threepenny Opera* when she collapsed on the stage as a
result of a stroke. She died twelve hours later in a hospital.
She was thirty-seven.) Turning to native work, the Phoenix
next mounted a fascinating revival of Dion Boucicault's *The
Octoroon* with its astonishingly clear family-album prints of
life in Southern plantation and slave society. The promised
new play was not forthcoming, and Walter Kerr wrote, "If

we can't have good new plays, we can at least be grateful for bad old ones." As an exercise in reviving history, *The Octoroon* was the Phoenix at its schoolroom best.

One actor in a thousand is suited to the role of Hamlet. The Phoenix was fortunate to have such an actor in its own company in Donald Madden. On Broadway he had succeeded Kenneth Haigh in *Look Back in Anger*. For the Phoenix he had played Hotspur, and he had appeared in both *She Stoops to Conquer* and *The Plough*. Madden had youthfulness, good looks, an athletic figure, and faultless diction. Beneath the engaging exterior was an undercurrent of watchfulness—Madden had a quizzical, sideways way of looking at life —and controlled anger. His history-making *Hamlet*, which opened March 30, 1961, had a run of twelve and a half weeks, or 101 performances. It was not the record, but he had tied John Barrymore's run in 1922 and was only a performance short of the record run for an American actor set in 1912 by John E. Kellerd. Nothing in Phoenix history aroused quite so much interest as the youthful Hamlet of Madden, and box-office business was never brisker.

Despite this landmark production, the Phoenix once again was forced to reassess its position. Phase Four was upon it. The very success of the big-name classics pointed to one of the theater's worst drawbacks. Hambleton reflected on the expectation of doing new work: "If we tried to do primarily new plays we wouldn't have a ghost of a chance. Remember that this is a theater with 1,200 seats, not 200. If we do anything too special, we're in real trouble, because we don't begin to fill the house."

The Phoenix was inhibited by the size of the theater from undertaking the kind of risks that alone can keep a theater alive and responsive. The size of the Second Avenue building had become a burden. As costs rose, they found themselves more and more looking for plays to suit the theater. In eight years in its downtown location the Phoenix had

mounted forty-four major productions and had presented
many showcases and special attractions. The annual deficits
averaged more than $100,000. Now some form of retrench-
ment seemed necessary. Putting it positively, rather than
search for an idea to fit the theater, it wanted a theater to fit
the idea. Norris Houghton came in on the discussions. He had
been in Russia on a cultural exchange mission and had
brought home some theatrical projects he thought suitable
for a revised Phoenix.

Hambleton located a new theater on East Seventy-fourth
Street in the Upper East Side heart of its subscription terri-
tory, a handsome, well-equipped theater back to back with
the old Bohemian National Hall, with its vast creaking uncar-
peted ballrooms used for rehearsal space, and just across the
street from the busy Jan Hus Playhouse. The Phoenix move
would bring new life to a potentially lively uptown theater
center. But the change to reduced quarters meant jettisoning
the permanent company—and giving up the second and
third years of the Ford grant subsidizing actors' salaries. It
meant dropping the permanent director. Stuart Vaughan's
work was over with *Hamlet*. His best efforts had been with
Shakespeare, with Graham Greene's *The Power and the
Glory*, and with Sheridan's *She Stoops to Conquer*. For a
brief few seasons he had given New York its first acting company in many years. In the future a different director would
be hired for each project. Vaughan left for a year of study in
Europe. Fittingly, the last production in the old theater was
one of Guthrie's—*The Pirates of Penzance* brought down
from Stratford, Ontario, at the outset of the new season.
Uptown, the Phoenix immediately shifted focus from the
classics to new work. To secure newer plays, the Phoenix
sometimes had to go into partnership with other producers
who had tied up the rights to desirable work. It did so with
Caroline Burke Swann in order to present N. F. Simpson's
One-Way Pendulum. The Phoenix followed with Shaw's
Androcles and the Lion and *The Dark Lady of the Sonnets*,

and Houghton's European investigations bore fruit in *The Policeman* by the Polish playwright Slawomir Mrozek. It was a director friend of the Phoenix management, Daniel Petrie, who brought it Frank D. Gilroy's *Who'll Save the Plowboy?* and enabled it to introduce its first significant American playwright. Gilroy spoke in the language of the postwar generation. Later he was to write *The Subject Was Roses*. They were slight, spare scripts, but the voice was that of an impassioned and personal playwright who wrote in the revealing autobiographical vein of O'Neill. Before *Plowboy* the Phoenix had committed itself to joining Roger L. Stevens in a production of Arthur L. Kopit's exhaustively titled *Oh Dad, Poor Dad, Mamma's Hung You in the Closet and I'm Feelin' So Sad*. Kopit was a Harvard undergraduate when he wrote the play. It came to Audrey Wood's notice and began to create interest in New York theatrical circles. To make room for this play, the Phoenix had to move *Plowboy* to a downtown off-Broadway house, possibly hurting its run.

Oh Dad, Poor Dad opened with great éclat. It was a precocious parody of avant-garde work, brilliantly produced, directed, designed, and acted. The play was set in the lush lobby of a Caribbean hotel where Madame Rosepettle, played by Jo Van Fleet, had taken her inept son, Jonathan, played by Austin Pendleton. In the anonymously uniformed squad of six bellboys were two actors later to make names for themselves off-Broadway—Jaime Sanchez and Barry Primus. In his direction Jerome Robbins exploited the play's possibilities of physical movement to the fullest and injected the sort of visual humor one later associated with Mike Nichols in *Luv* on Broadway. In the trick set designed by William and Jean Eckart, chairs and sofas collapsed spontaneously, pictures dropped, and a man-eating Venus flytrap snapped viciously at passersby. Jo Van Fleet had a wearyingly long monologue, but the play rose to a hilarious climax when a saucy Barbara Harris set out to seduce the backward Jonathan. From a pouting little girl she suddenly blossomed into a sexual tigress, the gooey baby talk sliding into suggestive insinuation as she stripped off her little-girl party dress down to her panties and took the alarmed Jonathan to the floor. It was the perfect image for the hot, writhing sex of adolescent fantasy.

In *Oh Dad* the Phoenix had a surprise commercial success and an unbroken run of thirteen months. Commercially this production was another high-water mark equaling that of *Once Upon a Mattress,* but it broke the continuity of multiple productions in a way that contravened the purposes of the theater.

Throughout its history the Phoenix had occupied an anomalous position somewhere between Broadway and off-Broadway in size, somewhere between New York and the regional theater in sophistication, somewhere between the commercial and the art theater in audience appeal, drawing upon the most intellectual and serious-minded of the Broadway audience and the most affluent of the off-Broadway, somewhere between the contemporary theater and the classic in the thrust of its programming and in the volume and quality of its productions. By adaptation and structural change the Phoenix repeatedly found the means of survival. Conforming to constantly shifting economic conditions, the Phoenix remained open to its best possibilities.

Because of the continuing run of *Oh Dad, Poor Dad* in September, 1962, the Phoenix decided to delay its regular season, but hoped to have the best of two worlds. The so-called "experiments" would go into the East Seventy-fourth Street theater. Classics would be produced in a second theater downtown, the 1,700-seat Phyllis Anderson on Second Avenue, eight blocks south of the Phoenix's old home. Once having engaged the city's student audience with Shakespeare in significant numbers, the Phoenix was anxious to resume contact with them. Stuart Vaughan returned to direct Hal Holbrook in the Raymond Massey role in *Abe Lincoln in*

Illinois and, as a second production, *The Taming of the Shrew*. The schedule was Tuesday through Friday in the late afternoons and weekend performances at conventional times for the general public. But it was impossible to balance up all the economic factors in a venture of this complexity, and the Phoenix was unable to sustain it beyond the initial two productions, well cast, well acted, and well directed though they were.

The following fall of 1963 the Phoenix regained full scheduling control over its uptown theater but yanked a production of *The Imaginary Invalid* in order to team up once again with a Broadway management—Kermit Bloomgarden and Philip Barry, Jr.—to present James Saunders' *Next Time I'll Sing to You* directed by the English Peter Coe and casting James Earl Jones opposite Estelle Parsons. But it opened at a bad time—just after the Kennedy assassination —and closed after twenty-three performances. After the first of the year the Phoenix attempted a Burt Shevelove adaptation of a William Gillette farce, *Too Much Johnson*—a work of considerable wit and style—but it, too, failed to get over. It was then that the Phoenix's association with Ellis Rabb's APA—Phase Five—commenced. The excuse for the initial contact was a project not then ready for execution. The Phoenix management had become interested in *War and Peace* in a stage adaptation by Erwin Piscator which had been done at the Schiller Theater in Berlin with great success in 1955. The play was produced in London by the Bristol Old Vic under the direction of Val May. Norris Houghton had seen it there in 1963. Hambleton and Houghton recognized that the intricacies of the work demanded the talents and training of a company of players well accustomed to working with one another. Such was the APA.

Twenty strong, the company came back to New York from Michigan in March, 1964. They brought four pretested and refined productions: Pirandello's *Right You Are (If You*

Think You Are), staged by Stephen Porter; George M. Cohan's *The Tavern,* staged by Rabb, which had been seen two seasons before at the Folksbiene Theater off-Broadway; Molière's *Scapin* and *Impromptu at Versailles,* low comedy and high comedy translated and staged by Porter; and Gorki's *The Lower Depths,* staged by Rabb. Members of the company included Nancy Marchand, Joanna Roos, Jane McArthur, Clayton Corzatte, Keene Curtis, Paul Sparer. But there was a notable missing name—Rosemary Harris was in England at the Chichester Festival playing with Laurence Olivier in *Uncle Vanya* and would be staying on to play Ophelia for the British National Theater in London.

The partnership began—on one side, the talent, the programming, and the artistry, a skilled and confident company anxious to move out of the peripheral theater and prove itself in the theater capital; on the other side, the in-place theater management that could deliver the building, the playing machinery, and the audience in New York.

A running pattern was established the following season. The APA would have a break-in period at its fall home base in Ann Arbor to mount the new shows and put them in smooth running order. Its New York season would commence in early December and continue through March, or longer if the demand held up. The prospect of an APA season brought many old Phoenix subscribers back into the fold. To start off the season the Phoenix independently produced *Dr. Faustus* directed by Word Baker with a large cast headed by Lou Antonio and James Ray. The APA's own season opened with a stylishly played *Man and Superman,* and Rosemary Harris rejoined the company to play Giraudoux's *Judith.* Miss Harris was an actress of personal radiance, a brilliant highlight to an accomplished company. By midseason the build-back of Phoenix subscriptions had reached 7,500.

War and Peace, in many respects, was the most interesting production the APA-Phoenix attempted, and one of the most challenging. How could one fit so vast a historical panorama to the confining stage? Within the company proper were all the main performers needed to portray Tolstoy's characters —Donald Moffat as the Soldier Prince Andrei Bolkonski, who is separated by the war from his fiancée and finally mortally wounded at the Battle of Borodino; Rosemary Harris as the lovely young Natasha Rostov; Sydney Walker as the fierce-eyed but sentimental old Prince; Keene Curtis as Napoleon, giving an uncanny impersonation in stance, and voice, and bearing; Ronald Bishop as the good-hearted but vacillating Pierre, who is Andrei's friend and also falls in love with Natasha. Into their lives the war weaves its way inexorably, jarring and transforming friendships and old attachments. Against the vast backdrop of the Napoleonic invasion small scenes were played: Sydney Walker as the Prince scolding Natasha with mock severity for not learning her lessons better. The corner details in the tapestry were sewn with as much care as the centerpiece, and this equal attention to foreground and background gave the production human and historical verisimilitude.

Rabb, the director, was interested in the project for its overwhelming production challenges. As writing the work was undistinguished, but as a concept for a production it was unique. Platforms of different height separated the Russian forces from the French. Single banners unfurled to the fanfare of trumpets signified the massing of armies. A tilted chessboard with oversized pieces displayed the alignment of forces along the Borodino River. Perhaps the most successful innovation was the use of an adaptable narrator, Clayton Corzatte, in a dinner jacket, to speed up the narration, introduce the characters, and occasionally step into the scene to play the part of a minor character. The trained APA actors made Tolstoy's great novel come alive.

Financially the Phoenix found itself sinking back into the same old difficulties it supposedly left behind in the downtown theater. It now had the financial burden of carrying a permanent company even larger than the one before but supported by a theater with a considerably smaller gross capacity. There was no way off-Broadway with its 299-seat ceiling could sustain a company of twenty on a long-term basis. Even with capacity houses the deficit was again approaching $100,000. Hambleton and Rabb felt it was time to make the assault on Broadway. There were artistic reasons as well as financial compulsions in support of such a move and an undeniable drive for wider public recognition. They opened negotiations with the Shuberts to rent the Lyceum, the ideal Broadway house for repertory because of its vast scene docks and storage space and its honeycomb of dressing rooms on either side of the stage rising in tiers like the boxes at the opera. Daniel Frohman had built and equipped the Lyceum to house a repertory company in 1902, but not until the days of the APA-Phoenix was it to be used exactly as intended. No theater in New York was more spacious or better suited to this purpose until the Vivian Beaumont in Lincoln Center was opened in 1965.

Needed foundation grants to support the move to Broadway, especially a large sum requested of Ford, failed to come through. It was agreed that APA would hold together for a year, sustaining itself through out-of-town engagements, while Hambleton mounted a fund-raising drive of sufficient size to assure a five-year period of repertory. During the past season on East Seventy-fourth Street they had opened three big productions, each involving serious artistic risks, both with the critics and the audience, and each gamble they had won. Now they had to accept the added hazard of losing that carefully gathered momentum by being absent a whole season. Writing in the New York *Times* in June, 1965, Howard Taubman suggested the difficulties they faced: "The impetus for the founding of resident professional companies in the United States shows no sign of lessening. While the trend is encouraging, there is a danger that must not be blinked. It is now too easily forgotten that a solid, permanent company cannot be expected, except in the rarest of circumstances, to be self-sustaining."

A final performance of *Man and Superman* wound up their extended season in early September, and Ellis Rabb spoke indefinitely of the future. Once again it seemed like the end. "With this kind of project," he said, "we have gone as far as we can go until new circumstances challenge us or until I and the rest of the troops learn something we just don't know at this time."

There were, inevitably, intracompany strains. Paul Sparer and his wife, Nancy Marchand, severed their five-year-old connections with the APA and went their own way in August. Rabb, while not alluding specifically to this break, spoke understandingly of the difficulty: "We take the talent we've got and we wear it out, we burn it up." Of Sydney Walker, who had played probably more big roles in a shorter period than anyone in the company, he said, "The number of hours he's worked, the number of parts he's played over the last three years is a phenomenon in his profession." For the actors the APA-Phoenix was their whole life. One of the secrets of their success was simple to the point of obviousness: they simply never stopped rehearsing. Once, a day or two before reopening their production of *School for Scandal*, which at that time they had been rehearsing and playing for five years, Rosemary Harris turned to Rabb and asked, "Have you really canceled that run-through for tomorrow? I feel under-rehearsed." The APA policy was never to say finished.

Out in Ann Arbor at the beginning of the new season the Phoenix mounted a production of Kaufman and Hart's *You Can't Take It with You*. The irrepressible Hambleton pronounced it good enough to bring in. Against the possibility of a repertory season at the Lyceum he had raised some money from 500 Phoenix subscribers and friends—funds held in escrow when the Ford grant fell through. By raising the balance of a $45,000 budget from among the twenty Phoenix board members, he was able to open *You Can't Take It with*

You at the Lyceum. There its success unlocked the doors to the APA's return to New York in November, 1966, for a thirty-week season with seven major productions. Ford eventually came through with a substantial grant of $900,000—one of its largest to an individual theater organization—to be spread over the following three seasons. APA-Phoenix had three seasons at the Lyceum. Even with augmented audiences on Broadway and, on the whole, extraordinarily fine notices, the deficits continued to mount. The annual cash outflow exceeded $2,000,000. The payroll for stagehands owing to the continual scene-shifting requirements of repertory became a staggering burden and accounted for an unreasonable proportion of total costs. For the final, killing season, the stagehand bill was reported to be $304,000. Compare this to the $597,000 paid to all the artists involved—the actors, directors, and designers.

A poorly received final production of *Hamlet* with Ellis Rabb in the title role seemed to be the *coup de grâce*. But the difficulties went deeper than any one production. A widening separation developed between the artistic side represented by Rabb and the business side represented by Hambleton, symbolized, perhaps, by the width of the Lyceum Theater, which separated Rabb's office at the back from Hambleton's at the front. In the middle of most artistic breakdowns, economics is usually a factor, and in the demise of APA-Phoenix money worries were the chief cause.

As APA gradually dispersed around the country, Hambleton, in New York, lost no time in reasserting the identity of the Phoenix. So long as he was there, the day of his theater was not over. Prepared to operate either on Broadway or off Broadway, he commenced functioning essentially as a Broadway manager. Into the ANTA Theater on Broadway he brought a revival of *Harvey* starring James Stewart and Helen Hayes. Hambleton had always been able to persuade big names to work for the sake of a presumed theatrical idealism. The following season, 1970–71, he returned to the Lyceum with a Stephen Porter-directed *School for Wives* in the immaculate Richard Wilbur translation. Brian Bedford won a Tony Award for playing the foolish trusting husband. At the Good Shepherd-Faith Presbyterian Church adjacent to Lincoln Center, in a production directed by Gordon Davidson, the California director-producer who got his start stage managing at the Phoenix, Hambleton co-sponsored Father Daniel Berrigan's moving confessional documentary *The Trial of the Catonsville Nine*. This was the Phoenix's nearest approach to dealing directly with the issues of the day.

In the middle of managing his season in 1971 Hambleton was hospitalized with a painful back and underwent an operation for a slipped disc. He returned to the job as soon as he was able, smiling his quizzical smile, rising with some stiffness from behind the broad desk he keeps upstairs in Frohman's old quarters in the decaying Lyceum—testimony to the extraordinary continuity that is still alive in certain quarters of the New York theater—and hobbled down the hall past the handsome French windows above the Lyceum marquee where Times Square pigeons flutter on the rococo colonnaded balcony. Carelessly, as if trying to deny his limitation by ignoring it, he moved rapidly along the corridor on his cane to the elevator to make a lunch date concerning his next show. In the years since 1953 the Phoenix, measured by any standard, not alone off-Broadway's, had made of itself an enterprise of great pith and moment. Hambleton had never lost the name of action.

Seven

Regional Theater

There is a close and significant correlation in time between the beginning of off-Broadway and the first meaningful stirrings in the regional theater. The earliest of the regional theaters in the late 1940's and early 1950's coincide with the first signs of off-Broadway activity and both the regional theater and off-Broadway had a common rationale—an anti-Broadway bias, a shared distrust of commercial standards; in New York a conviction that an alternate theater could be established free of the economic restrictions of Broadway and elsewhere in the country a hope that audiences could be induced to patronize a theater of their own rather than wait upon road tours of New York origin. The regional theaters (or rather, in place of "regional," which carries the wrong connotation, the "resident professional theater," signifying a local awareness, in cities across the country, at about the same time, of the desirability of indigenous theater institutions) were cast in the image of off-Broadway, never in the image of Broadway.

The earliest of these theaters are among the strongest today. They sprang from local impulses, from the steadfast determination of some one individual: Margo Jones, perhaps the first to gain national recognition, establishing her theater-in-the-round in Dallas in 1947, or, then more obscurely, Nina Vance, who founded her Alley Theater in Houston the same year. In their early philosophical conversations, Margo Jones used to say, "Nina, what do you want to *do* in the American theater? Just what is it you want to *do*?" But for Nina Vance it was enough simply to have a stage, to do the plays, and she did not look to the theater for the fulfillment of some abstract and swelling idea that might alter history. "Do?" she would reply testily, for these two Texans both had impatient ambition and a flinty independence. "I don't want to *do* anything." And in truth she set out, as she put it, to prove only a few things: "That good taste in Podunk is the same as good taste in Houston; that Houston and Podunk both should have good theater and that the standards of good theater should be the same everywhere."

Much the same controlled ambition led Mack Scism to found his Mummers Theater under a carnival tent in Oklahoma City in 1949 and Zelda Fichandler her Arena Stage in Washington in an abandoned movie theater in 1950. Later on, theaters were conceived in the civic consciousness of the townspeople and housed more handsomely from the start, particularly as arts centers came into vogue. But the earliest theaters were one-woman shows. Without exception each was the outgrowth of the extraordinary impulses and talents of an individual. The opening of theaters in Houston and Dallas, Oklahoma City and Washington corresponds roughly with the off-Broadway opening of Circle in the Square in 1951 by Quintero and Mann and the Phoenix in 1953 by Hambleton and Houghton. The record discloses theaters of more antique origin. The history of the Cleveland Playhouse goes back to 1916, and the Pasadena Playhouse was started in 1917. Again the correspondence in time between these events and the appearance in New York of the Washington Square Players and the Provincetown Playhouse in that earlier flowering of the off-Broadway spirit seems hardly accidental.

In the cities of the Southwest and to some extent Washington, the opening of permanent theaters was evidence of a general cultural awakening. Almost the whole cultural development of Houston occurred in a rush of outsize Texan enthusiasm in the decade before the Alley Theater came into being. Art galleries had begun popping up like corner drugstores only five years before. The interest in theater—a theater for performing the classics, the new European plays, modern American work, and, when possible, the product of new playwrights—grew alongside the interest in music, in art collections, and the increased flow of traffic to the cultural capital of New York. Rich Houstonians would think nothing of flying up to New York for a weekend of theater and gallerygoing. From a literary standpoint, the theater took inspiration from the American playwriting renaissance of the 1940's, which was to die out in the 1960's; already in the 1950's the theaters in Houston and Washington and elsewhere were preparing themselves to be the conduits of new American writing talent in the 1970's.

Later theaters had a less specific germination. Resident theaters that came along in the 1960's, like the Tyrone Guthrie in Minneapolis, Seattle, and the New England theaters in Hartford, New Haven, and Providence, were part of a more generalized national awakening of interest in theater. Many were started by complete outsiders, who either invited themselves in or were brought in at the invitation of civic groups. Two New York producers, Oliver Rea and Peter Zeisler, were determined to set up a large repertory theater somewhere outside New York. They interested Tyrone Guthrie in their plan and canvassed the country for a likely location. They settled on Minneapolis where large-scale community support seemed assured.

In the development of the whole movement the ubiquitous Ford Foundation has played a mammoth role. Through an imaginative variety of grant programs, starting small and ending up, in some cases, very large indeed, Ford tested the ground and coaxed and urged the movement along in the hope of raising *professional* standards for theater outside New York. Individual grants have been awarded directors to study theaters outside their own cities and often outside the country. Playwrights have been subsidized to work directly with resident companies. Project grants have been established to support the salaries of actors willing to commit themselves to full seasons of strenuous repertory away from the more commercially alluring center of New York. In one or two cases there has been deficit financing to cover the operating losses of theaters through ticket subsidy. And very large grants have been made for the building of new theaters so elaborate and costly in design, but so closely tailored to the artistic needs and capabilities of each theater's director and staff, that they could be either the breaking or the making of the entire movement.

Chief architect and moneyman of Ford expansion has been W. McNeil Lowry, a former English professor and Washington newspaper chain correspondent who has headed the foundation's program in the humanities and the arts from the beginning. Lowry initially made a careful survey of the possibilities for theater everywhere in the country, looking especially for artistic potential outside New York, whose Byzantine theater structure and devious workings, particularly in the commercial realm, he very early despaired of influencing. Small travel grants in the late 1950's to such directors as Nina Vance (Lowry had visited Houston as early as 1957) and Mack Scism in Oklahoma City enabled Lowry to discover where genuine talent lay and, once having located it, to develop it. Lowry got to know all the serious theater figures in the country—directors, producers, leading actors, designers, promising playwrights, front-of-the-house managers, even journalists. He developed two guidelines or principles to determine Ford's grant policy for years to come. First, permanent resident companies, not excluding New York, were "the chief hope for the advancement of serious American drama." The Phoenix was to be included under this heading. Second, the strength of any theater depended ultimately on a person—on the talent and drive of the producing

Off-Broadway's gifted Sada Thompson, with John Dodson, in Circle in the Square's 1961 production of the Dylan Thomas play *Under Milk Wood,* which was directed by William Ball.

Friedman-Abeles

Another skeleton awaits in the closet for Jo Van Fleet as Madame Rosepettle in the Phoenix' 1962 production of Arthur L. Kopit's *Oh, Dad, Poor Dad, Mamma's Hung You in the Closet and I'm Feelin' So Sad.*

Henry Grossman

Liza Minelli leads the line in a scene from the musical *Best Foot Forward,* in which she made her stage debut in 1963.

In rehearsal for O'Neill's *Desire Under the Elms* at Circle in the Square in 1963, Rip Torn comforts Colleen Dewhurst while a wounded George C. Scott bellows behind them.
Friedman-Abeles

J. D. Cannon and James Earl Jones playing brothers in the South African Atholl Fugard's two-character *Blood Knot* at the Cricket Theater in 1964.

layton Corzatte as Hector Malone and osemary Harris as Violet in the 1964 PA-Phoenix production of Shaw's *Man nd Superman*.

James Keson

The monstrous papier-mâché figur
in *Motel*, one of the three sati
pieces that made up Jean-Claude v.
Itallie's *America Hurrah* in 1966.

Off-Broadway's acted-out anger at the war in Southeast Asia was physicalized
in Megan Terry's *Viet Rock* at the Martinique Theater in the fall of 1966.

director. "A true theater," Lowry said, "never starts with a building but with the fanatical determination of one driving talent (nowadays usually a director, but sometimes a playwright or an actor)." Consequently, Ford has stepped in with substantial theater-building funds, as in Houston and Oklahoma City, only when convinced of the strength of the resident artistic leadership. Again in an address in Houston in April, 1967, Lowry said, "To make any difference in what happens in the creative life of the United States, everything we do must bear witness to the fact that art begins and ends with the artist and the artistic director."

Even with talented leadership the resident theaters beyond New York had two great problems to contend with outside of the ever-present burden of fund raising. One was the problem of asserting a personal artistic identity when one's monopoly position as the only theater in town persuaded one continually to the generalized function of being all things to all men. In the theatrical capital of New York a hundred flowers bloom. All within the same season and utilizing the same actors, in their choice of plays, the resident theaters needed to reconcile competing demands: to be comprehensive and intensive at the same time. On the one hand was the pitfall of being the theatrical supermarket stocked to accommodate a wide audience and on the other that of catering too personally to the artistic director's taste. The theaters which strayed in this latter direction historically have seen serious leadership struggles develop between the director and the board of trustees.

Second was the problem of attracting and holding a company of good actors against the competitive pressures of the East and West coasts. In 1959 Ford devised a program to test the sincerity of the often-heard actor's expression of preference for repertory. Four theaters were picked to receive a three-year matching, or challenge, grant to underwrite the annual contracts of ten company actors at the level of $200 a week. The theaters were the Alley, the Arena, Herbert Blau and Jules Irving's San Francisco Actor's Workshop, and the Phoenix in New York. Lowry said, "Everywhere in the country they are crying 'repertory.' The real question is, do the actors mean it enough to leave New York. Will they go to Houston and San Francisco and Washington? We're calling their bluff."

Aside from its short-term benefits, the program contributed to the acceptability of resident theaters as places to work for a widening pool of performers. Within the benefited companies jealousies inevitably developed between the "Ford" actors and the regulars. But in retrospect, the program significantly upgraded the acting standards throughout the movement. Naturally, today, Gordon Davidson at the Mark Taper Forum in Los Angeles, discounting his own enviable record as a director, has an easier time finding exceptional actors than Word Baker might at Cincinnati's Playhouse in the Park, even crediting his wide acquaintanceship with actors, and New York will remain the actor's unforsakable home, to which he must return, if not often in body, always in spirit.

For a while Lowry and the Ford staff, which had done its homework well, expected the assisted theaters eventually to become self-supporting. That was rather wishful—and Lowry's major mistake. But the error was understandable. Foundations are not so constituted or endowed as to be able to exempt their beneficiaries from the facts of life. "The Ford Foundation," said Lowry in 1962 as he announced grants totaling $6,100,000 to nine favored theater companies, "will not go into the indefinite deficit financing of theater companies." All the chosen companies, he anticipated, would find a break-even point at 75 percent or less of capacity, eventually. In a progress report two years later he hedged his bet: "The ability of non-profit theaters to attain artistic and economic continuity still remains to be demonstrated." By 1967 he had thrown in the towel on financial self-sufficiency. In his Houston address, quoted above, he appended this admission, "By now we all realize that artistic organizations and groups of

truly professional quality and with a professional repertoire
cannot be expected to reach permanent self-support at the
box office, from tuitions or from the sale of memberships,
even those who may have been the beneficiary of a significant
philanthropic grant for a stipulated period of years."

The theaters themselves cannot look to the foundations for
continuing support, but there are now good indications that
the National Endowment for the Arts, first under Roger L.
Stevens and next under Nancy Hanks, has accepted a continuing, if limited, responsibility for the health of the new
cultural network. During the first five fiscal years of the endowment, 1966–70, a total of $1,400,000 was committed to
resident professional theaters. In fiscal 1971 the amount committed was $1,100,000, and by fiscal 1972 the endowment in
one year was allocating more to these theaters than it did in
the first five years put together—$1,500,000 divided among
thirty-six theaters.

Ford's real accomplishment was to force the issue of local
responsibility. In the beginning, not unexpectedly, noti-
fication of a Ford grant tended to dry up the sources of local
giving. Why would anyone need a rich uncle if he had Ford?
But in the long run, by raising the ante, the foundation
encouraged the community to accept a continuing commitment to theater. From the financial standpoint, it remains to
be seen, of course, if cities will accept theaters on an equal
basis with libraries, art galleries, and symphony orchestras.
From the artistic standpoint, still to be demonstrated is the
ability of the theater to survive as a cultural landmark while
preserving its free artistic spirit.

In Washington, Houston, and Oklahoma City especially,
these landmarks are not only highly visible but ineffaceable.
The theaters are now housed in substantial, unusual-looking
modern plants for which there is no architectural precedent,
each containing two theaters of varying seating capacity and
utility. In January, 1971, Zelda Fichandler opened the

$1,500,000 Kreeger Theater as a connected addition to her Arena Stage, christening it with the American premiere of the British comedy *The Ruling Class* by Peter Barnes. "Theater buildings by themselves do not matter," said Mrs. Fichandler in a dedicatory address, "because the theater event is an explosion of life and can take place anywhere. The essence of theater as an art is the storyteller looking around at his audience and beginning to speak. . . . On the other hand, if a theater building is right for its time and function it can matter most of all."

The main brick and concrete part of the 796-seat Arena Stage with its offices, kitchens, and rehearsal rooms was put up in the fall of 1961 to become then the biggest new theater built for a permanent professional company. Originally housed in a movie theater, the Arena Stage had next occupied an old brewery in the Northwest section of Washington to which still clung the stale aroma of long-since-emptied kegs of beer. The arenalike staging area had seen many previous uses—a hospitality hall, a basketball floor, an icehouse, a clubroom, and the shipping department where the kegs were loaded onto wagon carts.

By contrast, the new Arena, as indeed is each of the big new resident theater buildings, was tailored to the hour-by-hour walking and working habits of the director, staff, and company, and Mrs. Fichandler's office was so situated near the stage that she could look out on rehearsals and performances from her desk. Architect Harry Weise had worked from tapes of lengthy staff sessions and a file of filled-out questionnaires specifying what everyone wanted in a theater, down to a box-office window of a height that would enable the ticket seller to sit while the buying customer stood. In Houston architect Ulrich Franzen studied the work patterns of the Alley staff before designing the new $3,500,000 complex in downtown Houston. Of the two theaters inside, the 300-seat Arena stage is modeled most closely after the original playing space in the converted factory building on Berry Street Miss

Vance occupied from 1949 to 1968. The other is a "multi-space stage" facing a fan-shaped auditorium seating 800 in which sections of stage at several acting levels surround the audience. A Ford grant of $2,100,000 in 1962, half construction, half developmental, started off Houston's building campaign.

A similar two-part grant of $1,250,000, later supplemented with $535,000 in additional funds to cover rising building costs, assured the construction of the new Mummers Theater in Oklahoma City. Local contributions came to $750,000. The Mummers, designed by John M. Johanson, is visually the most remarkable of the new theaters—three interconnected circular buildings of varying circumference joined in a construct of blocks, connecting pipes, inclined ramps, and rectangular vertical columns. Brightly colored, it looks at a distance like a creative plaything for an advanced seven-year-old. Largest of the circular sections, the 592-seat Space Stage Theater, was opened in December, 1970, with Edward Mulhare playing the Paul Scofield role in *A Man for All Seasons*. The 240-seat Arena Theater is patterned after the stage in the Mummers' former home in a one-story warehouse building in an industrial part of town—a gesture of respect for the workable past.

In Oklahoma City, ever since as an Oklahoma City high school English teacher Mack Scism founded the Mummers Theater in 1949, he had a building fund which varied from a few hundred dollars to a few thousand. As the home of ballerina Maria Tallchief, Oklahoma City was dance-conscious, and major foreign companies such as the Royal Danish Ballet used to play the vast 6,000-seat Municipal Auditorium. For a time Scism's theater found house room in the auditorium's Mirror Room, but it took agonizing years of mostly ignored pleading for him finally to graft a theater onto the city's cultural skin. Perhaps the fear of renewed neglect accounts for the flamboyance of the new theater's design. It is one building among the busy oil rigs ringing the town that cannot be ignored. Scism first came to the notice of the Ford Foundation in 1959, when he received one of Lowry's director's grants. He took the summer in Stratford, Ontario, to study Shakespeare techniques. "We've been so isolated here," he said. "We've never done any research preparation. We've just hauled off and done things. But the chance to observe how other people have managed has helped a great deal. We know all the shortcuts now."

In the summer of 1960, still on the grant, Scism continued his education by visiting theaters throughout Europe and spending time with Joan Littlewood in London and Jean Vilar in Avignon. In the United States he worked with both Nina Vance and Zelda Fichandler, regional American Joan Littlewoods. The Ford-financed foreign travel of American resident theater leaders has helped assure a European orientation to the American resident theater movement. Rejecting the commercial standards of the New York theater, the traveling directors took their cue from the great publicly supported repertory theaters of Europe—the company of regular performers, the classic repertoire, the artistic leadership of a Max Reinhart or Helene Weigel, schools and training programs, long rehearsals, the cultivation of a full and rich professional life within the walls of one respected and community-supported institution. They aspired to be the Comédie Française rather than the Theater Guild.

To these indigenously begun and managed theaters— Washington, Houston, Oklahoma City, and San Francisco in the days of Blau and Irving—there is, however, a native American grass-roots spirit. No matter what the size of the town, Nina Vance believed, the basis for its theater should be the best possible use of local people. Until his new theater came, Mack Scism resisted going Equity and drew his acting talent from a 100-mile area surrounding Oklahoma City. When the Arena Stage became too big for one-woman management, Zelda Fichandler's husband, Thomas C. Fichandler, resigned his position as an economist with the Twentieth

Century Fund in Washington to supervise the administrative and financial operations full time. Still, the flow of repertory actors around the country, the thrust of Ford support, the interchangeability of jobbed-in directors militate against a theater's chance to develop a uniquely local character. It was optimistic to expect that actors, designers, directors, technicians, and playwrights could be located in plentiful enough supply in each town, even on an amateur basis, to staff a theater. As a result, a national, transcity theatrical structure has been superimposed on these theaters, tending to obscure local character and spread a certain programmatic sameness throughout the movement. To some extent the success of the parts was to depend on the success of the whole. Again the Ford staff, in its wisdom and with its cash, anticipated the interdependence of these emerging groups by setting up the Theater Communications Group in 1961 as the central intelligence agency of the movement. TCG keeps each theater informed of what the others are doing. It provides professional consultation on subscription drives and arranges exchange visits of directors and staff members among the theaters. It has raised central casting to a high level by conducting annual two-day mass auditions attended by everyone—all with the ultimate objective of the steady professionalization of theater nationally. TCG, today an association of thirty-three resident theaters including four based in New York, is presided over by Hartney Arthur, an experienced and wise theater man who has worked on three continents and is the unseen catalytic agent for many key theater moves throughout the country.

The most advanced, the most successful, and financially the best managed theater in the movement is clearly Zelda Fichandler's Arena Stage in Washington. It enjoys, of course, the advantage of being situated in the second most cosmopolitan city in the country, drawing on government employees, members of Congress, and the diplomatic corps for audience to support a balanced theater program of European stage literature, modern American plays, Broadway successes, and new work. It is near enough to New York readily to bring down visiting directors of such note as Gene Frankel, Alan Schneider, and William Ball. (Zelda Fichandler has herself directed about a quarter of the 165 productions in nineteen seasons.)

Mrs. Fichandler has not let Broadway's judgment influence her own. Like off-Broadway, the Arena Stage has had considerable luck in taking plays that were either dismissed on Broadway or unsuccessfully produced there and making good on them. Lawrence and Lee's *The Gang's All Here* and Robert Anderson's *Silent Night, Lonely Night* fall into this category. A considerable body of new work has come out of the Arena—Josh Greenfeld's *Clandestine on the Morning Line*; two shorter plays by Millard Lampell, *The Lonesome Train* and *Hard Travelin'*; Loring Mandel's *Project Immortality*; Howard Sackler's *The Great White Hope*, directed by the Arena's Edwin Sherin, with James Earl Jones and Jane Alexander (who had played in *Saint Joan* at the Arena two seasons earlier), in the season of 1967–68; and Arthur Kopit's *Indians*, directed by Gene Frankel the following season, both of which were subsequently produced on Broadway and staged by the same directors with much of the Arena's casting intact.

Certainly the myth that no new work comes out of the resident theaters—a myth perpetrated by Broadway producers unable to accept the possibility of any new theater of consequence being started outside their jurisdiction—can no longer be supported. But this was so even before New York began receiving the new work of the Arena Stage, Gordon Davidson's Mark Taper Forum in Los Angeles, Robert Brustein's Yale Drama School, and New Haven's Long Wharf Theater.

It was, for example, Nina Vance's Alley Theater in Houston which first produced Paul Zindel's *The Effect of Gamma Rays on Man-in-the-Moon Marigolds* in May, 1965, the last

year of the old Alley, before the move into Ulrich Franzen's
new plant. The Alley has even put on Broadway commercial
successes before they got to Broadway: Ronald Alexander's
Time Out for Ginger in 1950. And it had done James Lee's
Career in 1955, a year before it was produced off-Broadway.
Texas, in fact, has had something of a record in starting new
plays: Margo Jones in Dallas had produced both Tennessee
Williams' *Summer and Smoke* and Lawrence and Lee's *In-
herit the Wind* before the plays reached Broadway. Lawrence
and Lee, more than most playwrights, have been persuaded
of the value of a regional tryout, and they use the system to
their advantage.

The determined and driven individuals such as Nina Vance
who have started theaters have voracious appetites—for good
plays, for design, for talented actors, for ideas. But they are
also pragmatists. "I get what I call the hot dog and caviar
trade," Miss Vance has said of her audience. "On the one
hand, young people come to the theater, which is fine and
encouraging. And on the other hand, we get the kind of
person who can go to New York theater any time he wants
and whose standards of quality are consequently very high."
She made a point of staying close to her audience, of being
ready to throw on the moneymaking certainty when she felt
she had lost the audience's ear with serious work, and therefore it was with reluctance in 1961 that the Alley turned to
subscription and foreclosed the possibility of abrupt midseason schedule changes to hold the fluctuating audience attention.

Practically all resident theaters today are on subscription,
for subscription is obviously the best technique for weaning
audiences from the hit-only psychology of Broadway theatergoing and inducing them to identify their loyalties with
the institution, not the play.

In some cases the artistic direction of the theater was so
assertive and strong that the wishes of the audience, even
could they have been articulated, were of secondary impor-

tance. The Actor's Workshop in San Francisco had a four-teen-year history marked by considerable achievement, all with very little concrete support from the community. The theater was an extension of the forceful personalities of its founders. Jules Irving and Herbert Blau, both native New Yorkers, both highly verbal and articulate about theater, were professors at San Francisco State College when in 1952 they decided to start a theater dedicated to ensemble playing in a loft behind a judo academy. They had "no clear social motivation" at the time, Blau assures us in *The Impossible Theater*, published by Macmillan in 1964, but it seems clear in the years that followed they did only the work that interested them: Brecht, the Absurdist writers, Pinter's *The Birthday Party*. Their *Waiting for Godot*, directed by Blau, with Irving playing the slave, Lucky, came to the York Playhouse in New York in the summer of 1958 prior to playing the Brussels World's Fair. They had acquired quite a reputation by the time they received the call in January, 1965, to take over the Lincoln Center Repertory Theater from Robert Whitehead and Elia Kazan. Their departure signified the end of the Actor's Workshop. There was a brief interregnum when the director John Hancock was brought in to carry on, decimated though the company was by the wholesale borrowings of Blau and Irving for New York. Musical chairs has been a favorite game among the resident theaters. In the summer of 1966 Hancock left San Francisco to become artistic director of the Pittsburgh Playhouse vacated by William Ball and his American Conservatory Theater after a disagreement with local authorities. Ball, who had been casting about for a place outside New York to sustain his huge operation—not only a theater but a conservatory—thereupon was welcomed to San Francisco. Ball's spirited ACT, through which flows some of the finest theatrical talent in the country, has had headquarters there ever since, keeping two theaters busy, the small 600-seat former home of the Actor's Workshop and the larger 1,500-seat Geary, once a tour house for road attractions.

Ball in many respects is the most interesting figure in the resident theater movement, a brilliant director, something of a faddist, one of the first to promote the Alexander Technique for stimulating psychic health through muscle control, and a Nijinsky in juggling actors, directors, and multiple-play repertory schedules. Handsome to the point nearly of prettiness, he has a personal magnetism that is both masculine and feminine and enormously appealing to actors: on the one side an almost acrobatic athleticism, on the other a brooding sensitivity lightened by quick flashes of intuitive thought. He is perhaps the one true theatrical genius of the movement. Vast as it is in staff and company and program, ACT remains very much one man's circus. National in scope and personally run, it does not belong in the category of the indigenous theaters which have been discussed earlier.

The second significant category of resident professional theaters is that of the community-inspired theater—those theaters that came into being not so much as the result of the theatrical vision of an individual as of the cultural aspirations of the community. The Center Theater Group in Los Angeles, Seattle, Milwaukee, and the no-longer functioning Theater of the Living Arts in Philadelphia belong in this group.

In Gordon Davidson, after many years of theatrical fumbling, Los Angeles had at last found a director-producer of talent and energy to galvanize the theatrical resources of the West Coast. Davidson got his theatrical training in the East, as an apprentice at the American Shakespeare Festival in Stratford, Connecticut, as a stage manager for the Phoenix, as an off-Broadway producer, and in the Southwest as a visiting opera and theater director in Texas. Sensing that the real growth in theater was taking place outside New York, Davidson in 1964 joined the UCLA Theater Group, which Abbott Kaplan had founded in 1959, signing on as an assistant director for a production of *King Lear*, and staying to become managing director. He first made national news directing a production of *The Deputy* booked coast to coast. In 1967 the Theater Group left the UCLA campus and moved into the Los Angeles Music Center—the 2,100-seat Ahmanson Theater for major productions and big tours such as the Royal Shakespeare Theater and a possible starting point for Broadway shows; the 750-seat Mark Taper Forum for less commercial theater. The more flexible Forum under Davidson's supervision, opening on April 14, 1967, with John Whiting's *The Devils* with Frank Langella and Joyce Ebert, has produced the more interesting work. A high percentage of Davidson's projects have worked their way East, giving him the reputation in the 1970's of the most exciting young director in the resident theaters. He produced Derek Walcott's *The Dream on Monkey Mountain*, which had been seen at George White's Eugene O'Neill Memorial Theater Foundation in Waterford, Connecticut, and was subsequently done by the Negro Ensemble Company in New York; *In the Matter of J. Robert Oppenheimer*, done at Lincoln Center; the Reverend Daniel Berrigan's *The Trial of the Catonsville Nine*, done by the Phoenix Theater and Leland Hayward; and *Murderous Angels*, Conor Cruise O'Brien's controversial reconstruction of what may have happened between Patrice Lumumba and Dag Hammarskjöld in the Congo crisis of 1961. In addition, Paul Sills' *Story Theater* might never have made it to Broadway but for its success at the Forum under Davidson's management.

Other theaters go about their work more quietly on the surface but with internal disruption. The Seattle Repertory Theater was a community-inspired project arising out of a real estate surplus left by Seattle's World's Fair—an 800-seat theater the city was reluctant to see demolished. Stuart Vaughan was hired as artistic director to organize a company, and the Seattle Rep opened in November, 1963, with *King Lear*. Vaughan survived two and a half seasons to be succeeded by Allen Fletcher, previously the artistic director of the American Shakespeare Festival, and Fletcher, in turn, recently was succeeded by W. Duncan Ross, an English-born

director who had been in the Drama Department of the
University of Washington. In the season of 1970–71 Ross
induced Richard Chamberlain, television's Dr. Kildare, to
play *Richard II*, a stroke of casting that brought the theater
out of the red into the black. Ideally the theater is pro-
grammed to run on annual budgets of three-quarters of a
million dollars, up to 75 percent accounted for by subscriptions and single ticket sales.

Many of the big-name directors have had a try at Milwau-
kee. The Fred Miller Theater was started by a group of
Milwaukee citizens with funds of just over $100,000. William
Ball, Ellis Rabb, Allen Fletcher, Paul Shyre, and Adrian
Hall at one time or another attempted to make Milwaukee
go. More recently the 500-seat theater in the Performing Arts
Center enjoyed a period of continuity under the leadership
of Tunc Yalman. In 1971 a new phase began with Nagle
Jackson, a vigorous theater director in his early thirties who
has seen service with the Oregon Shakespeare Festival, Ball's
ACT, and has directed productions at, among other places,
the Mummers Theater in Oklahoma City and the Hartford
Stage Company. Jackson is regarded as potentially the most
exciting newcomer in the movement.

The opening of the Theater of the Living Arts in Philadelphia was tied in with the cultural rejuvenation of downtown Philadelphia, with large-scale restoration work in the
Society Hill section, with the desire of Philadelphians to
recapture a more graceful past and reassert a new cultural
independence from New York, and with the belief that the
city should no longer continue exclusively as a tryout town
for New York but should sustain its own theatrical activity.
An old South Street movie house of 500 seats in a renewal
area of new apartments and reconditioned houses was converted into a legitimate theater. The Theater of the Living
Arts opened in January, 1965, under the artistic direction of
Andre Gregory. Gregory was thirty at the time but had a
wide and sophisticated knowledge of theater, then more theoretical than practical. He had spent time on the experimental

frontiers, a co-producer of *The Blacks* off-Broadway, an assistant director at the Actor's Workshop in San Francisco,
manager of the American theater program at the Brussels
World's Fair, an assistant at the Seattle Rep, an observer for
a season with the Berliner Ensemble, the most admired theater company of so many American directors in the 1950's and
1960's. Restless, experimental, curious about new theater
techniques from whatever direction, Gregory began making
news with his fresh staging of familiar work or Broadway
hand-me-downs. In his second season, Anouilh's *Poor Bitos*,
which had been something of a bore on Broadway, exploded
with contemporary ideas on the Living Arts stage—electronic
underscoring, Mozart interspersed with congas, sun-gun
lighting trained on the audience in scenes of abrupt transi-
tion, use of such "now" materials in costuming as vinyl and
animal furs, and even an early outbreak of stage nudity, a
single bared breast in a sensual scene. Gregory was eager to
incorporate the contemporary into his productions—sounds,
sights, materials, customs, ideas—and he was willing to go to
the limit with the new kind of stage material coming out of
New York. Eventually Gregory, pursuing his own artistic inclinations, went beyond the tolerances of his Philadelphia
audiences. Disagreements and misunderstandings arose between the theater management and the board of trustees.
The break came in February, 1967, soon after Gregory
opened Rochelle Owens' *Beclch*, a primitive piece whose
crudities the author excused as taking place in an "Africa of
the mind." As a result, he later said, of differences with his
board over artistic policy, money, and communications, Gregory left in early 1967, and the theater, now defunct, was
unable to recover from this blow. Gregory, personally, has
moved on from his Philadelphia into new realms of theater.

In contrast with Philadelphia the New England theaters in
Hartford, Providence, and New Haven resulted very largely
from individual initiatives, the artistic director picking out

the town rather than the other way around. Jacques Cartier was teaching drama at Smith College in Northampton, Massachusetts, when he began looking around at the possibilities. In the mid-1960's Hartford had strengthened its museum and music resources. It had its own university. The reclaiming of the downtown area through the elevated Constitution Plaza building complex above the old riverfront slum streets had been fully realized. But the city lacked a resident theater project. Cartier worked persuasively with some of Hartford's well-disposed civic leaders, who were ready to help with the project both financially and architecturally. Across from the tall new office towers on Constitution Plaza, angled against the backs of some of the older stores on Main Street, was an old warehouse which an interested local architectural firm remodeled with a small open stage. The Hartford Stage Company opened with *Othello* in April, 1964. Civic support has been strong, and each succeeding season the theater's ties with the community have grown firmer. Katharine Houghton, a Hartford-born actress who got her start off-Broadway and in a film appearing with her aunt and namesake, Katharine Hepburn, has appeared with the company. Several Hartford Stage productions have been considered for transfer to New York. Cartier resigned in June, 1968, to pursue further projects of his own and in 1971 took over the direction of the New Orleans theater. The Hartford theater continues securely under the leadership of Paul Weidner. Size is the theater's main economic burden. In a 206-seat theater there is no conceivable break-even point. But plans for a new, larger theater in downtown Hartford are under way.

Providence in 1971 also had a building program to renovate a downtown movie theater as a new home for the seven-year-old Trinity Square Repertory Company headed by Adrian Hall. One local foundation had pledged its entire anticipated four-and-a-half-year income of $200,000 to the project. Hall's company, operating out of several different theaters in town, is one of the best integrated in the country, many of its members having had earlier associations with him in New York productions.

A native of Texas, Hall had trained under Margo Jones in Dallas. A guest director in the resident theaters, he has also staged a number of off-Broadway productions, including *Orpheus Descending*, the musical *Riverwind*, O'Casey's *Red Roses for Me* and *House of Breath* by his fellow Texan William Goyen, this last play about the self-searchings of a Southern family put on by Hall in Providence first with a white cast and then with a black cast in the same evening. Among new works attempted was the musical *The Grass Harp*, which had its premiere in Providence. In 1966 Providence was one of three theaters picked to receive special federal funds from the National Endowment for the Arts and the U.S. Office of Education to test, through actual performance, the feasibility of incorporating live drama into the curricula of secondary schools. The other selected theaters were New Orleans, then run by Stuart Vaughan, and the Inner City Cultural Center in Los Angeles, then headed by Andre Gregory and David Lunney after they together left Philadelphia. In Providence's case, the grant totaled $535,000 over three years. For the actors, besides upgrading production across the board, the project was a stimulating extension of their regular work. Performing before schoolchildren was lively, something of a risk, usually unpredictable in response, but never failing in some sort of response, never bland and indifferent.

In New Haven the Long Wharf Theater is located in a new market development near the harbor and can be viewed fleetingly from the perimetric Connecticut Turnpike as it skirts southwest New Haven. The Long Wharf got started about a year after Hartford and in much the same way. Its young founders, Harlan P. Kleiman and Jon Jory, dividing the business and artistic functions respectively, had both taken courses at the Yale Drama School but had no deeper connections with the city other than their faith in its ability to support a theater even in competition with Broadway tryouts at the Shubert and Robert Brustein's Yale Drama School. Their extraordinary self-assurance—Kleiman aged twenty-four, Jory, twenty-six—as they started fund raising in New Haven derived in part from a successful summer stock season at the Clinton Playhouse farther east on the shore of Long Island Sound. In ten months they raised enough money to erect a thrust-stage theater of 440 seats and begin production. Their energy was prodigious. If they had a fault, it was in trying too much too soon—children's theater on top of the regular program, classes, school-touring plays, in their second summer an entire festival of new plays. A financial crisis ensued in 1967, eventually solved by an emergency local campaign, but in that year Kleiman resigned to take up producing in New York and Jory to be a free-lance director. They were succeeded by Arvin Brown, who has already overseen the transfer to New York of several projects of Long Wharf origination including *A Whistle in the Dark*, which came to off-Broadway in 1970, and the Robert Anderson one-acts *Solitaire, Double Solitaire*.

The most renowned of all resident repertory theaters begun by outsiders is, of course, the Tyrone Guthrie Theater in Minneapolis, which in nine seasons has undergone several changes in command and is now in the charge of Michael Langham. The Guthrie's ties with Stratford, Ontario, where Langham hails from, have always been strong—Guthrie himself; Tanya Moiseiwitsch, the theater's principal designer; Glasgow-born Douglas Campbell, who was Guthrie's first successor; and Langham. Guthrie's first season in 1963 brought in actors of national repute such as Hume Cronyn, Jessica Tandy, Zoe Caldwell, and George Grizzard to perform an ambitious schedule, classical and modern—*Hamlet, The Miser, The Three Sisters,* and *Death of a Salesman*.

The new 1,400-seat open-stage theater had the advantage of expert assistance in every department and an unprecedented outpouring of civic support, including more than $2,000,000 raised regionally by John Cowles, Jr., and Roger G. Kennedy. From the beginning the theater aimed at a national importance and aspired to the position of first repertory theater in the land. Guthrie carried with him very much of a world view, traveled as he was, cozily familiar in his tennis sneakers with stages in England, Canada, Ireland, the Continent, Israel, and New York. Succeeded by Campbell in the 1966 season, Guthrie still returned paternally to his offspring, notably in 1967 to direct *The Oresteia* of Aeschylus in a new adaptation by John Lewin, a resident playwright, under the title *The House of Atreus*. Guthrie improbably cast Douglas Campbell in the role of Clytemnestra, Lee Richardson as Agamemnon, and the Canadian-born Len Cariou as Orestes. This first professional production of the trilogy was brought into New York in the fall of 1968 for eleven performances at the Billy Rose Theater.

Guthrie is now dead; the founders, Oliver Rea and Peter Zeisler, both have left; so have several succeeding artistic directors. Change is part of the normal rhythm. All theaters need to renew themselves periodically. Sometimes the fresh sense of adventure every theater needs to sustain interest is maintained by building programs, sometimes by a change of face. Whether the resident theater movement can be supported indefinitely is still open to question. As Jules Novick, the critic most knowledgeable about these institutions and their work, concluded in his book *Beyond Broadway* (Hill & Wang, 1968): "They were started as acts of faith; nobody knew until they tried, whether the major cities of this country contained large enough potential audiences to support theaters. And nobody knows yet. It stands to reason that in some places the answer will be no. Some weeding out must take place. The arts in general have failed to secure an important place in our national life, and theater is no exception. If our prosperity holds, many of the resident professional theaters may well prosper also; but if there is a depression, these costly institutions are likely to be found expendable."

Our prosperity has not held, but the theaters seem to be clinging on. Perhaps the energy and community commitment that went into the creation of institutions such as the Guthrie, the Alley, the Arena Stage, the Mummers, the Center Stage, and the others will carry them into the foreseeable future.

Eight

Off Off-Broadway

Theater is always reaching back to its innocent sources. Off off-Broadway sought the purity of the simple theatrical partnership of author, director, and actor working with their heads together on the script. Off off-Broadway was like Circle in the Square in the days of its innocence, before it was discovered, when the actors and directors lived and worked together, communal fashion, in their double brownstone off Sheridan Square intent upon the work and oblivious to any presumed critical standards. Ted Mann, whose normal professional curiosity takes him to the off off-Broadway theater perhaps two or three times a week, once said, "When I go there, I feel I'm looking at myself ten years ago." Off off-Broadway recalled the Living Theater's early peripatetic search for a stage from loft to living room. Ellen Stewart's Cafe La Mama suffered similar seasonal uprootings as a result of municipal harassment.

Off off-Broadway was in the tradition of George Cram Cook's Provincetown Players in its ambition to remain small, avoid commercial temptations and pressures, resist professionalism, and do the work. Like George Cram Cook, such off off-Broadway sponsors as Ellen Stewart, Joe Cino, Al Carmines at the Judson Poets' Theater, and Michael Allen and Ralph Cook at Theater Genesis were catalysts of talent. The whole of their drive was to create the conditions of possibility and preserve the amateurlike interrelatedness of the theatrical process whereby the playwright himself could participate in all phases of the production from casting and costuming to setting the lights.

Commercialism creates a distance between the writer and the work, interposing the producer, the business manager, and the publicist and establishing standards of success unrelated to the original impulse. First and last the purpose of off off-Broadway was to serve the writer and give him a hearing. The importance of the writer is emphasized before every curtain at La Mama when Ellen Stewart appears to deliver her catholic and unvarying greeting. Ringing her cowbell at the start of each performance, with a slight dip to the audience and a little abrupt shake of her handsome head, Ellen announces, "Good evening, ladies and gentlemen. Welcome to La Mama ETC [Experimental Theater Club] dedicated to the playwright and all forms of the theater." The language each time is identical, followed by the names of the play, the author, and the director.

Geographically, off off-Broadway was as hidden and as scattered as off-Broadway was in relation to the central theater. It occupied nontheatrical real estate in the Village and East Village—coffeehouses, lofts, cellars, and hospitable churches. A sense of community was developed around these little stages. Theater Genesis was started by the Reverend Michael Allen at St. Mark's-in-the-Bouwerie at Second Avenue and Tenth Street initially because he wished to make his neglected church meaningful to the members of the East Village artistic and intellectual community. In this respect St. Mark's was quite unlike St. Clement's Church with its American Place Theater across town on Forty-sixth Street between Ninth and Tenth avenues in the midst of what was once called Hell's Kitchen. St. Clement's, although it lay athwart the theater district, had no natural constituency living in the immediate area, and in fact its near neighbors remained hostile to the parish's principal activity of theater despite the repeated efforts of the St. Clement's people to interest and involve them. The deliberately nontheater character of the real estate was a hallmark of off off-Broadway, and when off off-Broadway groups such as La Mama and Robert Kalfin's Chelsea Theater Center raised themselves out of the church or coffeehouse class and established themselves in headquarters of their own, in real theaters—La Mama in a remodeled four-story building on East Fourth Street and Chelsea in the Brooklyn Academy of Music—they began in their behavior to resemble off-Broadway more than off off-Broadway. To remain as it meant to be, off off-Broadway continually was forced to resist the natural escalating tendencies of theater.

Off off-Broadway made its first appearance in the coffeehouses of Greenwich Village in the late 1950's. At first taking the simple form of impromptu poetry readings by writers and actors, off off-Broadway would not for a few more years be identified as a distinctive theater phenomenon. The first of the off off-Broadway impresarios was Joe Cino who opened his coffeehouse at 31 Cornelia Street in December, 1958, and soon thereafter began encouraging patrons and friends to hang their paintings on his walls and read their poetry for regulars crowded around the small round tables in front of his tall espresso maker. Poetry led to dramatic readings and dramatic readings to staged miniproductions put together on zero budgets. Sometime later Caffe Cino's proprietor began to put his own imprint on the programming by choosing from among many volunteers and concentrating on new one-act plays. No one was paid except from the proceeds of a passed hat. There were no sets, just the words and the performers. Within the next few years other coffeehouses followed suit—Take 3, Cafe Manzini, Phase 2, and others.

Still it could not be said that this activity constituted an alternate theater to off-Broadway. Michael Smith of the *Village Voice* dates the true beginnings of off off-Broadway to September 27, 1960, when Alfred Jarry's *King Ubu* opened at Take 3 on Bleecker Street with a statement of theatrical self-awareness by the sponsors. It was also in 1960 that Ellen Stewart opened her Cafe La Mama in a cellar on East Twelfth Street. From the outset the emphasis was on the play. The coffee was more of an official subterfuge. License problems ensued for Ellen Stewart. She was forced into three or four moves before settling in the long loft above a cleaner's at 122 Second Avenue. Like Joe Cino, she seldom read submitted scripts and picked her writers more or less by hunch and intuition. Each author was left to be his own producer.

What made this system so attractive to writers was the instant possibility of seeing their work staged and the clear exemption from any form of censorship or commercial coercion. By the early 1960's off-Broadway had developed caution and the encrustations of an incipient commercialism. Productions were not so readily available to new playwrights. Off off-Broadway became the place to go to get a hearing. Paul Foster, one of off off-Broadway's best-known playwrights, author of *Balls*, a play whose only two visible characters were ping-pong balls swaying under the spotlights, once told John Gruen, an astute observer of the East Village scene and author of *The New Bohemia* (Grosset & Dunlap, 1966), "Off off-Broadway allows you to set your own pace. It does not have to please the audience—you can test out an idea. It gives you a chance to fail. And if you choose, you can be involved with your work—and that of others, twenty-four hours a day."

Off off-Broadway allowed a writer to go to the outer limits of his material. No theme or situation was beyond permissibility. There were plays about sexual deviation in all its forms. Homosexuality was frankly treated. One of the more interesting exercises in the exposure of hidden sexuality was Lanford Wilson's ambiguously named *The Madness of Lady Bright*. It consisted of a long monologue in which an aging homosexual named Leslie Bright looks back on his numerous flickering love affairs and his earliest relationships with his sister and mother. As performed by Cris Alexander off-Broadway in 1966, the play was also an acting tour de force, pathetic, poignant, and memorable. In the companion piece *Ludlow Fair*, Ann Wedgeworth and Sasha von Scherler gave interesting performances as two women in trouble over the same man. On these two rather slight plays alone Lanford Wilson showed himself to be one of the most talented of the newer playwrights.

There were dramatizations of sadomasochistic experiences and solemn instances of bestiality. Rochelle Owens in 1967 used the theme of sodomy—a man frankly in love with a pig —in *Futz*, a fable that anticipated the "male chauvinism" cry of women's liberation in the 1970's. In all this, off off-Broadway anticipated the flood of frankness to come in the off-Broadway theater. Lanford Wilson dealt with the after-midnight lunch-counter characters to be found at one of the seamier intersections of upper Broadway in his long, verbally intricate script *Balm in Gilead*. The play, tossing together an odd assortment of riffraff—dope pushers, pimps, prostitutes, addicts—anticipated some of the scenes in the later film *Midnight Cowboy*. Sam Shepard's *The Rock Garden* was a 1966 play about parents speaking guardedly but suggestively about sexual matters although the boy was open and explicit. Michael Allen, of St. Mark's, defended the play against its critics in an interview with Douglas Davis in the New York *Herald Tribune* (February 6, 1966), "The play is dominated to the end by the parents, whose conversation is filled with subtle sexual imagery, hypocritically disguised. The boy is franker than they are, that's all, and maybe he thinks sex is not evil. I believe this whole generation of young people is saying to us in effect, 'Look, you use beautiful words and do ugly things; we'll take ugly words and make beauty out of them.' " To the off off-Broadway playwright, the Absurdist writers Beckett, Genet, and Ionesco were traditional theater.

A casual, drop-in kind of audience formed around the little theaters and grew accustomed to paying the membership fees to attend the shows at La Mama. Younger than off-Broadway theatergoers, they were students, artists, writers, *Village Voice* readers, agents, uptown professionals anxious to get the new theater line early. It was an audience that went to be "shook up, intellectually and emotionally."

The spread of off off-Broadway into other locations such as lofts and churches signified its coming of age. In the fall of 1961 Al Carmines became the assistant minister at the Judson Memorial Church on the south side of Washington Square and soon after opened the Judson Poets' Theater. He had identified a need for new theater outlets, and, as a composer, he was pursuing his own strong talents and interests. The Judson sponsored some heady experiments, especially in the musical form, and Al Carmines himself was the composer of several shows with extended off-Broadway runs. He wrote the music for Rosalyn Drexler's *Home Movies* in 1964, a sort of satirical revue from the underground, and himself unapologetically played one of the characters, Father Shenanigan. Rosalyn Drexler's off-center humor—she was novelist, painter, and sometime lady wrestler—intrigued Orson Bean, the actor-comedian, and he sponsored the off-Broadway production, staged by the Judson's principal director, Lawrence Kornfeld. Carmines' 1967 musical version of Gertrude Stein's *In Circles* was also moved to off-Broadway in 1968, but by far his most ambitious musical effort to date was *Promenade*, written with Maria Irene Fornes, which Edgar Lansbury and Joseph Beruh produced in their new Promenade Theater in a hotel on upper Broadway. Another Judson work to gain wider recognition was Ronald Tavel's *Gorilla Queen*, a take-off on Hollywood's jungle epics of twenty years before. Tavel had achieved a certain fame as the author of such underground screenplays as Andy Warhol's *The Chelsea Girls, Vinyl,* and *Hedy L,* and his musical extravaganza was transferred to Paul Libin's Martinique Theater in the spring of 1967.

At the Judson the smaller plays were done in the choir

loft, and heavier productions, such as the musicals, in the church's main hall. There was never any assumption of church-imposed restrictions in the nature of the material. Michael Smith quoted Carmines as saying, "God can take care of himself. This is the first article of Judeo-Christian religion: we don't have to protect God. We don't create God. We can do a decadent play or a cynical play that's totally nihilistic, with the feeling that we can be exposed to it without secret weapons—without having to think of some way in your mind of defending yourself."

Now a number of theaters were to find sanctuary in churches. The Hardware Poets Theater, begun in 1962 by Elaine and Jerry Bloedow, Peter Levin, and Audrey Davis, was given a home in the Good Shepherd-Faith Presbyterian Church near Lincoln Center, where some years later Father Daniel Berrigan's *The Trial of the Catonsville Nine* was to be performed. In 1964 the most substantial of these theaters, the American Place Theater founded by Sidney Lanier, began life in St. Clement's Church, a neglected parish and a new theater saying their vows together, each intending to complement the other, the theater using the church sanctuary, the altar rolled aside to open the stage. In the same year Theater Genesis opened in St. Mark's-in-the-Bouwerie on the second floor of the parish house and began presenting the plays of Leonard Melfi, Sam Shepard, Charles L. Mee, Jr., Sally Ordway, and Tom Sankey. In 1965 Robert Kalfin, planning a new company in the theater-poor Chelsea area of Manhattan, was granted workshop space in St. Peter's Church on West Twentieth Street, later shifting to the Church of the Holy Apostle on West Twenty-eighth Street. (The move to the Brooklyn Academy came in 1968.)

Chelsea was operated by Robert Kalfin on a policy of doing new work with meaning—plays in Kalfin's judgment that spoke to their time. Kalfin's acute ear accounts for the particular liveliness of his theater. He put on *Black Quartet*, the plays of Ed Bullins, Ben Caldwell, LeRoi Jones, and

Ronald Milner, and Jones' *Slave Ship* in 1969, a searing, nearly wordless history of the black coming to this continent. *In White America* six years earlier had supplied verbal descriptions of slavery in transit aboard the rampantly crowded transports. *Slave Ship* was the experience itself, a physicalization of the voyage in which the wordlessly moaning actors were chained tightly within two compressed layers of staging representing the deck, from which they looked out incriminatingly at the minority of white members in the audience, offering strangled pleas of "Help me" and untouchable held-out hands. Kalfin brought over the modern English writer Edward Bond, author of *Saved*, a play set in a mean British working-class district in which there is a scene of gratuitous violence, a baby in a baby carriage being stoned to death. Visiting the Chelsea in its fourth-floor room at the Brooklyn Academy is never the same experience. Kalfin and his executive director, Michael David, change the room to suit the needs of each play. Solid support has come from his board of trustees, headed by Oliver Rea, who personally produced both *Slave Ship* and *Saved* off-Broadway.

The churches were never less than entirely open regardless of the character of the material presented. That generosity of attitude held even when the content was pointedly anticlerical. Leonard Melfi has said, "I've never felt so free in my life as I have writing for St. Mark's. I have a theory, you know, that sexual fantasies are a necessary opiate for the people, so to speak, and most of my plays are sexual fantasies. But the church plays them without a whimper."

One Sunday at St. Clement's Church, at the invitation of the Reverend Eugene A. Monick, members of Joseph Chaikin's Open Theater performed a specially improvised scene as part of the morning service. It was called "Sunday Morning Improvisation." The actors lined up facing the congregation, forming another congregation, and began singing a hymn in the manner of sedate parishioners. Gradually they let their hymnbooks fall. Their thoughts slid visibly from the supposedly sanctimonious to the frankly curious and then into outright salaciousness. In a Pirandello-like switch the solemn ranks disintegrated. The church coffee hour that followed became a barnyard of sniffing animals exploring each other sexually.

Chaikin's brilliant Open Theater—of which, of course, this stunning image was only an offhand gesture—represented another dimension to the off off-Broadway movement. This dimension was the personality-centered experimental workshop: the Open Theater, Richard Schechner's Performance Group, Andre Gregory's Manhattan Project, even John Vaccaro's Theater of the Ridiculous whose heavily made-up performers, their transvestite finery sprinkled with sequins, their rouged faces painted in gold dust, formed the oddest and most outrageously behaved company to be found anywhere in the off off-Broadway scene.

Time to do the work was the possession these groups guarded most jealously against the encroachments and intrusions of the regular theater world. Gregory, utilizing foundation grants and facilities at New York University, rehearsed a small company for more than a year before showing his *Alice in Wonderland* to the public. His driving impulse was not to allow conventional economic considerations to hinder or impede the work. The outcome was a startling *Alice*, the extreme physicalization of events happening in the moonlit landscape of the mind, thickly textured and glistening with sweaty detail.

The most articulate of off off-Broadway directors is Richard Schechner, former editor of *The* (Tulane) *Drama Review* and an aggressive propagandizer for his ideas. With his *Dionysus in 69, Makbeth,* and *Commune*—where the audience's minimal contribution was to take off its shoes on entering the house—Schechner did pioneer work in setting up an environmental theater. In his Performing Garage on Wooster Street, in a district of narrow cobblestone streets and gloomy warehouses, a different audience framework was constructed for each production. Usually it consisted of a rambling scaffolding of multilevel platforms, ramps, balconies, and porches surrounding a trespassing stage that wandered here and there into the audience's preserve. The deliberate intention was twofold: to expand the range of the performers and to heighten the awareness of the audience by surrounding it with action, forcing it to look at the stage experience with fresh eyes. Schechner has written (the New York *Times*, December 13, 1970), "Theater is an unliterary art, a here and now experience. Its finest expressions are immediate, gestural, involved, inclusive, and participatory."

As editor of the intellectualized *Drama Review* Schechner made it his business to be in touch with the avant-garde wherever it appeared. He was an early admirer of the Polish director Jerzy Grotowski and in 1965 was the first to publish material on Grotowski in this country. Frankly borrowed from Grotowski are the shaping of the theater to conform to the character of the play, the use of psychophysical conditioning exercises for the actors, and the "collaging" of the text. Writing of the *raison d'être* of his group, Schechner has said, "You see the problem is to make a theater, not cast a play. Americans are terribly unskilled at making theaters—there have been precious few in our history. We are good at business: producers, director-entrepreneurs, agents hold our theater together. Take the regional theaters, for example. These are nothing other than collections of administrators who keep a certain consistency in policy, but none in the company taken as a whole. Regional styles vary from blandness to academically experimental to Broadway tryout. These theaters are the slaves of the middle class culture that owns them."

To Schechner, whose expressed intentions usually outrun his stage achievements (which is the norm), holding a theater together, let alone making a theater, proved to be a harsh and difficult experience. The price of his rigorous experimentation was bitter dispute and company defections commencing after the *Makbeth* failure in 1970.

In 1970 the Open Theater suffered an internal splintering

equivalent to that of Schechner's group and continued with
a reduced company. It is Joseph Chaikin, with his sedulous
disregard for popularity, who has been the purest experimen-
talist. Chaikin operates almost wholly outside the system. He
has sought no financial help from the Establishment (although National Endowment for the Arts grants to the Open
Theater through fiscal 1972 totaled $102,000) and has made
no effort to interest the foundations. Public performances are
given only sporadically, usually benefits for a group or cause
such as the Black Panther Legal Defense Fund in which the
activist-inclined members have a political interest. Like
the Living Theater and La Mama, it has had several successful European tours. Sometimes through college tours the
Open Theater raises money for itself; otherwise, keeping expenses to the minimum and using only the cheapest loft
space obtainable, it exists mysteriously by self-support.

Generally, when its work surfaces in the regular theater, it
is through the channel of some other theater organization
like La Mama. *America Hurrah*, the work Jean-Claude van
Itallie had completed when he first met with Chaikin, went
into La Mama from the loft and emerged from La Mama for
a long off-Broadway run in 1966–67. *Viet Rock*, Megan Terry's powerful, partly improvised "folk" piece on American
involvement in Vietnam, was handled in much the same way.
Megan Terry worked closely with the Open Theater actors,
culling bits of dialogue out of the week's news, framing in
the language of current usage the speeches of her military,
her civilian, her Senatorial witnesses, her son at war, her
Mom at home, her Hanoi Hannah, and her lonely sweetheart.
All the clichés of war were introduced but in a startlingly
contemporary way. With music, the play opened at La Mama
in the spring of 1966 and was transferred to off-Broadway in
the fall.

In no sense, however, did off off-Broadway consider itself
a tryout place. The playwrights and the directors were interested more in the process than in the final product. Gregory

finding physical metaphors for mythic tales; Schechner spatially rearranging the actor-audience relationship; Chaikin discovering a dramatic notation for timeless themes of life and death; van Itallie developing methods of direct playwright-performer collaboration. At La Mama Tom O'Horgan, with his musical background, choreographic sense, and visual imagination, exhibited the most free-flowing experimental techniques. *Hair, Lenny,* and *Jesus Christ Superstar* on Broadway all bear the marks of O'Horgan's early off off-Broadway experimentation. In Paul Foster's *Tom Paine,* developed at La Mama and produced at Stage 73 in March, 1968, a play using historical figures to illustrate the modern dilemma of the nonconformist liberal, O'Horgan deliberately left passages in the play open for improvisation and even for audience talk-back to the actors. Process was at the heart of most of this experimentation, down to the clicking of tongues and panting of breath in the Open Theater's production of *The Serpent,* the verbal rhythms built into sexual suggestion in the Biblical recitation of the "begats." How to renew theater, going back to the beginning, starting from scratch, was what off off-Broadway was about.

Most prolific of all the off off-Broadway stages is Ellen Stewart's Cafe La Mama. Getting the new playwrights a hearing, putting the scripts on, has been her all-absorbing concern. Since the earliest days her unremitting zeal has accounted for production after production, Thursday through Sunday, literally hundreds of plays through the years. Now, in her new building four blocks south of busy St. Marks Place, two plays are in progress at once, one upstairs, one down in her piggyback theaters. All this activity helps validate the claim made by Richard Barr, Albee's producer, that in the 1960's and 1970's there were more produced playwrights in New York than anywhere in the world. Out of La Mama have come some of the star writers of off off-Broadway: Jean-Claude van Itallie, Paul Foster, Ruth Yorck, Tom Eyen,

Julie Bovasso, David Starkweather, Sam Shepard, Lanford Wilson.

The one personality to emerge over the years of ceaseless work, however, is not a writer, or even a director or actor, but Ellen Stewart herself. She came to New York from New Orleans in 1950, and although she still betrays a trace of the Creole accent of her upbringing, she creates her own milieu. She is of her own place. Coming to town, she moved into the retail clothing and then the fashion world of New York, working in a Fifth Avenue store, a Brooklyn bathing suit factory, becoming a free-lance designer. She had natively the chic of the fashion world and a modellike litheness, dressed in suede pants and simple blouse and wearing hand-wrought earrings. She is black in a predominately white world, but one's reaction to her, as she steps in front of the audience and gives a momentarily diffident shake of her head, is never the color difference. Although she is richly black, one's first response to her is not "Negro." If "charismatic" were a word to be applied acceptably but once to a person in the present-day theater, it ought to be applied to Ellen Stewart. As "La Mama" in person, aside from the sense of fun and sense of humor, she is ferocious in the support of her playwrights. She thinks nothing of telephoning an agent at one thirty in the morning if the commercial possibilities of a script suddenly occur to her. She has no private life to speak of. Her large but essentially one-room apartment at the top of the La Mama building is a public hall for the La Mama people.

What she has not learned about East Village real estate, about moving, about dealing with municipal authorities is not worth mentioning. Her first cellar was lined with bricks hand-carried from Bellevue Hospital's construction site ten blocks uptown. On the next move she pleasantly instructed her audience at the end of the performance to pick something up as they left and carry it out. Her colleague Joe Cino saw his coffeehouse destroyed by fire on Ash Wednesday, 1965. Cino himself died in April, 1967, and with him went off off-Broadway's first theater. Municipal officiousness frequently threatened to do Ellen Stewart in too. In 1966 Actors' Equity saw fit to crack down on the coffeehouses and workshops by not allowing Equity members to appear unless they were paid off-Broadway minimums. No off off-Broadway theater could have survived one week under such requirements. Equity, for reasons of falsely aggressive unionism in a field where unionism cannot usefully be everywhere applied, was interfering with the necessary informality of theatrical arrangements. But Equity finally consented to a showcase or workshop code still in effect that permits Equity performers to appear in carefully limited productions where no formal admission is charged and where a maximum of ten performances are given.

Recognition for La Mama that did not come from home came from abroad. Ellen Stewart took her troupe to Europe in the winter and spring of 1965 on the first of a number of trips that were to show La Mama's work quite widely abroad. La Mama first performed in Paris at the American Center for Students and Artists. The following fall, by demand, the La Mama troupe, besides Paris, visited Denmark and Sweden. La Mama made its own arrangements. This was no State Department-sponsored tour of acceptable and politically safe work. It was the American avant-garde that appealed to the Europeans, a feeling that they were seeing what was really happening in America, and if it was iconoclastic, if a little blood was spilled at America's expense, so much the better.

La Mama moved up to off-Broadway in April, 1966. Theodore Mann, who had been watching the work from his vantage point at Circle in the Square, and his associate Paul Libin presented *Six from La Mama* at the Martinique. Among the six short plays that made up the evening were *Thank You, Miss Victoria* by William Hoffman, a man's gratitude to an employment agency for securing him a job as a male secretary to an aggressive female executive and ending up on the floor in submission to her; *This Is the Rill Speak-*

ing, Lanford Wilson's evocation of family life in a Tobacco Road kind of country past; and Leonard Melfi's *Bird Bath* about a poet and a waitress meeting at the cafeteria cashier.

In the late 1960's the foundation grants began coming to Ellen Stewart ("If I hadn't gotten a grant," she said, "I would have had to move to Europe"). The extra funds enabled her to move in 1969 and renovate 74 East Fourth Street at a cost of more than $100,000. From this recharged power station, like the rest of off off-Broadway, and like the Living Theater which was the real forerunner of off off-Broadway, she continues to send shock waves through the conventional theater.

Nine

The Living Theater in the World

Julian Beck was the John the Baptist of the avant-garde carrying the message of revolution to come. With his sunken cheeks and wide, stretched forehead he was perfectly cast as the prophet, a scholarly wandering Hebrew moving with urgent eyes among the people, knowing something they did not. The fringe of long hair falling away from the circle of baldness gave him a premature venerability. He had an ascetic's disregard for his lank, long-limbed body. Humor and gentleness flickered in the quick eyes; intensity and zealousness never left them.

In every important respect the Living Theater was the precursor of off off-Broadway. It had the same vulnerability to the law and led the same unsettled existence, and like off off-Broadway, it was always more concerned with dramatic process than with the final staged product. In life-style and choice of work, the Living Theater, perhaps more accurately than any off-Broadway theater, prophesied the future. At the end of the 1950's *The Connection* foretold the developing national concern over dope addiction of a decade later. In the early 1960's the repressiveness of *The Brig* prefigured the present-day concern for society's treatment of prisoners and the rethinking of our automatic assumptions of the evilness of the man behind the bars and the goodness of the gatekeepers.

As time passed, the zeal of the Living Theater was directed to revolution, a peace-loving, nonviolent revolution to overhaul society which reached its fullest dramatic expression in its loosely structured marathon work of the late 1960's, *Paradise Now*. As a member of the audience—that no longer so easily defined term—one anticipated the trip to *Paradise Now* at the Brooklyn Academy of Music with less pleasure than apprehension. Advance reports of the work stirred a certain unease. What demands would be made of one? How much "participation" was expected? Would one, indeed, be called upon to take off one's clothes? Would one find oneself, against nature and decency, wanting to? Was one's curiosity about the latest venture of the Living Theater a little voyeuristic? I admired the Becks and wanted to respond. But did that mean submerging my identity in a mass of dirtily dressed hippie youth and becoming one with them? The natural conclusion to the evening of indeterminate length, I had read, was to take to the streets. Did I have to join the revolution?

The Living Theater had been gone from New York for four years when it returned in the fall of 1968. In that time the Living Theater had performed new works of communal company authorship in cities throughout Europe, sometimes encountering audience disapproval and police interference. Now these works were to be shown on American college campuses and at the Academy.

Up the aisle of the auditorium and into the marble lobby of the Academy came a more haggard-looking Beck than the one I remembered from years before, dressed in a wild, ragged costume. Shouting questions to a colleague trying to keep up to him, he rushed roughly through the curious entering audience, inquiring about the size of tonight's house and bearing down on the box office disconcertingly like an anxious uptown producer. One refrained in such circumstances from greeting him for old times' sake. And, besides, possibly he was in character and the play had already begun.

Paradise Now actually begins with the members of the company coming purposefully up the long sloping aisles of the Academy and shouting harshly into the ears of the aisle sitters:

"I am not allowed to travel without a passport! I am not allowed to travel without a passport!"

"I am not allowed to smoke marijuana! I am not allowed to smoke marijuana!"

"I am not allowed to take off my clothes! I am not allowed to take off my clothes!"

This last is the cue for the actors to strip to the briefest sort of underwear and in some cases to nudity. For the rest of a gymnastic and frequently tumultuous evening they remain in these flimsy costumes. During an early performance, sitting in the auditorium, Richard Schechner read "cannot" for "not allowed to" and removed all his clothes to disprove the proposition to his own satisfaction.

The performance was like a freely structured religious service, a modern Dionysian rite, in which the audience was encouraged to take part. The actors willingly made room on the stage for the bolder members of the audience, who formed rings to watch the acrobatics of the performing cast. The structure of the performance was a series of rites—guerrilla theater, which included the shouted epithets; prayer; study; "universal intercourse" practiced for the achievement of sexual freedom; and so on. At the top of the ladder was the creation of the revolution. Speeches from the stage that could be clearly understood were rare, except when a powerfully built black actor went into a lengthy harangue about the Ocean Hill-Brownsville community school board dispute in Brooklyn then in the news.

Given its freedom, the audience moved about, changing seats at will, squatting in the aisle, advancing to the stage to engage cast members in bilateral discussion. One robust and handsome woman of about twenty-four, dressed in a midnight-blue skirt and turtleneck blouse, lay on her back at the edge of the stage clutching an infant to her chest. Not seeming to address anyone in particular, neither audience nor actors, she denounced the company for the tameness of the performance. She shifted position to the aisle, where she began breast-feeding her child. Later she called out her comments from the back of the house. The onstage audience built up massively when the rite of universal intercourse was lengthily performed—the actors paired off around the stage and going through choreographed copulatory motions. There was an awed silence in the theater in the instant before orchestrated shouts signified a prolonged and gigantic climax.

Later actors held aloft real dollar bills and set fire to them, chanting, "Burn the money! Burn the money!" At this point the young woman in blue, still cradling her child, shouted angrily from the rear of the auditorium, "Fuck the money! Burn the theater!"

The evening worked its way elephantinely to an indeterminate close. So long as the audience lasted, the actors had the energy to endure. At some point the initiative had passed to the audience, and theater was being made like love by everyone present.

Weirdly disorganized though it seemed, *Paradise Now* drove straight back to the earliest impulses of the Living Theater and connected up. The anarchistic spirit, the pacifist beliefs, the search for solutions outside the system, the esthetic explorations were all there in the beginning. To the Becks money was always the prime evil. Long before they were burning bills on the stage of the Brooklyn Academy they were flushing money down a barroom toilet in the 1961 *Jungle of Cities* in their tiny theater on Fourteenth Street. The role of the audience was always a matter of deep exploration. In *Many Loves* in 1959 one of the characters anticipates *Paradise Now* by crying out, "The audience is the play!" A thread of absolute consistency runs through the history of the Living Theater.

The theater had not one prophet but two. Judith Malina was an equal partner with her husband, Julian Beck, and at

times the more eloquent spokesman. Since the late 1940's
they had been involved in theater together. They had known
each other as teen-agers. Born in New York on May 31, 1925,
Beck attended Horace Mann School for Boys in Riverdale
and went to Yale. So far everything was on a sane middle-
class track. But he left Yale before graduation to attend the
College of the City of New York and, again by leaving, rejected the formality of graduation. He was by then a confirmed philosophical anarchist, and Thoreau and Gandhi
were his guides. Judith Malina, the daughter of an actress,
was born in a theater in Germany and developed undif-
ferentiated instincts for theater on both sides of the curtain,
artistic and managerial, coming from long familiarity. An
actress and a director, co-manager of the theater, Judith,
with a face sad or gay as a clown's, was small, almost frail, but
possessed of enough iron to direct men in brutal plays such as
The Brig. Artistically, Julian and Judith complemented
each other, he as designer and director, she as director and
versatile actress who in the same play once portrayed a young
girl and a ninety-six-year-old woman.

The theater's experimental interest in producing poetic
drama and avant-garde writers derived from Julian Beck's
knowledge of art. He had many friends among modern artists, both musicians and painters. As a painter himself, Beck
was affiliated with the Leo Castelli Gallery in New York.
Among the early sponsors of the theater were poets Lionel
Abel and Jean Cocteau, the composers John Cage and Alan
Hovhaness, the choreographers Merce Cunningham and Erick
Hawkins, and the painters Willem de Kooning and Betty
Parsons. Initially, carrying his portfolio of stage designs, Beck
had gone to Robert Edmond Jones for advice on starting a
theater.

After performing at the Cherry Lane and then in a loft at
Broadway and 100th Street—each time being closed down
by city authorities—the Becks decided to find a theater of
their own. It was two years before they located suitable space
on the second and third floors of a large corner building on

the Avenue of Americas and Fourteenth Street, another six months to get the plans approved, another seven months to remodel. The new theater opened auspiciously on January 13, 1959, with *Many Loves* by the poet William Carlos Williams, who years before had seen the Living Theater at the Cherry Lane and had written the Becks a letter of praise.

The new theater was reached by a steep narrow staircase from the street, opening into a lobby in which visually the most prominent feature was a sculptured water fountain fashioned out of twisted pipe. On the walls there was usually an art exhibit, and to the right of the lobby the doors leading into the narrow 162-seat theater. One more flight up were scene docks and dressing rooms and the Becks' cluttered office, a desk for Judith and another for Julian. Having a theater of their own allowed them to keep a company and present verse drama in repertory. The new theater was opened on a subscription base of 260 and was to be supported entirely by memberships, contributions, and admissions. By summer there were three plays ready for repertory: the popular *Many Loves*; Paul Goodman's *The Cave at Machpelah*, which had music by Ned Rorem and dances by Merce Cunningham; and a jazz play with hip jargon. Reflecting on the variety represented, Judith Malina said, "I have no objection to the extent of the experiment. I'm very permissive. Anything is all right so long as it is interesting and has life. That's why we called the theater The Living Theater."

They were to find a meaningful statement of their own aims in Artaud's denial of the separation between culture and life in his book *The Theater and Its Double* (Grove Press, 1959):

> We can begin to form an idea of culture, an idea that is first of all a protest. A protest against the senseless constraint imposed upon the idea of culture reducing it to a sort of inconceivable Pantheon, producing an

idolatry no different from the image-worship of those religions which relegate their gods to Pantheons. A protest against the idea of culture as distinct from life— as if there were culture on one side and life on the other, as if true culture were not a refined means of understanding and EXERCISING life.

The jazz play was *The Connection,* and it was to make the Living Theater internationally famous within a few weeks of its opening on July 15, 1959. The play by Jack Gelber dealt with a sensational subject in new dramatic terms. Dope addiction was depicted with such realism that some members of those first audiences to see the play had a sickening sense of participation, a suspicion of complicity in some unnamable crime. The form was entirely new. There was no curtain as an accepted line of demarcation between actor and audience. All the action takes place in Leach's pad, the squalid living room of an apartment belonging to the main character, a role handled with a kind of straight-off-the-street authenticity by Warren Finnerty. The actors are discovered onstage, sitting on the floor, slumped over, arms hugging knees, waiting. A mood of timelessness is evoked by Freddie Redd's intentionally monotonous jazz score played onstage throughout by his quartet. There is minimal action, no expected effort by the actors to "engage" the attention of the audience, no exposition. Various devices are used to induce the audience to accept the "reality" of what they are watching.

Throughout the first act the "actors" are waiting for a "fix." Cowboy is coming with the stuff. It will be administered to each one in turn in the bathroom in the second act. Around this meager plot and "slice of junkie" life realism, Gelber erects an artificial frame. We are introduced to the "producer" of an avant-garde film to be made of the action, to the "author," and to the cameramen. The supposed payment to the "real" actors being filmed is the fix that is arriving in the second act. The subject matter of this play, the

frankness with which junkie life was depicted at a time when
it was merely being whispered about, made most of the news
for *The Connection*. From a technical artistic standpoint,
however, at least as interesting to the Becks was the manipu-
lated rearrangement of the audience's relationship to the
stage action.

Dealing with so unexplored and so contemporary a theme,
Gelber had no desire to write naturalistically or use any of
the normal stage conventions. Understandably, perhaps, the
daily critics were harshly critical of *The Connection*, while
the weekly critics and foreign critics such as Kenneth Tynan
were full of praise. There was nothing "likable" about the
characters or pleasant about the experience; there was, at one
remove, much to admire in the technique and presentation.
It was not just dope Gelber was dealing with; it was the sense
of loss and abandonment in modern life.

Some critics approached the play defensively, as an attack
on the literary theater that was familiar to them. Thus Walter Kerr in a Sunday piece in the *Herald Tribune*, after
Judith Crist reviewed the play unfavorably in the daily:

> There is a serious and genuine undercurrent running
> beneath the styles and anti-styles of our time, an under-
> current that honestly distrusts art as art, a conviction
> that whatever is organized must therefore be falsified.
> It has led—not only in experimental drama but in other
> media as well—to a notion that truth is never to be found
> in meditation, and certainly not in premeditation, but
> only in what pops out on the spur of the moment, only
> in what is wholly or at least partially improvised. A
> craftsman can lie, but a reflex cannot.
>
> I would like to put down one of the reasons why this
> disturbs me. In the case of *The Connection*, when all
> that is unwritten is taken away—the long, suspended
> silences, the itching choreography, the experience of
> physically enduring the passing time, the half-hour or

so of jazz—is there very much left beyond some intentionally ordinary lines and a road-map for the director?
I have a feeling that the distrust of art, because art may
distort the truth, may in the end leave us with very
little to hold in our hands.

Kerr's reasoned argument is a brave defense of worthwhile
and enduring dramatic values, but it overleaped its time. By
its omissions it illustrates perfectly the repeated and damaging failure of the daily critics to provide us with any reliable
road maps to where off-Broadway was heading in the years of
its most rapid advance. It is extraordinary that in the above
two lengthy paragraphs Kerr should not once have mentioned the play's attempt to comprehend and illuminate a
hidden social evil not before dealt with in terms of such
dramatic realism. Nor did Kerr or other critics bother to
consider the play in the perspective of the Living Theater's
serious explorations into the role of the audience. In the
light of the historical importance of the Living Theater, and
of *The Connection*, this was a serious failure. It is no isolated
example. Time and again the New York critics, whatever
their bias, failed to spot or rarely paused to consider the
social significance or intention of what they were seeing.
They were, most of them, reviewers without any framework
of values outside of their own initial and well-trained responses to a piece of stage material. Reacting to isolated impulses,
they seldom bothered to analyze the purpose or aims of the
productions held fitfully up to their appraising eyes. Writing
on a daily basis, viewing work nightly, they scarcely had time
to credit the intention or weigh the enormous artistic compli-
cations of the stage form. As a result, they tended to separate
everything they saw into simple success and simple failure,
and some possibly flawed but significant work in the light of
history was simply passed over. But the Becks and their production survived the initial slighting critical reception, and
lesser critics than Kerr such as Jerry Tallmer at the *Village*

Voice and Henry Hewes on *Saturday Review* were not so
delinquent. Nor, characteristically, did Harold Clurman, that
artful and seasoned campaigner, miss the significance of *The
Connection.*

It was *The Connection,* so particularly New York in its
data, that opened up Europe to the Living Theater. As usual
the entire financing was left in its hands. In order to accept
an invitation to participate in the Théâtre des Nations in
Paris in June, 1961, they had to raise some $40,000. No gov-
ernment assistance was forthcoming. Fittingly the money
came mostly out of the art world that had given the Becks
some of their interested early sponsors. A month before departure time the painter Larry Rivers held an art auction
that included the works of Franz Kline, Grace Hartigan,
Richard Lippold, Robert Rauschenberg, Louise Nevelson,
Jasper Johns, and Willem de Kooning. There were also
drafts of Allen Ginsberg's poem "Kaddish." The auction
raised $20,500. Carrying a company of twenty-six and the
repertoire of *Many Loves, In the Jungle of Cities,* and *The
Connection,* the Living Theater played to enthusiastic audiences numbering 20,000 in Paris—half a season's audience at
home—and won the Grand Prix for best acting company at
the Théâtre des Nations. A five-week tour to Rome, Turin,
Milan, Berlin, and Frankfurt followed. *The Connection* was
everywhere the company's lead card. The State Department
money that year went to the Theater Guild's deluxe package
put together just for world touring, Helen Hayes in *The
Skin of Our Teeth* and *The Miracle Worker,* a hit at diplomatic receptions. The Living Theater played to the people,
the artists, and the intelligentsia. *Il Popolo* of Rome, the
organ of the Christian Democratic Party, editorialized, "We
must declare ourselves with the 'rebels,' the 'anti-Broadway,'
which is not only American but is also an international
movement."

This and a subsequent tour in the summer of 1962, adding
more countries, helped pave the way for the Living Theater's

future role in Europe during the years of exile. Foreign travel demonstrated how much more powerful an artistic force, bad or good, the Living Theater was than the critics at home had given it credit for. The new mobility, the world appeal were evidence that the little theater at Fourteenth Street probably was already obsolete for the Becks and their company when it opened only three years before. They had burst the walls of the small theater and found their audience in moving outward into the world traveling among the people. Nevertheless, in July, 1962, they returned home and resumed performances of their strongest production, *The Connection.*

The economics of the little theater were perilous. Raising money to mount a new production required an enormous exertion. For the sake of the box office it became necessary to rely primarily on proven work. In September it returned to Brecht to do *Man Is Man.* It was ironic that rights problems always prevented the Becks from doing any Genet—of all the modern European writers the one to whom they felt the closest affinity. Two years previously Stefan Brecht, the playwright's son, had made available *In the Jungle of Cities,* a play set in Chicago in 1912 that deals with a strange wrestling match between a rich Malayan lumber dealer and a young man in a bookshop before whom, as a form of bribery, the Oriental debases himself. The Becks saw themselves already then involved intellectually in the struggle for world power between East and West. *In the Jungle of Cities* had been a success, but *Man Is Man* was not, and the following spring, after further exhausting fund-raising attempts, the Becks put on what was to be their final show on Fourteenth Street. *The Brig* opened on May 13, 1963, and proved to be nearly as great a success as *The Connection.* Kenneth H. Brown's play dealt in semidocumentary fashion with the harsh disciplinary measures of the Marine Corps which he personally had experienced. The set was by Julian Beck, but he said the design was by the Marine Corps. Between the audience and the actors there was a close-link wire fence—the

fence of the outside compound. Behind it were the five double bunks for prisoners numbered one through ten, the
white-lined corridors requiring repeated disciplinary swab-
bing with real mops and real soap, the doors to the head, the
office for the four guards. The action of the play was simply
the repetitive daily routine of brig existence, monotonous,
noisy, and violent, the prisoners moving from bunk to head
to compound to corridor. The key phrase was repeated like a
litany, "Sir, prisoner number one requests permission to
cross the white line, sir." "Sir, prisoner number two requests
permission to cross the white line, sir." Such were the physical demands of performance that the actors were put through
daily drill to get in shape, and frequently there were injuries
requiring medical attention after each performance, like
football game casualties. Watching *The Brig* was a head-split-
ting experience: the pounding of feet in quick time, the
coming to attention, the endlessly repeated permissions. The
unrelieved unpleasantness was in itself the message of the
show.

Comparing *The Brig* with *The Connection* reveals more
similarities than differences. Both were repressive, airless,
closed in. The junkies in Leach's pad may seem to have
freely chosen their escape and exile, yet they are no less
victims of forces beyond their control than the prisoners in
The Brig. *The Brig* was the more explicit metaphor of a
repressive society. Both dealt with human existence at the
outer limits of endurance, one with the extremes of military
organization, the other with the extremes of a disorganized
and disintegrated society seeking escape through drugs.

In *The Brig* the Becks were deliberately testing the endurance powers of the audience. No one could sit comfortably, no
possible "enjoyment" resulted, but one carried away an unforgettable image. Once again the prophetic properties of
off-Broadway material at its best came through. For the attitudes implicit in *The Brig* were picked up in the early 1970's
by the radical lawyers in their defense of such prisoners as

George Jackson when they began using the term "political prisoner" to suggest that criminals were more the victims than the transgressors of society. The Becks for years had been saying that prisoners were not to be held accountable in a society that incriminated itself.

Erecting a prison on the Living Theater stage behind a chicken-wire fence held symbolic meaning for the embattled Becks. As anarchists and pacifists they took to the streets as early as 1958 and served their first jail sentences for refusing to seek shelter in a civil defense drill. At the time Judith Malina said, "Making that simple Thoreau-like gesture of disobedience changed everything for us. Going to prison was a frightening experience—yet fantastically enlightening. The girls in prison were mainly prostitutes. They were prostitutes because they were poor. Their crime was poverty; it was the Establishment against the innocent."

In early 1962 the United States was reconsidering its ban on nuclear testing in the atmosphere, and in March President Kennedy was to make his decision on the resumption of testing. The Becks organized a week-long General Strike for Peace and turned out the lights on Fourteenth Street. "If not I, who?" said Judith Malina. "And if not now, when?" A sit-down demonstration in Times Square was broken up by police with some forty arrests. Julian Beck suffered two fractured ribs and was taken to Bellevue Hospital. Shortly after this action, the Living Theater was vandalized. The phone lines were cut, and stolen tickets were later found scattered all over Greenwich Village. Beck issued a special plea to get their prizes and framed citations back. It went unheeded. In 1970, after their European episode ended, the Becks and the hard core of their company moved to Brazil to perform street theater. In the summer of 1971, after imprisonment for sixty-five days on a drug charge, they were expelled from Brazil and returned to the United States.

It was in a sense fitting that in 1963 their final production

at home was the Marine Corps play and that their difficulties
with federal authorities should have involved the nonpayment of the withholding tax on the actors' wages. Financially,
as we know, the Living Theater had never been strong.
Foundations by and large had overlooked its needs. Private
donations arrived in $100 amounts or less. In its entire life-
time, Beck estimated, the Living Theater had raised no more
than $200,000. And half that sum had been earmarked for
foreign travel. The weekly operating deficit had been running in the neighborhood of $500. Each time a new produc-
tion was put on, the cost, even considering Julian's frugal
reliance on string, used board, and odd bits of surplus material for the sets, was $7,500. For themselves the Becks had
never taken out of the theater more than $40 a week each.
They had been able to secure nonprofit status, but they never
seemed to have on hand enough for the legal fees to apply for
a tax-exempt status which would have relieved them of admission taxes. Yes, they admitted, this wasn't businesslike,
but their business was producing plays.

By the time the federal authorities finally intervened on
Thursday, October 17, 1963, in the celebrated incident that
closed the Living Theater, they were five and a half months
in arrears in rent. That, coupled with back taxes owed and
other debts, amounted to $50,000. The landlord had stayed
his eviction notice until Tuesday. The other leading creditor,
the Internal Revenue Service, claiming $23,000 mostly in
withholding taxes, was unwilling to delay any longer.

At three o'clock that afternoon IRS agents moved in.
They evicted some actors and seized and tagged the theater's
movable assets—costumes, scenery, desks, office equipment.
The Becks insisted they had never evaded payment. They
had fallen into arrears. The federal indictment was to charge
that over a twenty-two-month period Julian Beck had made
"numerous promises to pay the indebtedness which he failed
to keep." Beck put his priorities elsewhere. It was more important, he felt, to pay the actor his wage than the govern-

ment the withholding money. "It was a matter of insisting on art before money, before risk, before any other obligation. Any other obligation except one of life, death, physical harm, what not, is false anyway. The primary obligation is after all to the creator spirit, who when he whispers in your ear is to be obeyed. God or Mammon."

Julian Beck was perhaps not standing on the firmest constitutional ground. Radical interpretations of the law were rarer then. His subsequent actions, however, made certain inroads on popular assumptions of governmental responsibility. The Becks objected most strongly to the enforced cancellation of the night's performance because they had not been forewarned of the seizure.

Arriving for the evening performance of *The Brig* and finding the theater seized, some of the actors refused to leave. The sit-in, Beck later explained, resulted solely from the actors' wish to affirm their right to earn a week's wage. Then on Saturday night, as an act of civil disobedience, the company gave the unauthorized final performance of *The Brig*. It was the Living Theater's farewell after nearly 2,000 performances of twenty-three productions over a twelve-year period. Climbing in upper windows and entering through a rooftop door from an adjoining tenement, about thirty members of the theater, including the cast and author of *The Brig*, and an audience of some forty gained entrance to the theater, and the final performance went on.

The Becks were indicted in January, 1964. They were charged with impeding federal officers and with failure to pay their taxes. For a time *The Brig* production held together. Reorganizing themselves as Exile Productions, they played to an audience of a thousand in Philadelphia and had offers from England and Ireland. For a time Irving Maidman turned over his empty Midway Theater to them rent-free. The Becks were brought to trial in May, 1964. They represented themselves, sending up many an impassioned anarchistic statement to no avail. On May 25 they were found guilty. Beck was sentenced to sixty days in jail; Judith, convicted on two fewer counts, to thirty. But they were permitted to postpone serving the terms until the following fall after they had fulfilled a London engagement of *The Brig*. By fall Beck had figured out a new role for the Living Theater as an itinerant group finding its audience outside New York.

Jail in the personal lives of the Becks became as significant a metaphor as jail was artistically on the stage of the Living Theater. The inside of jail became more meaningful to them than the free world outside. To a friend Beck wrote:

> Life in jail is very real. No one has to fake. I hear real speech all the time, and how I wish I could hear more of this kind of speech in the theater. Actors don't have to speak better than people. Nothing is better than people. As I write this I am sitting in a very ugly room in this jail but I find it, strangely, more beautiful than most of the settings I've seen in the past on the stages of London, Paris, Berlin, and New York. . . . Life is very dramatic. You don't have to fancy it up.
>
> I often think that if the people on the street would realize how the world we live in is a prison, they'd do more yelling and railing, too. The sad, perhaps tragic thing is that people do not realize they're not free. How thoroughly we have lulled ourselves with our pride into our brand of limited liberty. . . . Outside, people delude themselves because they don't see the bars.
>
> What remedy do I suggest? I guess I am recommending complete social restructure. Just changing a few auditions in the theater won't help. That's an illusion. How? No answer. But if enough people start thinking about the state of things we're in, we might find a solution, an action, together.

In the spring the nomadic new life of the Living Theater began in Europe. It developed entirely new forms. Its *Myster-*

ies and Smaller Pieces, mixing yoga exercises, *tableaux vivants,* and spoken political slogans, opened in Paris in October, 1964, its *Frankenstein* in Venice in September, 1965. Wherever it went, it stirred audiences sometimes to violence and often drew the police. There was a new passion and a new rebelliousness. " 'Paradise Now' is our motto," cried Judith Malina. The expression was a double word play on Milton and on the "Freedom Now" of the civil rights movement. "I demand of each man everything! I want total love. I want no governments. I want no armies, no police, no warfare. I want no money. I want love as our standard!"

When the Becks returned to New York in 1968, it was with a theater flying banners. Artaud had said in words they once measured into their credo: "If there is still one hellish, truly accursed thing in our time, it is our artistic dallying with forms, instead of being like victims burnt at the stake, signaling through the flames." As makers of theater they had burst the walls and merged with life. Their protest from the stage had spilled into the street. In *Paradise Now* the play was "no longer an enactment but the act itself." The audience at the Brooklyn Academy of Music became the actors, and the actors took their places in the audience. The action swept into the lobby, and the company marched into the streets. But the attempt to join activism to art resulted in their mutual destruction, and in the end only the Becks were left, signaling through the flames.

Ten

The Importance of Being Edward Albee

Edward Albee more than anyone else opened up off-Broadway to new writers. It was partly his visible success that gave encouragement to new writers: the suddenness of his acceptance and the extent of his fame on the basis of a quite slight output. It was also the quality and character of his writing that alerted the theater and excited and challenged his contemporaries. For he had opened a new vein of dramatic writing, skeptical, sardonic, quarrelsome, contemporary. The two qualities one first notices in Albee personally—his humor and his distrust—permeate his work. They set the tone for a decade of playwriting. I remember Albee's reaction some years ago when I held out a paperback copy of his play *Who's Afraid of Virginia Woolf?* for him to autograph. He looked at me, smiling his quizzical smile, and said, deprecatingly, "Are you sure?" I felt he suspected me of flattery. Or that he questioned the value of such a perfunctory formality. Or that I was embarrassing him into assuming the role of the Great Playwright. Albee never let a seemingly straightforward gesture in others go unquestioned. He was concerned with hidden motives; he generally suspected the worst; he always put one on guard. It was this very edginess that made his writing strike sparks: the argumentative style, the suspicion. It was only when he got around to metaphysical subjects as in *Tiny Alice* and *All Over* that his style seemed to lack its old bite.

In view of his influence and the association of his name with off-Broadway it is remarkable how brief the off-Broadway connection was. The off-Broadway plays were all presented within a fifteen-month period in 1960 and 1961. Up to 1972 he had had no new work produced off-Broadway since *The Death of Bessie Smith* in March, 1961. Thereafter, beginning with *Who's Afraid of Virginia Woolf?* in October, 1962, all his plays were done on Broadway. *Virginia Woolf* capped and confirmed the off-Broadway promise. It validated the numerous knowing critical judgments pronounced from the earliest days of his career and made a very wide public aware of the seminal importance of off-Broadway.

Albee came along at a particularly fortunate time in the development of off-Broadway. Much was due to the key role the producer Richard Barr played in his career, beginning with *The Zoo Story* in January, 1960. For although Albee's first production of this play by a chain of casual circumstances happened to be given in Berlin, it was Barr's recognition of his talent at precisely the moment Barr had recognized the enormous potentiality of the off-Broadway theater to develop such talent that gave Albee his true start. Remarkably, Albee and Barr have remained in partnership for more than a decade—possibly the longest continuous playwright-producer relationship in the American theater. "I started with Edward Albee," Barr has said. "He fell into my lap, and that was the beginning of a lifelong professional association and friendship." The relationship had a definitive influence on off-Broadway in the decade of the 1960's. Physically they were curiously dissimilar—Albee of medium height, compact, dark, collegiately good-looking; Barr, tall and bald, sharp-featured behind his glasses, like an eager and curious research chemist.

In 1959, just prior to *The Zoo Story* production, Barr had been canvassing the possibilities of off-Broadway for many months. Late in 1959 he decided to strike out on his own. He resigned from the Broadway production office of Bowden,

Barr, and Bullock, which had revived *Hotel Paradiso* and had sent out a number of tours of *Auntie Mame*, to devote his time to new playwrights and to off-Broadway. There were to be no revivals in the future. Unwilling to assume real estate obligations, he decided at first not to settle in a single theater but to remain in a position to negotiate for any of them and, if necessary, for more than one simultaneously. He wanted to do the plays one after the other as quickly as he was able to finance them. Barr was tired of Broadway's compulsion for hits, its subordination of the judgments of taste to the pressures of time and to the availability of name writers, name directors, name stars, name everything. Wonderfully proficient though it was technically—the professionalism of Broadway in such matters as sets, costumes, and choreographed movement was unmatched—it was woefully barren of new creative ideas. Barr saw the other arts—painting, music, and dance—moving far out in front of a laggard theater, scrambling to repeat past successes. Only by uncovering the new writing could the theater catch up. Barr wanted to interest young painters, choreographers, and musicians—all of whom were so much ahead of the theater in their ideas and techniques—in the stage as another outlet for their work. Barr was impressed with the amount of new writing talent he had been able to find, all untouched, most of it in the one-act form in which Tennessee Williams and William Inge and Thornton Wilder had taken their first steps. In the last three months of 1959, as he was getting ready to begin, Barr had read more than fifty new authors, Albee among them. The premiere performance of *The Zoo Story* was given in Berlin on September 28, 1959, but Barr, knowing nothing of Albee at the time, became aware of the script quite independently the following month. It was sent to him by the director Edward Parone, then in the William Morris Agency. Barr was struck by the quality of the writing. Barr tends to believe that playwrights spring full-blown, like Venus at the break of dawn. If the quality is lacking in the first script, it will never appear, however much experience and training may assist new writers to learn the rules and master the craft. In *The Zoo Story* Barr could discern a defined and assured future. At the time, for personal reasons, he had been reading deeply into the history of religion and philosophy and studying Kierkegaard. Existentialist thought was freshly in his head, and Albee's play seemed to fit the scheme. Jerry, the protagonist in the two-character play, was in fact a "spiritual hustler." Barr optioned the play at once for $125 at a time his available cash resources for options were running out. He had not yet met Albee. The very heart of his whole new enterprise was to be the primacy of the playwright. Edward Albee's career was about to begin.

Richard Barr's career goes back to the late 1930's. Graduating from Princeton University in 1938, Barr joined Orson Welles' Mercury Theater and had an acting part in Welles' famous Martian invasion radio broadcast on October 30, 1938. He was an assistant producer on the film *Citizen Kane*. During the war Barr produced training films for the Air Force. Getting out, he went to the City Center as a director. In March, 1959, when Bowden, Barr, and Bullock decided to present Nathaniel Banks' *Season of Choice* at the Barbizon-Plaza, they regarded themselves as the first Broadway management ever to go off-Broadway.

By striking out on his own, Barr intended to keep the overhead down to one person, himself, and pick up his financial supporters and limited producton staff as he went. He decided on a name, Theater 1960, and the opening production, a double bill consisting of *Krapp's Last Tape* by Samuel Beckett and *The Zoo Story*. His first co-producers were H. B. Lutz and Harry Joe Brown, Jr. The double bill opened at the Provincetown Playhouse on January 14, 1960, the first play directed by Alan Schneider, the second at first by Milton Katselas but then by Barr and Albee jointly when they intervened to complete the job. Both sets were by William Ritman, who with Schneider was to become an integral part of the Barr-Albee setup for many years to come. The plays were an immediate success. Financed for $5,200—there were only three characters between the two plays—the production repaid its backers dollar for dollar in thirty-nine days with $3,000 in surplus. Donald Davis, the Canadian actor, played the solitary old man eating bananas and listening to tape-recorded memories in Beckett's fragmentary piece. In *The Zoo Story*, the chance encounter of two men, one of whom has just visited the zoo in Central Park, William Daniels played Peter, a proper and dignified publishing executive in his early forties, and George Maharis played Jerry, a slightly younger, poorly dressed, more shiftless, more voluble wanderer who insistently intrudes on the privacy of Peter as he reads a book at his accustomed place on a park bench. Lee Strasberg once explained that the crackling dramatic tension in an Albee play came from the playwright's refusal to take even the flattest statement of fact at face value. If one character announced that he was going to sit down in a chair, another character would ask why. In the first line of his first play, Albee seeks an argument:

JERRY
I've been to the zoo. (PETER *doesn't notice*) I said, I've been to the zoo. MISTER, I'VE BEEN TO THE ZOO.
PETER
Hm? . . . What? . . . I'm sorry, were you talking to me?

No innuendo, no inflection pass unnoticed by Albee. Wary of being surprised himself, Albee delights in the off-balancing remark that surprises his audience, his adversary. Albee is master of the startling idea at the end of a sequence of relatively mundane thoughts. Thus Jerry says, "I don't talk to many people—except to say like: Gimme a beer, or where's the john, or what time does the feature go on, or keep your hands to yourself, buddy." Or, in *The American Dream*, where Mommy addresses her visitor Mrs. Barker,

"Would you like a cigarette, and a drink, and would you like to cross your legs?"

These were more than mere stylistic tricks. The device of excessive frankness was thrown like a firecracker into the subdued hum of conventional polite discourse. The tone was part of the message, and Albee purposefully was using it both to penetrate the screen of social hypocrisy between people and to dispel the blandness of naturalistic writing in the theater.

Whether he consciously intended the comparison, Albee in Peter and Jerry had sketched the two converging personalities of the modern American man—Peter who is struggling to accept society as he finds it, incomplete though it may be (he is given two daughters but no male heir), and Jerry, the alienated, bewildered, cut-off younger rebel who has no clear vision of what he is rebelling against. The play had a marvelously contemporary ring to it; Albee, writing directly out of the pressures of his time, anticipated the widening divisions and dissatisfactions in American middle-class life.

Albee's second produced play, in May, 1960, was a very brief sketch, *The Sandbox*, which he had written on commission for the Spoleto Festival in Italy. He had already written *The Death of Bessie Smith* at this point and was working on *The American Dream* and its no-nonsense characters, Mommy, Daddy, Grandma, Mrs. Barker, and Young Man. For *The Sandbox* Albee had simply borrowed three of the *Dream* cast—Mommy, Daddy, and Grandma—and placed them in a different environment. Directed by Larry Arrick, *The Sandbox* opened at the Jazz Gallery at 80 St. Marks Place on May 16, 1960, with Sudie Bond, a young actress with a remarkable vocal facility for playing the very old, cast as Grandma as later, and so felicitously, she would be also in *The American Dream*. It is virtually impossible to recall this play without hearing once again the matter-of-fact twangy accents of Sudie Bond saying such lines as "Old people are very good at listening; old people don't like to talk; old people have colitis and lavender perfume. Now I'm going to be quiet."

Barr had begun with a Beckett play, and in the years to come he was to do Ionesco, Pinter, and Betti, most of them not once but several times. Despite his readings into Existentialism, Barr had no very strong philosophical reasons for this interest in the modern European writers. They were there, they were good, and not enough good American playwrights were around. His second production was Ionesco's first full-length work, *The Killer*, about a benevolent and compassionate man's attempts to turn off death in a "radiant city" of tomorrow in which a killer is loose. For this futuristic play Barr had an opportunity to test the integration of the more "with-it" arts into the stage. The abstract painter Ilse Getz did a collage backdrop of New York City. Allan Kaprow, the artist and composer, built a special sound filter to run metropolitan static through on his electronic sound track giving off a continuous urban hum. And Todd Bolender, the dancer and choreographer of the New York City Ballet, worked out movement while Barr himself directed the production overall. It was an altogether interesting but not altogether successful production, despite Hiram Sherman's sensitive performance as Ionesco's running character Berenger and despite the handsome contributions of the modern artists.

It was in 1961 that Barr's new theater idea really began moving with productions of Richard Hepburn's *The Sudden End of Anne Cinquefoil* (January 10), *The American Dream* (January 24), *The Death of Bessie Smith* (March 1), *Gallows Humor* by Jack Richardson (April 18), and Samuel Beckett's *Happy Days* (September 17). By this time Barr had formed a lasting producing partnership with Clinton Wilder, also a Princeton graduate and a onetime Broadway producer who, like Barr, was interested in searching for the sources of a more contemporary theater and who, with Barr, felt that off-Broadway could become a showcase and training ground for new writers. Barr and Wilder met in Europe in the summer of 1960 and in the fall planned a most economically conceived production schedule in which all the above plays, together with a small opera, *Bartleby*, on which Edward Albee and composer William Flanagan had collaborated, and the Valerie Bettis Dance Theater, were put on for less than $25,000, or little more than most off-Broadway producers were then spending to put on one and a half productions. (Barr once calculated that the total bill for Albee productions through *Who's Afraid of Virginia Woolf?*, which was modestly produced with no out-of-town tryout for $45,000, had come to no more than $58,100, counting revivals. And yet, unluckily, in 1969, when they attempted to move their tested off-Broadway repertory of Beckett and Albee to Broadway, they suffered losses of $100,000 inside four weeks.)

One year after *The Zoo Story*, *The American Dream* opened at the York Playhouse with Jane Hoffman as Mommy, John C. Becher as Daddy, Sudie Bond as Grandma, Nancy Cushman as Mrs. Barker, and Ben Piazza as the Young Man—a cast that became practically an Edward Albee stock company. In his generation Albee was the first dramatic satirist to mount a large-scale attack on American self-complacency. His own description of the play was "a stand against the fiction that everything in this slipping land of ours is peachy-keen." His primary target was the foundation of the family, its matriarchal structure, the assumed obsolescence of the old at one end of the scale and the emasculation of youth at the other. The figure of the Young Man is represented as the emotionally damaged and unfeeling but physically perfect twin of an "unsatisfactory" adopted boy the family had mutilated and disposed of. Albee, himself an adopted child, viewed the hierarchical family structure both in personal and in representational terms. It is Grandma who has the last word of the evening, winding up the play just as the fatal cycle of birth and parental destruction of the wished-for child begins to repeat itself. "Let's leave things as they are right now," she says. "... while everybody's happy ... while everybody's got what he wants . . . or everybody's got what he thinks he wants. Good night, dears." With the American flag displayed on the set, Albee's *Dream* was the most mordantly antipatriotic play of its day.

In March, Albee's *The Death of Bessie Smith* with Lee Richardson as the hospital intern, Rae Allen as the nurse, and John McCurry as a Negro orderly opened at the York Playhouse to play with *Dream*. Alan Schneider was the director. Here Albee, approaching his theme obliquely, for Bessie Smith herself never appears as a character, probes some of the causes and symptoms of a diseased society. The play was a reflection in white and black of the event of Bessie Smith's death in 1937 from injuries in a car accident after she was refused admittance to a Tennessee hospital. With obvious sexual urgency Rae Allen played the neglectful admissions nurse who pays attention to all her own needs, frustrations, angers, and desires but ignores her clear professional duty.

At the start of the new season in September, 1961, Theater 1961 (now Barr and Wilder) put on its first show at the Cherry Lane, the small Commerce Street theater which was to become its headquarters for a number of years. The play was Beckett's *Happy Days*. Ruth White, buried up to her neck in a mound of earth, delivered the near monologue of complaint, the litany of despair that is the burden of the play. Her companion, the occasionally glimpsed John C. Becher, had only six lines to speak. As director Alan Schneider continued the uniquely close association he has had with Beckett's works in this country. Beckett was greeted with a cheerful opening line from Walter Kerr in the *Herald Tribune:* "Well, happy days are gone again. Beckett is back." Kerr in company with many actors argued that the nonuse of the stage in *Happy Days* and the nonuse of the actor's body was antitheater. But Beckett was trying not so much to reform theater as to rethink the purposes of life and make the stage conform to his new insights. Perhaps the validity of Beckett's disembodied monologue lay in the dramatic shock value of having everything familiar and helpful taken away and attention directed to the actor's speaking voice. Albee himself was to go Beckett one better with his short play *Box*, in which no actor appeared and only the taped voice of Ruth White was heard. The Barr-Wilder-Albee theater (for by now Albee in name had become part of the management) put on a new *Happy Days* for thirty-two performances in September, 1965, with Madelaine Renaud speaking the role in French for the first half of the run and Ruth White resuming in English for the second half.

Beckett was paired with Albee, Beckett was paired with Pinter, and Beckett was played alone. In early 1964 Beckett's *Play* was combined with Pinter's *Lover*, and in March *Play*, performed by three actors in ash cans, continued to run with the addition of two new plays, LeRoi Jones' *Dutchman* and Arrabal's *Two Executioners*. Albee was categorized with the European Absurdists—Ionesco, Beckett, Arrabal. In February, 1962, the Barr-Wilder management presented a repertory of nine plays under the Theater of the Absurd heading, including Beckett, Kenneth Koch, Jack Richardson, Genet, and Albee. By this time, however, Barr felt the Absurdist trend had run its course. To be sure, the Absurdist playwright's method of raising questions without demanding answers was exactly suited to the intellectual climate of the 1960's, disturbed as it was by the uncertainties raised by nuclear science and early space probes, and it had usefully freed playwriting of the domination of time and place conventions. But the plays attracted only the intellectuals and not the general public. The future suggested a return by the American playwrights to more conventional forms. The following October Albee was to go to Broadway with his first three-act play, *Who's Afraid of Virginia Woolf?*

In the summer, to reinforce their off-Broadway activity by

giving it a base, Barr and Wilder took out a five-year lease on the Cherry Lane, which for the previous seven years had been under the management of one of off-Broadway's pioneers, Noel Behn. There, continuing to do Beckett productions directed by Alan Schneider, they produced the first plays of William Hanley, *Mrs. Dally Has a Lover* and *Whisper in My Good Ear* and in a series of evenings in the winter of 1965 a platoon of new playwrights, including Sam Shepard, Paul Foster, Lanford Wilson, Frank Gagliano, Lawrence Osgood, Joseph Morgenstern, and Kenneth Pressman. Some of these writers came out of the Playwrights Unit which Barr, Wilder, and Albee, thanks to their good fortune with *Virginia Woolf*, had set up in November, 1963, in the Village South Theater on Van Dam Street. Their aim was to provide the playwright with actors, a director, a place, and an audience. Rehearsed productions were given before invited audiences on Sundays. The unit has been directed by Edward Parone and more recently by Chuck Gyns, first on Van Dam Street and later, until 1971, when the $50,000 annual budget became too burdensome to keep a building going, on East Fourth Street in David Ross' old home. Albee contributed not only money, but also his own time and enthusiasm. He spoke of the activity in these terms:

"I think we can offer these playwrights something a commercial theater cannot: the place and time to experiment and develop without the cruel pressures of the hit-or-flop syndrome. We think it possible that in giving these playwrights the chance to extend themselves we may also be giving them the chance to expand the horizon of the theater as a whole."

In six years the Playwrights Unit put on eighty-five plays, but neither Barr nor Albee would claim more than a handful of discovered talent. Of the twenty-one plays that have emerged into commercial production, the two most arresting were LeRoi Jones' savage one-act drama *Dutchman* and Mart Crowley's *The Boys in the Band*, both presented under Barr's management. From their workshop, *Dutchman*, staged by Edward Parone, went to the Cherry Lane in March, 1964, with Jennifer West as the provocative white girl and Robert Hooks as the quiet, properly dressed black she encounters on the subway. In this deceptively simple and altogether public setting (the subway, by implication, is the only place the races mix) the private erotic fantasies of the white girl are enacted overtly while the black stranger struggles to maintain his composure and contain his anger. When his hatred finally erupts against him and he is knifed in the empty subway car, another aspect of the utility of the set is apparent (open the door and dispose of the body and another unsuspecting black enters). In its economy of character and detail and in its bitterness, *Dutchman* recalled Albee's *Zoo Story*.

Barr and a new partner, Charles Woodward, produced *The Boys in the Band* at Theater Four on April 14, 1968. No play had ever told so much about how homosexuals live and play among themselves, nor had homosexuals ever been shown with such knife-edge accuracy or with such compassion. Financially, it was far and away the most successful show outside of the Albee plays Barr had ever produced. It was, in fact, one of the ticket scalper's shows of that season. In this realization, beginning in December, 1968, the producers boosted the ticket price to the highest level in off-Broadway history—in the first seven rows of the orchestra from $5.95 to $10. The world renown of Crowley's play alone would seem to justify all the time and effort that went into the Playwrights Unit.

LeRoi Jones has sacrificed his writing career to political activity in his home city of Newark. Of the other members of the Playwrights Unit there would seem to be an assured future for no more than perhaps five or six, and none has appeared of Albee's skill and standing. Barr estimated that in twelve years he had probably read 5,000 scripts and that he would regard all but 50 as virtually worthless. Barr and Albee would rightly maintain that such long odds against excellence are only to be expected in the theater.

For the immediate future, while the signs point to plays of more political and social orientation, Barr questions mostly the ability of the new playwrights to find an adequate metaphor for their concerns. Through Barr, and in his own activities, Albee has remained more personally and usefully involved in the theater than any playwright of his time. He cheerfully engages the drama critics in dubious battle, difficult though it is for one so viscerally affected by reviews to advance any credibly disinterested arguments. Although critics are not above reproach, an attack by a playwright usually improves their position. Still one is tempted to cheer from the sidelines when Albee strikes back. He lectures frequently on university campuses and keeps himself open to general discussion. His partner, Barr, whose main idea in 1960 was to make the playwright once again the star, has in his part strengthened the hand of the author. Albee's success, in turn, has bolstered Barr's position as a versatile producer working constantly on three levels, off off-Broadway, off-Broadway, and Broadway. Succeeding Harold Prince in 1967, Barr had the most statesmanlike administration of any president of the League of New York Theaters in recent times. Barr made the original suggestion that led to the formation of the Theater Development Fund to use nonprofit money in the assistance of the commercial theater through ticket subsidy and audience development. He put through the seven thirty curtain on Broadway, changing patterns of theatergoing, and the "limited gross" contract, ameliorating union demands in Broadway theaters when a producer voluntarily cuts back on his earning potential by rescaling ticket prices in the house.

Whatever accommodations can be made at the top, Barr and Albee are aware that new writing at the bottom alone feeds the theater. The Playwrights Unit, even homeless and economically restricted, will probably remain integral to their operation, for it keeps them reading plays. It keeps them in touch with the new trends in writing, and it keeps them looking for a new Edward Albee.

Julian Beck and Judith Malina, co-founders of the Living Theater, in December, 1964, just before they were forced to close.

Kenneth H. Brown's *The Brig,* in 1963, was the last play performed by the Beck's theater in New York.

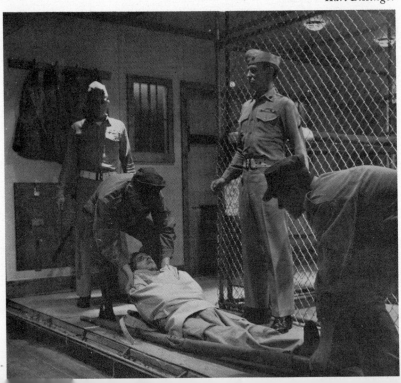

First important success of the Ameri
Place Theater at St. Clement's Church
Robert Lowell's *The Old Glory* in 1964
the scene (*below*) from *Benito Cer*
Lester Rawlins as Captain Delano hol
gun on Roscoe Lee Browne as the s
Babu. (*Left*) Frank Langella played
noble captain of the Spanish slave shi
Martha Hol

n Handman, director of the American
e Theater, and his colleague Michael
an, in costume for Ronald Ribman's
Journey of the Fifth Horse in 1966.
Martha Holmes

Dustin Hoffman as the robed
and fish-chopping Immanuel
in Ronald Ribman's *Harry,
Noon and Night* at the American Place Theater in 1965.
Martha Holmes

(*Above*) Seated in a subway car in LeRoi Jones' *Dutchman* are Robert Hooks and a provocative Jennifer West in the 1964 production at the Cherry Lane.

(*Below*) Left to right, Karen Johnson, Bob Balabain, Skip Hinnant, Riva Rose, Bill Hinnant, and Gary Burghoff in the 1967 musical *You're a Good Man, Charlie Brown*.

Eleven

Off-Broadway Comes of Middle Age 1964–1969

Economics dominated the vocabulary of off-Broadway concerns in the middle 1960's. As off-Broadway grew in professionalism and public acceptance, it began to acquire more serious money problems owing to the inexorably rising costs of production. The old dilemma was present in a new and more menacing form: Would off-Broadway have to become a "real" theater like Broadway, or could it remain, as George Cram Cook would have preferred, a place to do your own thing?

Albee would remind the overly ambitious, in their enthusiasm for off-Broadway's rare successes, of the true state of affairs. He spoke in December, 1964: "Off-Broadway is a losing economic proposition. The actors are not in it for money. The producers are not in it for money. The playwright is not in it for money. The off-Broadway theater simply has to be subsidized by the actors, the producers, the playwrights, the directors."

A new Equity settlement had boosted the actor's minimum weekly wage from $50 to $60. Though the wage was hardly exorbitant, this modest breakthrough sent the producers into one of their periodic moods of depression. Over the short lifetime of the off-Broadway theater preproduction costs had risen from an average of $1,500 to $15,000 and weekly operating costs had tripled—from $1,000 to $3,200.

The recurring contradictions of theater never seemed more troublesome: fixed seating capacities versus constantly rising costs; theater a handcrafted article which resists mechanization and gains nothing from computerization; the inability of ticket prices to keep pace with expenses; and, even with a product in great demand, no way to increase the unit rate of production—just one live performance a night and so many seats to be sold.

There was an advantage, furthermore, in the very smallness of the off-Broadway house. The principle of the small theater—the proximity of the stage intensifying the interaction between actor and audience—had by now become firmly established. No equivalent theaters were possible or in use elsewhere, and a defined and loyal audience had grown up in their support. It was never the expense-account audience and rarely the benefit crowd on which the Broadway theater depended. The core source was the Greenwich Village area and, in increasing numbers, tourists for whom off-Broadway was part of the Manhattan itinerary. It was an audience curious about theatrical experimentation, which preferred a daring failure to a safe professional success, which sought out revivals and was eager to see uptown flops reclaimed in smaller theaters, and which found pleasure in the recognition of new talent. For this last reason especially off-Broadway always attracted the theater people themselves.

And now the danger appeared to be an imbalance between the economics and the optimum size of the audience. The strain in the equation showed up in a statistical decline in the rate of production of off-Broadway shows. For a decade production had risen steadily, reaching a level of 100 shows in off-Broadway's tenth season, 1962–63. Over the previous five seasons off-Broadway had topped Broadway in numbers of shows produced, and the range of material was, of course, much greater. But a distinct falloff in off-Broadway production began in 1964, traceable directly to the worsening economics.

The slump caused a reshuffling in off-Broadway real estate. In the flush years of expansion, Irving Maidman, a West Side real estate developer who held important properties north and south of Forty-second Street from Times Square to the North River, had set out a string of little theaters on the south side of Forty-second going toward the Maidman-controlled West Side Airlines Terminal. They all took their names from his initial letter—Maidman, Mermaid, Masque, Mayfair. In five years he had never had a hit. The theaters were intended, partly, to serve the commercial purpose of improving the tone of the Maidman neighborhood, but finally conceding the theatrical odds, he began to unload. In another year he had liquidated this little Shubertian empire.

The Mayfair, on traveled Forty-sixth Street, went into burlesque, as some respected legitimate Broadway theaters such as the Hudson and Henry Miller's were later in their extremities to book blue movies. Uptown on the East Side Warner LeRoy turned his York Playhouse at Sixty-fourth Street, where Tennessee Williams' *Garden District* had played in 1958, into a movie house. Some years later, in the Swinging Sixties, and still more profitably, it became a popular "singles" restaurant, Maxwell's Plum, whose bar was nightly lined six-deep with single men and single girls eyeing one another across the smoky lamplit pickup pit.

Richard Barr, for one, was not entirely pessimistic about the general shrinkage in theaters and in production. He regarded it as a shaking-out process. "Off-Broadway is settling down into the hands of the professionals," he said.

Economics was partly the cause, too, of the emergence in the middle years of a number of institutional theaters, non-profit and otherwise: the American Place Theater, the Establishment Theater, the Negro Ensemble Company. Through the NEC and other outlets during this period were to come a series of plays dealing with the black life and the black experience in America. This phenomenon was really wholly unrelated to the racial composition of New York City, although in the decade of the 1960's the black population increased steadily, a total of 53.2 percent while the overall population of the city over the ten years shrank by 9.3 percent. There was no such thing as a waiting and expanding "black audience." But theater as an emotional outlet and as a platform for ideas has always been a more precious necessity of writers and actors than it has been a requirement of audiences, white, black, or mixed. Now, however, the stage offered itself as the readiest available sounding board for the anguish and shouted anger of the black world finding its voice and struggling upward for its rightful place in society. The stage became a megaphone of black militancy. As always in theater the impulse came first from the need for a means of expression—black actors whose talent was foreclosed by the limited opportunities of work in a predominantly white theater, black writers seizing urgently upon the most immediate and compelling means of expression, which has always been the legitimate stage. In the next few years the outburst of long-suppressed and long-withheld outrage and hurt produced not only strong black plays but also plays that transcended the presumed racial limitations of the material and made powerful the American stage. The urgency of message recalled the "fervent years" of Clifford Odets and Sidney Kingsley—the concerned 1930's written about by Harold Clurman. Off-Broadway was the principal beneficiary of this new eloquence, this renewal of theatrical power both in performance and in writing. Outside of the streets, the stage was the most effective platform of protest.

The possibilities for black playwrights dealing with black themes in the early days of the Movement first were dramatized in the great success of Lorraine Hansberry's *A Raisin in the Sun*, winner of the Drama Critics' Circle Award for best play in 1959. But *A Raisin* was a Broadway play and addressed itself largely to the white Broadway audience. In the middle years 1964–1969 off-Broadway was to produce ten shows for every six Broadway put on. The ratio of black plays off-Broadway as contrasted with Broadway, however, ran about four to one.

The character of the material was to vary widely. At the beginning of 1964 Langston Hughes' *Jerico-Jim Crow* played the Greenwich Mews Theater with its rousingly revivalist music and glorious sound. At the same moment Adrienne Kennedy's *Funny House of a Negro* conveyed the black experience in the terms of another generation. Langston Hughes was the sad lyric poet of the Harlem streets. Adrienne Kennedy used nightmarish images to describe the psychic confusions of being black. Right after these two plays came the South African playwright Atholl Fugard's *Blood Knot*, a two-character play set in a squalid shack of the Colored section of Johannesburg. The play examined the life possibilities of two black blood brothers, a darker and a lighter one. In the two roles James Earl Jones and J. D. Cannon gave compelling performances. *Blood Knot* could be thought of as a Third World play uniting the blacks of two continents through their common frustrations and feelings of hopelessness. Later, the NEC was to put on plays from Africa by blacks (Fugard was white).

The development of one of the theater's meteorically most brilliant directorial talents was tied in briefly but significantly with off-Broadway. In the spring of 1964, after one big success on Broadway with Neil Simon's *Barefoot in the Park*, Mike Nichols directed the four-character modern British comedy *The Knack* by Ann Jellicoe. Three young men played by Brian Bedford, Roddy Maude-Roxby, and George Segal, who was on the brink of a television and film career, shared a flat with a girl, Alexandra Berlin. Nichols described it as a "how-to-do-it" play—how to make out with a girl. Anglo-American in character, the play was a production of the Anglophile Establishment Theater Company founded at a time when many bright young English talents had flocked to New York and had made it in the then popular revues. The revues were soon to disappear from off-Broadway, although

The Mad Show, one of the most successful, was still to come, in the late spring Nichols' old partner, Elaine May, was to put on *The Third Ear* at the Premise, and Alan Arkin was to stage yet another *Second City* in the summer. Nevertheless, the topical revue, which depended so heavily on political comment and self-humor at the top levels of administration, was not to survive the Kennedy era in American life. No national administration since has had very much humor about itself, and the mood of grimness set in.

One of the most significant attempts by off-Broadway to bring authoritative and authentic voices to the stage to speak out on national problems in dramatic from was the American Place Theater. In the early 1960's Sidney Lanier, then assistant minister at St. Thomas Episcopal Church in New York City, spoke his concern for widespread reform in the church that might include the dispersal of large congregations such as were found at St. Thomas and their regrouping into small units intensely committed to specific goals. At the same time he found the theater expiring from lack of ideas and intellectual stimulus. An underlying assumption—not always to be validated—was that the theater would be refreshed if writers and thinkers accustomed to expressing themselves in other media were given the means to use the stage as their rostrum. On these two ideas St. Clement's Church as a theatrical parish and the American Place Theater, using the church's sanctuary and nave as a stage and auditorium, came into being simultaneously—both dedicated to assisting the theater to deal more directly with "the crucial themes of contemporary life." Through sharing a common building Lanier hoped further that theater and church could enter into "dialogue"—the word of the day. Liturgical experimentation would go forward in the church, theatrical experimentation on the stage—not so much with the stage form, for here the American Place was essentially conservative and literary, as with the method of working with writers to help them realize their ideas dramatically.

Lanier conducted the first service in St. Clement's in November, 1962. Three months later the American Place Theater was incorporated under the laws of New York State. The first play was an inspired and fortunate choice. Robert Lowell's *The Old Glory* opened on November 1, 1964, a play by one of the country's finest poets directed by Jonathan Miller, an English Mike Nichols who, like Nichols, had made his mark in a revue, *Beyond the Fringe*, who wrote for *The New Yorker*, was a highly verbal panel show participant, and, intellectually, was making quite a splash in New York theater and artistic circles. The title of Lowell's work covered two plays, *Benito Cereno* and *My Kinsman, Major Molineaux*, both drawn from literary sources, the first from a novella by Herman Melville, the second from a Hawthorne story set in the American Revolution about two youths looking for their British cousin in Boston. *Benito Cereno* was the more powerful work. Lester Rawlins played Delano, an idealistically upright New England sea captain in 1800 who comes upon a strange slave ship at anchor off the South American coast, its gear in disarray, its disheveled crew wandering the decks. The noble Spanish captain played by Frank Langella seems to be in the power of an unctuous slave, Babu, played by Roscoe Lee Browne. There are hints of mutiny. At last it becomes clear to the American captain that the slaves are in control. When Babu demands that Delano sail their ship back to Africa, Delano's concern turns to revulsion, and the play ends with a massacre of the slaves by Delano's crew. Here was a poet's projection of an historical incident into the present: Delano embraced the enlightened intentions and deeply embedded fears and guilts of white Americans toward the Negro enslavement, Babu expressed the militant rising up of the blacks and the shaking off of their enforced subservience. The co-directors of the American Place Theater, Sidney Lanier and Wynn Handman, could hardly have found a finer inaugural work.

The famous poet was followed at American Place by an exciting new writer, Ronald Ribman, with a remarkable first two plays presented a year apart—*Harry, Noon and Night* on March 17, 1965, and *The Journey of the Fifth Horse* on April 13, 1966. The first play, set in Munich during the military occupation of the mid-1950's, contained a visually shocking opening scene in which a prostitute making automatic wordless responses stands between a soldier and Harry, who alternately kiss, handle, and fondle her while casually conducting a conversation. In the middle 1960's this scene seemed especially shocking in the church setting. The St. Clement's Bishop's Committee, governing board of the parish, met with the author and Handman at their suggestion before the play was put on to review the artistic justification for material that in the context of the church setting might appear morally offensive. There was no interference or suggestion of censorship. The scene was clearly part of the intricate artistic fabric of the play.

An exceptional cast had been assembled: Joel Grey, later to become a major Broadway star in *Cabaret* and *George M*, in the title role as a visiting American journalist from an obscure magazine and an inept would-be painter; Richard Schaal, a later member of Paul Sills' *Story Theater*, as the soldier; Lynn Bernay as the provocative prostitute in an entirely physical performance. Scene two carried overtones of homosexuality and introduced two new characters, including Harry's crippled, lame German roommate, Immanuel, portrayed by Dustin Hoffman, who with his jumpy, feminine walk and oddly frantic fish-chopping gestures in the opening scene gave a performance that is indelibly fixed in memory. The other was Harry's brother, played by Gerald S. O'Laughlin, arrived on the scene from Ohio to bring his confused brother home, but too late to save him from arrest by the German police after a fit of presumed madness.

The Journey of the Fifth Horse was a larger work based on the Turgenev short story, "Diary of a Superfluous Man." Dustin Hoffman was again in the cast, again in the part of an ineffectual character, that of a junior, passed-over clerk in a publishing house whose control has been bequeathed to the lovely daughter of the dead owner, a part played by Susan Anspach. The two plays established the young Ribman as literarily the most exciting new dramatist at work in the theater, more imaginative, more skillful, and more poetic in his writing than any of his contemporaries. The play, directed with style and subtlety by Larry Arrick, was later redone for television.

For such a remarkable and original literary talent Ribman developed late. A native New Yorker, he went to Brooklyn College, where, by his own account, he was a poor and dilatory student, almost below the level of normal literacy, listless, unmotivated, and with no strongly developed intellectual interests. A desire to write was awakened by some English courses at the University of Pittsburgh, where he was graduated in 1954. In the Army of Occupation in Germany— the setting of his first play—he began writing for the first time, mostly rudimentary pieces such as press releases and announcements for the Armed Forces Radio. From that point his writing developed rapidly. Returning to Pittsburgh, he earned his PhD in English in 1962. For his "Magellan: 1521" he won a Borestone Mountain Poetry Award.

Of the contemporary English playwrights of this period Harold Pinter was the most frequently produced. The Barr-Wilder-Albee office had presented *The Lover* at the Cherry Lane at the beginning of 1964, a play in which Pinter visualized husband and wife playing different roles—husband visiting a prostitute, wife visiting a lover, the four roles united in the two persons of the marriage. And at the end of 1964 Pinter's *The Room* and *A Slight Ache* were done at the Writer's Stage under the direction of Word Baker. In the second play the undefined menace that overhangs so much of Pinter's work was embodied in a mysterious matchmaker who lingers all day outside the gate of the house of a respectable middle-aged couple conversing genteelly about such homey details as a wasp caught at the bottom of the marmalade jar. But by the end of the play the persistence of the matchmaker becomes unbearable. He is invited into the house, where he appears to supplant the dim and tentative husband. The married couple was played expertly by two accomplished actors, Henderson Forsythe and Frances Sternhagen. In time off-Broadway, with the collector's thoroughness, was to reproduce the entire body of Pinter's work, down to slight television sketches, such avid attention having been shown no other writer, American or British.

Early in 1965 Arthur Miller's *A View from the Bridge* was revived at the Sheridan Square Playhouse across the street from where his adaptation of Ibsen's *An Enemy of the People* was played in the Actors Playhouse six years earlier. Director Ulu Grosbard had directed two previous productions in stock, outside New York, with Robert Duvall playing the Brooklyn longshoreman who falls in love with a niece who comes to live in his house as his ward. Once again Grosbard cast Duvall, who this time researched his part of the actual New York waterfront. An attractive and exciting young actress, Susan Anspach, who was next to appear in the Ribman play, played his ward. With excellent acting, none of the play's initial impact was lost, and Grosbard's production had a long run of 780 performances.

Few important writers rise to prominence in other media without being encouraged to try the stage or without themselves being tempted to try the form. The rhythms of writing for the stage, the concrete realization of imagined characters, the technical demands of the craft—these are hard to master. Kerr, discussing Lowell's *Old Glory*, wrote, "Writers, distinguished writers, are not quite free 'to use the drama.' They must walk with it, attentive to its step." Joyce Carol Oates' reputation as a novelist of the first rank (*them*, 1969) was still to come when in 1964 Frank Corsaro, the director and a prominent member of the Actors Studio, asked her to dramatize some stories from her first published collection, *By the*

North Gate. Miss Oates at first resisted the idea, saying she didn't know how to write a play. Corsaro, a playwright himself, offered to help. Later William Gibson came in to assist her with final changes. *The Sweet Enemy* opened in February at the Actor's Playhouse but was not a success. The four-character play was about a Negro, his white daughter, a boy-friend, and a humanist professor. Miss Oates had written their exchanges as if they were four characters conversing around a table. "I wrote it more or less as prose," she said. "When you write a story, you don't have to visualize it. Very often it's just something going on in someone's mind. The stage is a much cruder form." Five years later her *Sunday Dinner* was to be done at the American Place Theater. Here she made actual use of the dinner table as a device for dealing with complex interfamily relationships. *Sunday Dinner* was not successful in dramatic terms, and Joyce Carol Oates has yet to write the play expected of one with her rare literary gifts.

Throughout the decade of the 1960's James Earl Jones was a remarkable figure in the off-Broadway theater. He was the second theater generation in his family; his father, Robert Earl Jones, was an actor, and father and son have acted in the same plays. Tall, deep-chested, gentle in manner privately, but with a bellowing voice to express outrage and anger, he is an imposing figure on the stage. Tirelessly, with inexhaustible drive and energy, Jones has taken role after role in small productions such as the two-character *Blood Knot*, in big ones such as *Othello* for the New York Shakespeare Festival in Central Park, in strong racial material such as *The Blacks*, and in regional family dramas such as *Moon on a Rainbow Shawl*. He was a powerful performer of whom in his formative period Edith Oliver of *The New Yorker* once said in a telling line of friendly criticism that he was already a potential star without yet having learned to be an actor.

After a summer in the park in the role of Othello, with Julienne Marie (whom Jones later married) playing Desdemona, Jones went into the Martinique Theater for a season's run in *Othello*, sponsored by Theodore Mann and Paul Libin. In May, utilizing the same cast, Mann and Libin opened a production of Brecht's early experiment in epic drama, *Baal*, to play in repertory with *Othello*. The same company of twenty-two actors, led by Jones and Mitchell Ryan and directed by Gladys Vaughan, performed the plays in alternation—Jones playing Othello and Ryan Iago and Ryan taking the title role in *Baal*, an animalistic and amoral man's journey through life, with Jones in the sexually equivocal second part of Eckart, who in one daringly explicit scene of considerable shock effect seizes Baal in his arms and kisses him full on the mouth. The alternating productions, splitting the playing week between them, were performed before audiences of high school students, a responsive and appreciative audience that had only one drawback. During the *Othello* performances they often held copies of the play open in their laps which made the actors nervous, recalling the story of Richard Burton's consternation at Winston Churchill sitting in a front row and audibly muttering the lines of the soliloquies during Burton's *Hamlet*. By summer the actors had to get back to work for Joseph Papp in the park and the run of the two big plays—a rare attempt at genuine repertory—ended.

In the middle 1960's some two-way traffic developed between the more established producing offices of off-Broadway and some of the better regional theaters. Developing the college and university market for the stronger off-Broadway material, especially literary works such as *Under Milk Wood* and *Desire Under the Elms*, was another source of recoupment for the fast increasing costs of production. After 497 performances *In White America* was $6,000 in debt because of losing weeks. A five-month tour among the colleges, where documentary drama, the classics, and readings were especially popular, made a profit that enabled *In White America* to be reopened at the Players Theater in May, 1965, for a limited return engagement. The Circle management, which was especially diligent about cultivating this developing market, in a turnabout gesture in the summer of 1965 brought in a production of the Theater Company of Boston. In one sense the company was an offshoot of the Circle. Its director, David Wheeler, had studied at the Circle school under Jose Quintero and had assisted him on *The Balcony*. Wheeler founded his own company in Boston in 1963. In a small room in the Hotel Bostonian it displayed considerable venturesomeness by introducing such playwrights as Pinter, Albee, Ionesco, Brecht, and Beckett. Wheeler's well-integrated company had done some plays by the English playwright John Arden so successfully that Arden allowed it to give the first American production of *Live Like Pigs*. Arden was an interesting contrast with his English contemporary Pinter. Where Pinter's focus narrowed onto the eccentricities of individuals within four walls, Arden's plays were constructed in more epic dimension. *Pigs* was a frequently unpleasant drama about two working-class families living as uneasy neighbors in a housing development in an English industrial city. Mann's importation provided an early example of how some theaters outside New York with permanent companies and committed directors could develop projects more fully than many commercial theaters in New York. A pipeline had been opened that was to flow New York-ward with increasing strength.

Another outside spawning ground of productions was the Professional Theater Program at the University of Michigan headed by Robert C. Schnitzer. In October, 1965, it sent *An Evening's Frost* directed by Marcella Cisney into the Theater de Lys. This was a staged reading of Robert Frost with Will Geer as Frost. Off-Broadway has always been hospitable to readings; the following month Bramwell Fletcher was to present his *Bernard Shaw Story* at the East Seventy-fourth Street Theater.

The off-Broadway slump continued. At the end of the 1964–65 season the charts and seasonal compilations showed fewer of everything—fewer new plays; fewer musicals, and *no*

real musical success all season; fewer revivals; and many
fewer revues. In fact, the topical revue so much in vogue
in the early years of the decade—the Premise, Second City,
the Establishment, etc.—had by now apparently died out.
Once-enterprising producers such as Judith Marechal had
suspended efforts to present new playwrights. "The emergence of Albee," she noted, "glamorized the new playwright
beyond reasonable expectations." Continuing into the fall of
the new season, the slump caused the demise of three more
playhouses, which turned to films. Constricting economic
conditions temporarily drove out many independent producers, without of course discouraging the hard core of regulars,
and also swung the spotlight to some of the new nonprofit
theaters.

The American Place Theater, maintaining its unusually
high literary standards, opened its second season with William Alfred's *Hogan's Goat*. Against a musty nineteenth-century backdrop the Harvard poet examined the moral dilemma of an able young Irish politician with a flawed past;
his relationship to his wife, his political allies, and his ready
enemies. Frederick Rolf played Hogan, and Faye Dunaway,
not yet a star, played his wife with a serene and suffering
beauty. The verse play was rich in a kind of imagery that
comes rarely to the stage, on or off Broadway.

Downtown at the St. Marks Playhouse, where *The Blacks*
had once played and where LeRoi Jones' *The Slave* and
The Toilet were put on in 1964, the foundations were being
laid for what was to become the Negro Ensemble Company.
Two of the founders, Robert Hooks, the actor, and Douglas
Turner Ward, an actor and playwright, joined up to produce
Ward's one-act social comedies *Happy Ending* and *Day of
Absence*. It took them eight months to raise the $8,000
needed to put this production in the St. Marks. Within the
next few years they were to receive more than $1,000,000
from the Ford Foundation for their NEC. In the two plays
Ward adopted the farcical style of dealing with bitter mate-

rial used by Ossie Davis in his *Purlie Victorious*. Ward described his *Day of Absence* as a minstrel show in reverse. Negroes in white face impersonated white Southern stereotypes and played out the whites' helplessness on a day all the Negroes mysteriously had vanished from town. The play was later done on public television for a national audience.

Circle in the Square, of course, was still going strong; no one was more persistent or more adept at threading his way through the economic labyrinths of off-Broadway than Theodore Mann. For the Circle Jack Landau staged a handsome production of John Webster's Jacobean horror play *The White Devil* with a superlative cast that brought together on the Circle's long three-quarter stage Carrie Nye, Eric Berry, Paul Stevens, Robert Burr, Maria Tucci, and Frank Langella.

The Establishment Theater, running counter to its early English bias, put an entirely American-style revue into its East Fifty-fourth Street headquarters. *The Mad Show*, with a score by Mary Rodgers, was performed in sketch and song by a new generation of revue talent: Linda Lavin; Jo Anne Worley, later a star television comedienne; and Paul Sands, later a member of Paul Sills' *Story Theater*. It borrowed its theme and iconoclastic attitudes from *Mad* magazine and, while not political, was contemporary in feeling. Ivor David Balding's Establishment Theater enjoyed fancy financial support from varied sources, which included the treasury of Joseph E. Levine. Possibly because he was New York-based, Levine was one of the few movie producers to make any kind of investment in the theater. He looked upon lively off-Broadway with its mixture of budding talent and competent middle-ground actors as a source for the movies. In this Levine was among the first of the movie moguls to sense that the "new reality" of contemporary films would require not only location shooting, but real actors, no more merely pretty faces. One of the first dividends of his investment was Mike Nichols, who had directed *The Knack* for the Establishment and was to direct *The Graduate*, a "make-out" film, for Levine. The acting "discovery" of that film was of course Dustin Hoffman, whom Nichols cast after seeing his performance at the Circle in Henry Livings' *Eh?* in 1966.

At one point Balding's Establishmentarian board directors included Levine; Edgar Bergen; Peter Cook, of *Beyond the Fringe*; John Bird; Eleanor Bron; Sybil Christopher, Richard Burton's former wife; Jeremy Geidt; and Jean vanden Heuvel. His company reached peak activity in the early spring of 1966. At twenty-seven, bright and ambitious, Balding enjoyed the confidence of financial supporters more mature and experienced producers might well have envied. By March he had *The Mad Show* running strong at the New Theater in its roomy Fifty-fourth Street building. At the de Lys he had opened John Arden's *Serjeant Musgrave's Dance*, a play studied admiringly in professional American theater circles. Uptown at Stage 73 he was sponsoring Jerome Kass' *Monopoly*, a series of brief but incisive character sketches. A second company of *The Mad Show* was to open in Los Angeles in May, and *The Knack*, the show that started all the success, was to reopen on tour in Chicago. In June Arnold Wesker's *The Kitchen*, a play of many voices as intricately orchestrated as Lanford Wilson's *Balm in Gilead*, with a cast of twenty-nine—one of the largest off-Broadway companies on record—opened at the Eighty-first Street Theater. Directed by playwright Jack Gelber, author of *The Connection*, this giant production came out of the Establishment-affiliated New Theater Workshop run by Stephen Aaron and included Rip Torn in its impressive cast. This was flood tide for Balding, the high-water mark of his Establishment Theater Company.

Beginning noticeably in the season of 1966–67, events at home and events overseas and the slow stirring of the American conscience began to be reflected in a new kind of material off-Broadway. There was a new anger in the writing, a reaction to the apparent indifference at the national level to the moral doubts shared by so many over our role in Southeast Asia. Some of the strongest plays of disillusionment were among the first on the scene. One early instance of the new growing antipatriotism that gathered in the colleges and was about to overtake the most disaffected elements of society was a flag-burning incident within a performance at the Bridge Theater in the East Village in April, 1966. The lawyer who sprang to the defense of Elsa Tambellini, the producer of the show in which the desecration of the flag occurred, was none other than William M. Kunstler, whose real fame as an advocate of the rebellious was to come in Chicago. In the ensuing litigation, Kunstler argued successfully for the "use of the stage to communicate symbolically."

Opening alongside each other in November, 1966, were Jean-Claude van Itallie's *America Hurrah* and Megan Terry's *Viet Rock*, both emerging from the off off-Broadway scene. But then in February came the most daring political satire off-Broadway has ever seen, Barbara Garson's *MacBird!* The thesis of the play was the revenge of a fictional Robert Kennedy against a fictional President Johnson for a presumed responsibility for the assassination of John F. Kennedy. Although at first privately printed, the play raised murky questions of criminal libel and sedition, the main characters lying under the thin disguise of "Robert Ken O'Dunc," "Ted Ken O'Dunc," and "MacBird," the title role brilliantly played by Stacy Keach. The play had the perhaps therapeutic but unfair effect of fixing blame for a crime that seemed insupportably monstrous. *MacBird!* was an extreme example of a deep national revulsion. As the most conspicuous beneficiary of the assassination of the President, Vice President Lyndon B. Johnson was the exposed lightning rod for the kind of unreasoned ire and blame-fixing expressed in *MacBird!* In its attack on Johnson the play also sought a retributive justice when the Vietnam War not only continued but expanded after Johnson in his election campaign seemed to promise solutions. Instead the days and months of escalation were upon us.

As for internal social problems, in *Fortune and Men's Eyes* at the beginning of 1967 off-Broadway explored a concern for the humanization of prison life four years before the killing of George Jackson and the Attica prison uprising thrust the problem forcibly into the national consciousness.

Off-Broadway, of course, still had its lighter moments and could turn its hand to a popular musical. One of the most financially rewarding musicals since *The Fantasticks* was that comic strip opera *You're a Good Man Charlie Brown* in March. Name identification, likability, familiarity (through daily syndicated reminders in newspapers) were promotionally in its favor. In the fall Bruce Jay Friedman brought a new kind of topical comic insanity into the theater in his popular *Scuba Duba*. Plays such as these two successes helped erase the strict distinctions between Broadway and off-Broadway. The professionalism of the better off-Broadway shows helped break down the old barriers between the two audiences. The powerful Play Selection Committee of the Theater Guild-American Theater Society, dominated by self-interested Broadway producers, still scorned off-Broadway shows as candidates for the much sought-after Guild subscription. But even here the cracks of accommodation would soon begin to open. The strict separatism of the two theaters was beginning to disappear. Every third year, when Equity negotiations came around, the actor's wage crept upward—this year to a minimum of $70 a week, rising to $75 in the final year of the three-year contract. The settlement of this issue in the late fall released a modest flood of new productions.

At the beginning of 1968 Israel Horovitz's startling and powerful *The Indian Wants the Bronx* opened at the Astor Place Theater. Overnight Horovitz became one of the most talked-about of the new playwrights. His long, menacing one-act play, set on an upper Fifth Avenue bus corner late at night, dealt with the kind of random, unmotivated violence —two street boys without provocation setting on a non-English-speaking turbaned Indian—that began to seem increasingly a part of city life. It was as if Horovitz had superimposed an inside-page story in the daily newspaper on the stage, recording all the unreported verbal exchanges. The shock properties of the stage were exploited in other ways. Off-Broadway was coming into its nude period. Here a new kind of experimentation tested the civil limits of what the audience could be induced to accept. An actress appeared in *Scuba Duba* in the bottom half of a bikini. In the Tom O'Horgan production of *Tom Paine* in March, 1967, two actresses were in loosely tied sheath dresses split at the sides which separated as they moved. At the end of the season Dan Sullivan would write in the New York *Times* of "neither the best season nor the worst but the barest." One of the *Tom Paine* actresses, Sally Kirkland, was later to break the no-clothes barrier by becoming off-Broadway's first serious dramatic actress to appear totally nude throughout an entire play when she played opposite Robert Drivas in Terrence McNally's *Sweet Eros* in November, 1968. For a good actress of star potential to throw in with the new nudity was in itself a comment on where theater was headed. All other means of commanding attention had been explored. Technique, content, training were of no use; all that counted was a search for the extremes of what the stage would allow.

In the emerging frankness the most talked-about play in the fall of 1967 was *The Beard*, which got to New York after achieving a certain notoriety in San Francisco. Employing an unending stream of obscene words, the play moved in its entirety toward a sexual act between a Jean Harlow figure and a Billy the Kid figure. Rip Torn directed this experiment, which in language use alone was credited by many with being a major breakthrough in stage freedom, a test case for which there would be many future beneficiaries. Possibly the lesson of *The Beard* was that anything was possible, anything permissible, on what was to become the freest of all stages. Hewing to its own line of literate drama, Circle in the Square opened the new season with *Iphigenia in Aulis* in November, 1967.

At the beginning of 1968, armed with a no-strings Ford Foundation grant of nearly half a million dollars, the Negro Ensemble Company commenced operations at the St. Marks Playhouse with Peter Weiss' *The Song of the Lusitanian Bogey*. Here was the realization of a hope Robert Hooks and Douglas Turner Ward shared in putting on *Happy Ending* and *Day of Absence* two years before. In a sense the origins of the company go farther back to the one-man Group Theater Workshop Hooks and the actress Barbara Ann Teer ran several years earlier for black street kids to channel their fears and frustrations into positive stage experiences. It was an experiment that foreshadowed the later flowering of street theater. Some members of that workshop, which Hooks operated out of his own apartment even while he accepted big parts in off-Broadway productions, they had been able to use in the first Ward plays. Now they had a regular theater, with a black company, black directors, black designers, a school attached, and a largely black management. In the first season they followed the Weiss play about the struggles between the black members of an African settlement and the white colonial workers with a black *Summer of the Seventeenth Doll*, transplanting the Australian play to Louisiana and exchanging sugarcane cutters in the story for black migratory workers. The third production was the Nigerian Wole Soyinka's *Kongi's Harvest*.

Though Ford was to renew its support, NEC did not have entirely clear sailing. There were problems of identity, problems of artistic leadership, criticism coming from both the black community and the white. Whites said total segregation within a theater was artistically harmful. Blacks complained about the "Negro" in the name and the location of the theater in a nonblack part of town. Some blacks questioned the origin of NEC's financial support from a white foundation. What the white community invariably ignored in considering the problems of any Establishment-supported black institution was the fragmentation of viewpoint within black society—an internal dissension blacks, perhaps with some justification, often suspected whites of fostering, as actress Ellen Holly, writing on a different aspect of the problem altogether, once suggested with her angry eloquence in a letter to the New York *Times* (September 15, 1968):

> The white press has played a historic role in fostering internecine warfare among Negroes. From time immemorial it has taught the rural Negro to be suspicious of the urban Negro, the Northern Negro to be suspicious of the Southern Negro, the dark Negro to be suspicious of the light Negro, the rich Negro to be suspicious of the poor Negro, and vice versa. . . .
>
> In my more paranoid moments I suspect a plot because I think that the white man knows that if we ever stop tearing each other to pieces, as we have been so beautifully counterprogrammed to do, and joined together against the *real* enemy, he'd be in for a bad time of it.

From among its "own people" NEC met with the most severe and disturbing criticism, for we had all come to a time when no one could do right, and every move was suspect. Barbara Ann Teer, who had helped Hooks some years before with his street theater work and was a part of the formative period of the NEC, soon left it to go to Harlem and head a Black Theater Workshop that was her own and was totally immersed in the black world. Ed Bullins never worked within the NEC at all but steered his plays through the American Place Theater and, later, the New Lafayette Theater run by Robert Macbeth. The common denominator of all these events, however, was a heartening one—recognition by blacks of the importance of the living theater as a vehicle for voicing the inexpressible and making tangible the untouchable.

At the American Place Theater Ronald Ribman's historical play *The Ceremony of Innocence* opened on New Year's Day, 1968. Donald Madden's subtle performance as Ethelred the Unready in the Danish-Saxon wars of the eleventh century caused Clive Barnes to express a wish to see Madden as Richard II, a role he would subsequently play for Joseph Papp in Central Park.

The rock sound in musicals came into American theater, beginning, of course, with *Hair* in October, 1967, at the Public Theater. Joseph Papp introduced a dozen or so rock songs into his updated version of *Hamlet* in December, 1967, and in January, 1968, came *Your Own Thing*, a stripped-down rock version of *Twelfth Night* reduced to the lovers Orsino and Olivia and Viola and Sebastian. Donald Driver, author of the book and the director, said in an interview with the *Times'* Lewis Funke that the rock music and lyrics by Hal Hester and Danny Apolinar "allows us to get closer to where we are in the world today in terms of political concepts, sexual concepts, protests against the Establishment."

One of off-Broadway's most enduring musical successes proved to be one of the simplest—the songs of the Belgian Jacques Brel. *Jacques Brel Is Alive and Well and Living in Paris* opened on January 22, 1968, at the Village Gate on Bleecker Street for a long run.

The sensation of the season was *The Boys in the Band*, which opened on April 14 at Theater Four, a case of the new frankness that eventually overcame its shock value and grew to be accepted for the eloquent playwriting that it was. That the bringing of Mart Crowley's play out of the Barr-Albee Playwrights Unit into commercial production by Barr and his partner Charles Woodward was an example of considerable professional courage tends to be obscured in retrospect by the enormous commercial success of the venture. The play offered a franker and fuller view of homosexual life and society than had ever been attempted on the stage. As a result, it has probably contributed to the more open and understanding view of homosexuality—to the humanization of homosexual life in the eyes of heterosexuals—that has characterized the new "enlightenment" of the 1970's. The play's point of departure is a birthday party given by Michael (Kenneth Nelson) for Harold (Leonard Frey) to which every invited guest but one unexpected arrival is gay. The byplay among the guests plunges the audience breathlessly into the world of homosexuals, their mornings and evenings, their loves and hates, and the agonizing guilt that overshadows the outcast life. The totality of the life depicted, the peopling of the stage with homosexuals, forced the audience to regard homosexuals not in a clinical sense, not in their uniqueness, but in their shared human weaknesses and common faults. It was a bitter, anguished play, but one of rare honesty and, ultimately, one of touching humanity.

The new frankness extended to social realism as expressed in *The Concept*, which came out of Staten Island's Daytop Village for the rehabilitation of narcotic addicts. The play was a faithful reenactment of life at the village, including such therapeutic self-help techniques then coming into vogue as encounter sessions and marathon groups. The story line followed the arrival of a new addict at Daytop and his assimilation into the group and charted the riptide of emotions that races through a marathon group, especially as one member's resistance is on the point of breaking. These were not actors but the real-life participants on the stage—ex-addicts every one—giving improvisations of their rehabilitation—directed scenes, polished up, perhaps, but improvisations nonetheless. Taken first to La Mama, *The Concept*, directed by Lawrence Sacharow, was brought to the Sheridan Square Playhouse by Mortimer Levitt and Arthur Cantor, with their profits returning to Daytop. Real life had become theater. The evening ended with the cast coming into the audience, holding out their arms for an embrace, and asking, "Will you love me?" Esalen had come East. The season ended at the two extremes of American classical drama and the American avant-garde with the Circle putting on Eugene O'Neill's *A Moon for the Misbegotten* and the bestiality of Rochelle Owens' *Futz* being brought to the de Lys.

Opening the 1968–69 season in the fall was Mel Arrighi's *An Ordinary Man,* a projection of the repressive countertactics that might follow the presupposed failure of the black revolution. Harold Pinter's two BBC television plays *Tea Party* and *The Basement,* each dealing in images of sexual fantasy, opened at the East Seventy-fourth Street Theater under the direction of James Hammerstein. In the first, Valerie French played the businessman's recurring fantasy of a seductive secretary, crossing her legs, smoothing down her dress, sliding around his desk like an adagio dancer. In the second, a man and his girl arriving in a rainstorm at his friend's one-room apartment take off their clothes and enter their host's bed, and for a moment there was male-female nudity in the half-light with *Oh! Calcutta!* still eight months off.

Throughout this period new plays on the black experience kept coming in. Out of Watts came the play about black political activism, *Big Time Buck White,* bringing a new kind of black militant hero to the stage. Right after the first of the year *To Be Young, Gifted and Black* opened at the Cherry Lane as a retrospective look at Lorraine Hansberry's life and work. In February Lonne Elder 3d's *Ceremonies in Dark Old Men* was produced by the Negro Ensemble Company and directed by Edmund Cambridge. Elder, an actor, wrote about the irregular coming to terms with life forced on people in unfortunate circumstances, using a Harlem barbershop for a setting, and the various accommodations made by the family of a former vaudevillian, the proprietor, whose shop is used for the illegal manufacture of corn liquor. The Chelsea Theater Center and Woodie King together produced *Black Quartet.* In May the Public Theater opened the most exciting of all the new plays about black life, Charles Gordone's *No Place to Be Somebody*, which was to win the Pulitzer Prize.

Off-Broadway was still interested in revivals and in recouping Broadway's losses. A new television-fostered interest in such escapist entertainments as the Busby Berkeley musical movies of the 1930's found a stage outlet in *Dames at Sea*, off-Broadway's *No, No, Nanette*. The Circle in January successfully revived Jules Feiffer's *Little Murders*, a one-week failure on Broadway in April, 1967. The old off-Broadway pattern was at work: rethink a Broadway flop in style and production, recast it, and put it before new audiences at another time. As director, Alan Arkin took the new approach to Feiffer's rather too-realistic fantasy of city life—gunfire just outside the triple-locked door, the "breather" on the telephone, the sexual dislocations of the children of one upper West Side family. In this revival the play found its true style and audience.

Elaine May was operating on the same satirical wavelength as Feiffer when she directed Gabriel Dell in her *Adaptation* and James Coco in Terrence McNally's *Next* at the Greenwich Mews in February. For her play Elaine May devised a television party game in which the markers were all real people vulnerable to most of the common psychological hangups. McNally wrote in comic terms of the indignities of undergoing an induction physical for the Army at the hands of a woman sergeant.

Throughout the winter and spring of 1969 debate raged within the elegant headquarters of the Dramatists Guild on the top floor of the Sardi Building over whether to accept off-Broadway playwrights for membership. Some of the older members, led by Sidney Kingsley, Arthur Schwartz, and Maurice Valency, whose contributions to the theater were mostly in the past, objected to a lowering of the barriers. Younger members regarded these holdouts as businessmen playwrights collecting royalties on past work, in no way connected with the current theater. Edward Albee led the fight

for the off-Broadway writers. Israel Horovitz and Leonard
Melfi testified to the lack of protection an off-Broadway playwright enjoys. Among the council members to support Albee
were Mary Rodgers and Muriel Resnik. At the deciding
council meeting on April 7 the opposition, all but Kingsley,
crumbled, and a special membership meeting on May 13
ratified the action of the council and approved amendments
bringing off-Broadway into the Guild for the first time.

The season was to close out with the fullest expression so
far of the new nudity—*Oh! Calcutta!* at the renamed Eden
(formerly the Phoenix) Theater. The kids were young and
beautiful; the audience was middle-aged.

Twelve

The Popular Theater of Joseph Papp

Joseph Papp turned fifty in 1971 at the beginning of the sixteenth summer of his New York Shakespeare Festival. A restless, commanding, Diaghilev-like figure, he had just come through his worst trial in a combative life and had emerged more vital, more powerful than ever, a dominant force not only in off-Broadway, but in all theater. Driven like Diaghilev to create theater without regard for the small inconveniences of cost or human interference, accustomed to dealing with difficult people and difficult stiuations, Papp was ambitious, animated, pugnacious, and given to feverish activity. Most of the decisions of the theater were his alone. Not himself a creator, not even predominantly a director, he was a discoverer of talent, a matchmaker of creative teams, and the sole chooser of the material his theater produced. Each part of the created production bore the essential stamp of his approval. He was blithely uninterested in money except for the result it could produce. The proceeds of one successful venture were put into the next. He dealt in immense sums, but money was meaningless to him until it was translated into what he alone valued, into theater.

Now, on his birthday, there was much to celebrate. No one threw himself more enthusiastically into the festivities, the speeches, the present giving, and the dancing of the fiftieth birthday party his colleagues were giving for him in the candlelit Anspacher Theater. Coatless, in an open shirt, putting down his ever-present cigar, he danced harder to the rock music and enjoyed himself more than anyone. He had got himself into one awkward speech and had thrashed his way humorously out of it like a bogusly drowning swimmer. Always sensitive to the feelings of artists, actors, and co-workers, the man of action in Papp never succumbed to sentimentality over himself. At the party it was difficult for him to accept a huge silver bowl and tray presented by the board of trustees without making some disparaging remarks about their utility to a cash-hungry theater, and Papp in his thank-you speech delivered from center stage—the short, boxerlike figure with hunched shoulders and the invariable shock of uncombed dark hair falling over his forehead standing there holding his inappropriate presents and playing to the audience—wobbled hilariously along the narrow line between courtesy to the donors and self-mockery. The dips and dives of the speech and the self-amused lunges to regain balance made the gallery of actors, colleagues, and friends roar with laughter, even if momentarily they may have been painful to the givers of the bowl whose generosity to his theater in other ways Papp would never forget. With attention focused on himself, this was the only way his controlled emotions would allow him to respond. Later when the playwright Robert Montgomery, whose *Subject to Fits* was then playing at the Public Theater, read a long, moving, poetic tribute of his own composition, Papp, marching to the stage again to respond, pulled the typed pages out of Montgomery's hand to keep them, and the rough, affectionate gesture was his only real revelation of how deeply he cherished the words.

During the boisterous evening there was little looking back, although his closest associate, Bernard Gersten, in his toast had taken a lovingly biographical glance into the half-forgotten Brooklyn origins of the leader. The whole thrust of the celebration was to look ahead to new things to do, to new plans and new plays. The Festival was close to completing the full canon of Shakespeare. The enormous Public Theater on Lafayette Street was more vital in the pulse and public appeal of its cultural programs, though naturally on a smaller scale, than Lincoln Center. It had seen works of its own origination go into profitable commercial production on and off Broadway—the rock musical *Hair*, whose world success has returned to the Public Theater royalties averaging well above $100,000 annually; *No Place to Be Somebody*, which won the Pulitzer Prize after the Public Theater subsidized its initial run at a substantial financial loss; and the musical version of the 1971 summer production of *Two Gentlemen of Verona*. With this last production the Public Theater made financial history. After its successful summer run in Central Park, a number of Broadway producers approached Papp to put the show on Broadway, and he was tempted to accept their offers. But to do so would be to share the profits, and for what? For a Broadway producer's skill in raising money? Papp personally had raised more money than most of them combined. For their producing acumen? The Public Theater was begining to originate more new American work than all of Broadway's producing offices together. From one member of their board of trustees, Mrs. LuEsther T. Mertz, over one lunch, Papp and Gersten raised the entire production budget of $250,-000 for the Broadway run, and Mrs. Mertz volunteered to put up the money herself not as an investment but as an outright gift so that from the first dollar *Two Gentlemen* repaid all its profits into the Festival treasury. It was perhaps the most extraordinary deal ever made by a non-profit theater, let alone a Broadway producer.

In the more remote future, at the time of the party, Papp was making plans to expand into a national theater with outlets outside New York for the best of the work developed on Lafayette Street. Yet, incredibly, all the future and all the past had almost come to an abrupt halt only two months earlier.

The time of trial arrived on a cold and cheerless March 11, 1971, downtown at City Hall. Many of the same celebrants at the birthday party had earlier shown up to support a faltering city measure that was then the only discernible key to the institution's survival in a bad financial time. Finally landing on the agenda of the Board of Estimate on this March day was the proposal for the city to appropriate $2,600,000 out of capital funds to buy the Public Theater building from Papp and lease it back at a nominal sum, thus enabling him to meet accumulated mortgage payments, debts, contractor's improvement bills, and provide additional capital for several years of production. A string of speakers had been assembled, and the Festival's supporters had begun gathering on the east walk of City Hall Park by ten o'clock—hours before the item would be called in a crowded day of public hearings. The gray, sunless sky drew all the municipal grayness out of the steps and walls of the formidably official City Hall, and gray police barriers stood before every walkway leading to the hall. People pleading an official reason for being admitted were merely waved on by clumps of patrolmen to the next barred entrance. Outside the barriers the group of supporters rallied before an open truck decorated with Festival signs and fitted with microphones and loudspeakers for the instrumentalists and performers borrowed for the occasion from the musical *Stomp*. Papp was especially restless and jumpy, waiting about for his time to come, and joked with friends and reporters with a kind of nervous bravado. At midday, after several hours' wait, while other groups of special pleaders were having their hour in the Board of Estimate chamber, Papp and two or three friends got past the police barrier to go to Room 9, the City Hall press room, and talk with a television reporter about the Festival's case. All the camera crews were out that day, many of them chasing the Boston housewife Louise Bruyn who that morning had reached Manhattan in her one-woman peace march to Washington, but Papp was still hoping for coverage on this day of his greatest need. As Papp and his party crossed the wide plaza to mount the front steps of City Hall, the tall, blue-suited figure of the mayor emerged, descended the steps, and strode alone across the empty plaza to his waiting car. From a distance, Papp called out more challengingly than in friendly greeting, "Hi, John! Today's the big day." The preoccupied mayor cocked his head in Papp's direction but was too far away to recognize him. Guardedly he smiled a half-smile, said "Hello," and continued purposefully to his car. With him, for a moment, seemed to go Papp's hopes. The mayor supported Papp's proposal, but he probably wouldn't be sitting with the Board of Estimate to argue in its behalf.

Papp shrugged off the unintended rebuff. In years of dealing with city officials he was much too wary ever to put all his political eggs in one basket. His political instincts were visceral and uncannily true. He had learned them long ago on the streets of Brooklyn. To keep moving, to keep on the offensive was to survive. Born in the Williamsburg section of Brooklyn as Joseph Papirovsky, the son of Eastern European working-class parents, he grew up among a mix of races and nationalities and early learned the survival tactics of street life. Here, too, he must have mastered the rapid-fire verbal delivery that brooks no interruption in conversation. These he combined with an eagerness to learn which sent him into the public library, where he memorized whole passages of Shakespeare, and a love of music which came from attending the free Goldman's Band concerts in Prospect Park. The two instincts—for survival in the streets and for learning—helped determine his course in the theater. Temperamentally, Papp was akin to his Brooklyn contemporary Norman Mailer. Papp was like an agile boxer slightly outweighed by his opponent but quicker witted and faster on his feet. Although Papp was not prone to the self-dramatization at which Mailer was so facile, they were alike in their pugnaciousness, their nimbleness, and their instincts for street fighting. On continual combat both thrived.

Papp was in an aggressive frame of mind when in early evening the buy-back item of $2,600,000 for the Public Theater building finally came before the Board of Estimate. Wearing on their coats the red-lettered "Save the Public Theater" stickers, Papp's followers and supporters crowded into the chamber. After some argument was advanced, sensing that all was not going well, Papp himself broke into the order of speakers to make his own case. Gersten noticed his antagonistic manner and remembered Papp's once saying that his political tactics were based on his earliest street lesson—the efficacy of the preemptive first strike: hit them before they hit you. His personal identification with his theater was absolute, and he sensed in the board an attack upon his person. Soon his antagonism drew hostile questions, and he was into a bitter exchange with the borough president of Queens who inquired why the city should pay for a Manhattan-based institution and what had it done for Queens. Papp replied sharply, "I was in Queens before you heard of it." After a day of listening and hours of droning municipal debate, the other board members pricked up their ears. Late in the day things were becoming interesting. The Queens member then inquired whether Papp's board of trustees included any representatives of his community. This was a tired refrain. Papp had heard it countless times before in making his appeals for citywide support. He was disgusted. Worn thin, his patience snapped. "I don't have to stay here and listen to any more of this crap," he said and turned and stalked out of the chamber. That might well have ended it for the day, if not forever, but Gersten, with nothing prepared but with all the figures in his head and now a great sense of urgency, went to the microphone and began in a new and calmer vein to restate the Public Theater's aims. Temperamentally, Gersten is altogether different from Papp, which may partially explain the success of their intimate ten-year collaboration as associate producer and producer, respectively, of the Festival. The soothed board con-

Barbara Dana and Dustin Hoffman in Circle in the Square's production of Henry Living's *Eh?* in 1966. From this stage Hoffman leaped into a major film career beginning with *The Graduate*.

Henry Grossman

The Circle's production of *Iphigenia in Aulis* in 1967 with the dark-haired Irene Papas and Jenny Leigh.

Friedman-Abeles

Friedman-Abeles

A failure on Broadway, Jules Feiffer's *Little Murders* was successfully revived at the Circle in January, 1969, with the Alan Arkin-directed cast including Fred Willard, Elizabeth Wilson, Jon Korkes, and Vincent Gardenia.

(*ove*) *Hair* on the stage of the Anspacher
ater, directed by Gerald Freedman in 1968
Joseph Papp's New York Shakespeare Festival
lic Theater.

George E. Joseph

ht) Joseph Papp at a rehearsal in the
pacher Theater in the Astor Library building
afayette Street.

Dan McCoy

(*Above*) Charles Gordone's *No Place to Be Somebody* at the Public Theater in 1969 won the Pulitzer Prize that season. (*Below*) William Atherton (center) in the title role of David Rabe's *The Basic Training of Pavlo Hummel* in 1970.

George E. Joseph

cluded with friendly questions. The combination of Papp's
fire and passion and Gersten's reasonableness may well have
turned the corner for the Public Theater, for a month later
the board, returning to the question, acted favorably, and
Papp this time shook hands with the borough president of
Queens.

Papp today stands at the head of a very complex cultural
institution. The base of its operations is his free Shakespeare
in Central Park with its various offshoots, the mobile theater
which visits the five boroughs, and the school touring productions. Annually these activities account for the employment of a large number of actors and the entertainment of
huge urban audiences. Equally important, indeed more important, have become the varied activities of the Public
Theater with its three legitimate stages, its film theater and
archives, its music room in the acoustically perfect Martinson
Hall, and its art and photographic galleries. In his theaters
Papp promotes new work and brings along new writers such
as David Rabe, who in the fall of 1971 had two plays running
side by side at the Public Theater, his *Basic Training of
Pavlo Hummel* in the Newman and his *Sticks and Bones* in
the Anspacher.

The history of Papp's theater has been one of rapid lateral
growth. It took Papp four years to get from his church workshop to the East River Amphitheater at Grand Street, where
the first outdoor free performances were given in the summer
of 1956, to Central Park. In the winter of 1957 he picked up
his initial foundation support, from the Doris Duke Foundation and the New York Foundation, and that summer built a
stage on the back of a truck to tour *Romeo and Juliet* to the
five boroughs. Papp's earliest concept was mobility: take the
theater to the people. In an interview with Murray Schu-
mach of the New York *Times* (June 23, 1957) Papp said: "I
made up my mind I was going to have a Shakespeare theater
that would go into congested neighborhoods. I had to reach

the thousands of people who live and die in their neighborhoods." But the creaking old trailer truck had trouble with underpasses and bridges and finally came to rest in the Belvedere Tower area of Central Park and would roll no farther. The remaining performances that summer were given at the lakeside site—home base for the Festival ever since. It would be seven years before Papp got a mobile theater going again.

In those earliest days Papp's director was Stuart Vaughan. Some of the Festival's acting stalwarts for years to come were even then beginning to appear: Colleen Dewhurst, J. D. Cannon, Roy Poole, Roscoe Lee Browne, Robert Gerringer, Patricia Falkenhain, George C. Scott. The Elizabethan background scores were being written by composer David Amram. Papp's staff expanded accordionlike in summer and contracted in winter. In the early days, on business matters, he relied heavily on Hilmar Salle, his general manager into the middle 1960's, when he was succeeded by David Black. His first designer was Eldon Elder. Already Papp was searching for some sort of continuity for the theater beyond its summer performances, possibly a winter series at the city-owned Heckscher Theater at Fifth Avenue and 104th Street. In January, 1958, Papp made his first request of the Board of Estimate for municipal funds and was turned down. The quality of his work had attracted critical notice, particularly the second summer's *Romeo*, which Walter Kerr said was in many ways the best he had ever seen, and Scott's brilliant performance reading the "Seven Ages of Man" speech as Jacques in the Heckscher Theater production of *As You Like It*. But there rose for the first time the bugaboo of municipal priorities that through the years was to haunt his efforts to make the city acknowledge its responsibilities for the cultural welfare of the people. A recession was in progress, the city was cutting down, and Mayor Wagner, addressing himself to Papp's request, said, "It's a worthy cause but we have to recognize it simply is not an operation of government. If we had $40,000 we could use it in areas of more direct benefit to the people. Things like taking care of unemployed people must come ahead of taking care of the Bard."

Momentarily Papp was tempted to charge admission. But he quickly put this thought out of his head, and the issue of admission was not to rise again until his celebrated fracas with Robert Moses a year later. The prices he would be forced to charge, Papp knew, "would immediately defeat the primary purposes of our existence—to reach large new audiences for the classics. What may seem an idealistic approach to the theater is in reality the most practical for what we are trying to build. Broadway and off-Broadway live in a world of romance; the quick buck, the overnight success, the one big break, here today and gone tomorrow—hardly a solid base for operations.

"I am trying to build our theater on the bedrock of municipal and civic responsibility—not on the quick sands of show business economics. I am interested in a popular theater— not a theater for the few. This is how I want our theater to stand (as the library does, free to its users), supported by two pillars—the city and private donors."

It was a statement that would stand without embellishment through the years. Papp was a practical visionary who read the signs correctly. In the spring of his second season he said, "Though we do not have enough funds to keep our curtain up right now, we have enough potential to keep it up for ten years."

Papp struggled gamely with inadequate funds through his third summer, putting on *Othello* and *Twelfth Night*, which he directed himself. Each night before the curtain he made an appeal to the audience for contributions but resented doing so. "We're supposed to be giving them free Shakespeare, and that's what it should be." In the winter, as a fund-raising effort, he staged a concert reading of *Antony and Cleopatra* with two of the most electrifying talents the Festival ever had, George C. Scott with his malevolent smile and Colleen Dewhurst with her enveloping earthiness.

Then came Joe Papp's first big fight, the contest with

Robert Moses, which Papp miraculously turned to advantage just at the point when quitting seemed his only course. As commissioner of parks Moses decreed that Papp's continued use of parkland as his theater site depended on his charging admission and rebating a percentage to the Parks Department to amortize costs of improvements and restore the trampled grass in the Belvedere Tower area, a responsibility, Papp did not fail to note, from which football, soccer, and softball players seemed to be exempt.

Down at City Hall Papp could count a few political allies, more anti-Moses, perhaps, than pro-Festival. He was adamant about not charging admission, and public discussion of the dispute, together with an avalanche of pro-Papp mail at City Hall, forced the mayor to take notice. In a hospital for a minor ailment, Moses, however, was unavailable even to the mayor. In the meantime, Papp's political past was being used against him in an unsigned letter circulated in City Hall. Along with other entertainment industry figures, the previous June Papp had been questioned by the House Un-American Activities Subcommittee. He testified that he had not been a member of the Communist Party since June, 1955, but invoked his constitutional privilege twelve times, as he later explained, "to protect myself and others from unjust abuse and persecution." The mayor chided Moses about the letter, and the battle continued to rage in the press. Papp was quoted as saying, "Mr. Moses hasn't been the same since he was hit on the head by a baby carriage," an allusion to a brigade of West Side mothers who succeeded in frustrating Moses' 1956 plan to turn a children's play area into a parking lot for the Tavern-on-the-Green.

It was now May and getting dangerously near final decision time for the summer program. While remaining obstinately opposed to admission, Papp was willing to try to find from other sources the money the Parks Department said it needed. Meanwhile, the city-sponsored Hudson Celebration Committee was proceeding rapidly with plans for open-air entertainment at the Wollman Skating Rink. The New York City Center had raised $300,000 to put on what Moses called "a genuine, outdoor, controlled, decently run theater run by responsible people." It crossed Papp's mind that the delays might have been forced by Moses in fear of the damaging competitive effect the free Festival could have on the admissions-charging Hudson Celebration.

Papp already had been obliged to drop one play from his schedule. By May 11 Wagner's opposition to Moses had weakened since the mayor's only recourse then seemed to be to fire his entrenched parks commissioner. After a reconciliation luncheon at the Players Club between Mayor Wagner and Commissioner Moses, Papp announced, "I think it's regrettable that the mayor has seen fit to disregard the feeling of thousands of New Yorkers and submit to Mr. Moses."

Papp was to make one last try. An appointment was arranged with Stuart Constable, Mr. Moses' deputy, for May 14 at the Arsenal, the ivy-covered Parks Department headquarters beside the zoo in Central Park. On Papp's side were Merle Debuskey, his earliest and constant associate, press aide from the first days of the Festival, and Robert H. Montgomery, Jr., of Paul, Weiss, Rifkind, Wharton & Garrison, the Festival's counsel. Papp opened the meeting by asking what the Parks position was. Constable, severe behind his walrus mustache, sat at his desk picking absently at a Band-Aid on his finger. The position was the same: the department would require $20,000 from the Festival for improvements and restoration of the grounds and an admission charge of $1 and 50 cents. Constable rudely brushed aside Papp's promise to try to raise the required sum. "The money's not important—we're not interested in money." What, then, were they interested in?

"There is no basis on which the Shakespeare Festival can operate in the parks," Constable blurted out.

"Is that a flat statement?" Papp asked, rising to his feet. "I don't understand." He then began reading laudatory letters about the Festival from Moses. Constable interrupted: "If you continue, I will get the police to eject you." With that the meeting broke up. Shortly afterward Constable and Moses together left to attend groundbreaking ceremonies for Lincoln Center. Three days later Moses declared the issue closed. It was not. On May 18 Papp sought a show cause order in Supreme Court on why Moses should not grant the Festival a permit to perform free Shakespeare in Central Park. He lost in this court and immediately appealed. In a unanimous decision handed down June 17, the appellate division found for the Festival, declaring that Moses had made "an arbitrary, capricious, and unreasonable decision," while granting his right to seek reimbursement for improvements.

Papp had won a tremendous victory——bigger than he may have realized. A man of lesser political instincts might pardonably have allowed himself a moment of self-congratulation. Papp never rubbed Moses' nose in his defeat. Instead he sent a telegram of friendly support and a request for Moses' assistance before the Board of Estimate. Moses later responded to this magnanimous gesture by pleading the Festival's case for a permanent theater facility in the park. The specified six-foot fence and asphalt paving on the theater site were paid for out of the $20,000 contributed by two private foundations later to figure even more significantly in the future of the Festival—the Edward L. Bernays Foundation and the Louis K. Anspacher Trust. Ranged behind Papp was an array of new supporters from all sections of the city.

During the whole controversy Papp had fought hard but never maliciously, and he had been careful not to burn his bridges. He had made high city officials look small, but he had never taken advantage of their pettiness. At one time or another both the mayor and Moses had acted more out of their own interests than the city's. Papp kept uppermost the duty he felt to his audience. In the end it was the court speaking that brought everyone to his senses.

The dispute had the ultimate effect of strengthening the Festival's position, of making municipal government more aware of its obligations, and of placing in Papp's hands, for his judicious future use, considerable political clout.

Now he could return belatedly to the business at hand. The summer program had been cut to just one play, *Julius Caesar*, with a cast of fifty-five that numbered Staats Cotsworth in the title role, Donald Madden as Marc Antony, Rex Everhart as Casca, John Harkins as Brutus, and among the anonymous "soldiers, citizens, and slaves" an actor named Jerome Ragni, later to become famous as co-author of *Hair*. Enormous public interest had built up over the delayed opening. Moses was invited but declined. Hundreds were turned away. The next day's notices unanimously praised Papp and the production. In this warmly gratifying aftermath Papp did nothing to draw attention to his victory. Instead he spent the day on the telephone raising the final $7,000 to see *Caesar* through its three-week run in Central Park.

In August Moses stood up in the Board of Estimate and requested $250,000 to build a permanent outdoor theater to the Festival's specifications on the Belvedere site.

The following year there was a new parks commissioner, Newbold Morris. On the opening night of the fifth season Papp shared billing with both Morris and the mayor, and an era of good feeling commenced. Stuart Vaughan had left the Festival to become artistic director of the Phoenix, and Papp himself directed *Henry V* with James Ray in the title role and Kathleen Widdoes as Katherine. Alan Schneider came in as the first outside director to stage *Measure for Measure*. Gerald Freedman directed a lively and imaginative *Taming of the Shrew*, mixing into the play's improvised opening a variety of styles, including burlesque, juggling, ballet, and opera buffa. Jane White was cast as Kate and J. D. Cannon as Petruchio.

Papp would now approach the city to accept responsibility for half the annual budget. Through the years he had never had much luck persuading the larger foundations to back him. The Rockefeller Foundation came in very late, and Ford repeatedly turned down his requests, thereby cutting themselves off from what by 1971 had become the most vital and interesting theater organization in the country. Ford turned Papp down ostensibly because Ford grants went only to companies that had demonstrated their ability to reach self-support at the box office. Practically no Ford beneficiary has been able to so demonstrate, but by the time this inevitability had been faced so much bad feeling had been engendered between Papp and the Ford officials that he probably would not have been given a grant anyway.

Papp was much too shrewd to count on support from any one given source no matter how promising. He had a natural suspicion of dependency on big foundations, whose decisions were reached in secret and over which the public had no control or influence. "On the other hand, were the government involved, one would, at least, have recourse to the system of checks and balances, to the principle that the government is responsible to the people. Under those conditions [wrote Papp in an article in the New York *Times*, July 24, 1960] it would be possible to cry havoc and petition our government for a redress of grievances. Admitting that interference is undesirable, but having the choice of private or government interference in the theater, it would seem that the latter is preferable. . . . The theater, like education, needs the security and comfort, if you will, of inclusion in a Governmental budget. It may be attacked. It may be cut. But it is there to be defended and fought for. Any discussion of freedom of theater without considering its permanency is largely academic.

"By making the theater a responsibility of the Government, it makes it also a responsibility of the people. Restricting the theater to private subsidy cuts it off from the mainstream of American life and perpetuates the growing separation of the theater from its vast potential audience."

Here was one of the most cogent arguments ever made for

government subsidy and support. There was nothing theoretical in it, only a direct and immediate application to Papp's affairs. He was looking for year-round continuity for his company. He recognized an obligation to the actors for their employment. He saw in statewide tours, supported at the state level, a means of accomplishing both objectives. Concurrently he would organize a company to tour among the city's public schools, supported at the municipal level. In December, 1960, Papp was voted $50,000 to send *Romeo and Juliet* on such a school tour, although at first the Board of Education dragged its feet on the proposal. The company rehearsed at the Heckscher Theater on upper Fifth Avenue and played its first break-in performances there with the dark-eyed Kathleen Widdoes as Juliet and Paul Roebling as Romeo. The first school audiences were bussed in. Gladys Vaughan had joined Papp as his assistant to manage this extension of the Festival's activities.

In winter, construction work started on the new theater by Belvedere Lake. One day while Newbold Morris was having lunch with George T. Delacorte, the publisher, Delacorte asked what he might do to help the Festival in the park. Morris suggested a gift of $500 to put on puppet shows, but Delacorte indicated his desire to do more. Within a few weeks of the lunch Delacorte had offered to put up $150,000 alongside the city's $250,000 to construct the theater that eventually took his name.

It was not ready by June, 1961, and the summer's program was shifted into the Wollman. The first production was *Much Ado About Nothing* with Nan Martin as the sharp-tongued Beatrice and J. D. Cannon as her lover, Benedick. The "common English garden party conception of the play" had been given a thorough shaking up by Papp, who as the director reset the play in a Spanish town with castanets and flamenco dancers specially choreographed by the Broadway jazz dancer Matt Mattox. Theoni V. Aldredge by this time had joined Papp's artistic staff as costume designer, and the

handsomeness of this production, and all future Festival productions, was hers. Late in the 1960's, Milo Morrow was to
become shop master and resident genius of the biggest costume department in New York. The handsome Miss Martin
was a flirtatious Beatrice in a long gray gown with black lace
collar and black curls piled saucily on her head. Here were
two lovers who meant business. Cannon as Benedick was a
lithe and dashing Don Juan. Sportive, witty, and shot
through with sophistication, *Much Ado* was one of the Festival's most stylish productions to date and a great critical
success. Papp for all his earnestness and combativeness
showed himself to have a light side as well, and the production established his credentials as a director with more range
than until then he had been credited with.

Papp knew his Shakespeare texts as if they were personal
to him, part of his vocabulary and inseparable from his
thought processes. An actor once himself—he had toured in
the national company of *Death of a Salesman* and hadn't
given up the idea of possibly, one day, appearing in one of
his own productions—he knew the way actors thought, knew
their apprehensions, and respected their bravery facing diverse outdoor audiences in difficult roles. He strove to reconcile Shakespeare to the American style of acting, not force
American actors into some preconceived English style of diction and behavior. "The typical English performance (with
the exception of Gielgud and Olivier)," he told Don Ross in
an interview in the *Herald Tribune* (August 2, 1959),
"places emphasis on reading and the sound of the words. The
typical American kind of acting is vital, emotional, and or-
ganic. The actor completely uses his being to express himself
in real live terms as a person, not just a figure on the stage."
His Shakespeare was robust, muscular, unfussy, and real. At
work in rehearsal, he was a restless, rapid-spoken, peripatetic
director, moving his actors around, injecting himself into the
scene, forming new patterns on the stage. No one was more
aware of the physical limitations of the outdoor arena. He
was a shrewd gauge of audience concentration: "Most people

have a breaking point in their attention span. They're grateful to have so much and then no more." And he could be self-critical: "We haven't pulled it together yet," he once said of a show he was directing. "The jokes are not timed. The quality of the scenes is too heavy-handed. There is a big hushy pause where you thought it was a joke. Something must be done."

Managing the Festival meant outwitting the weather. Overhead always hung the threat of a summer storm. Sometimes they felt they were working or playing "between the raindrops," as Bernie Gersten once put it. The opening of the brilliant *Much Ado About Nothing* was marred by rain. There was a break in the play of twenty minutes until the downpour subsided. When the play resumed, Cannon's opening line was, "Lady Beatrice, have you wept all this while?" The damp crowd roared. Amid the laughter came Nan Martin's answering speech, "Yes, and I will weep a while longer." Indeed, the show continued for only fifteen more minutes before the rain returned and halted it for good, just three scenes short of the end.

Planes crossing the skies on flight patterns northwest of LaGuardia Airport were another hazard making Papp long sometimes for the indoor theater Stratford, Ontario, enjoyed, "where there are none of these distractions that kill beautiful moments on the stage." Planes in that summer's *Richard II* were erasing five minutes out of the speeches every night. The hiked-up mikes killed subtlety. And Papp knew, too, that the special values of small performers were often lost, dispersed in the breezes, on the large open-air stage. But it could be wonderful as well. "Sometimes," Papp said thoughtfully, "I've looked up on a soft night when everything was quiet, and I've told myself we can't beat this any place."

The new Delacorte Theater was finished well in time for the following summer's plays, its alternate rows of yellow and apple-green seats, 2,300 in all, gleaming under a rehearsal sun. The opening play was *The Merchant of Venice* with George C. Scott as Shylock and Nan Martin as Portia. Papp himself was the director, assigning himself the double task of opening the new theater and opening the play. As always there were a myriad of last-minute worries, including setting special lights so WCBS-TV could tape a performance and the solemn and persistent objections aired daily in the papers by the New York Board of Rabbis to the supposed anti-Semitism of the play.

With his park base at last secured, Papp was free to expand in other directions. He was quick to seize his opportunities. In 1963 he proposed that a projected civic center in the City Hall area should include a 1,000-seat theater for the Festival. In March, 1964, he was able to get a $325,000 appropriation through the Board of Estimate—the largest sum to date—to be divided between his park program and his plan once again to put Shakespeare on wheels. The mobile theater idea, going back to the first days of the Festival, hadn't worked the first time, but Papp continued to worry that Central Park was not drawing audiences from all parts of the city. He tried busing people in, but the mobile theater—a completely equipped, self-contained portable stage that could be set up in any open area—was the better plan. Once again George Delacorte came forward with a gift of $35,000 for the stage truck. In transit the caravan stretched for two city blocks and included another big trailer truck, two dressing-room trucks that in place extended out like arms from the stage, a generator truck, a bus for the actors, a couple of station wagons, and two or three trucks to carry the folding chairs and the bleachers that provided seats for an audience of 1,500. Given a cleared area, such as a park or parking lot, the mobile theater could be set up in half a day.

Jack Sydow was commissioned to direct the first production, *A Midsummer Night's Dream*, with Ellen Holly as Titania, Ted van Griethuysen as Oberon, Clifton James as Bottom, and Yolanda Bavan as the First Fairy. Everything was in readiness by June 29, 1964, opening night in Harlem's Mount Morris Park, the only question mark being the audience. Would they come, and would they respond? Papp knew the neighborhoods of the city and was optimistic. "Word spreads rapidly when there are invaders coming," he told the assembled company in a pep talk before the opening. "To us these are the audiences of the future. We're breaking new ground. We're hitting people who respond because they don't know how the play ends. We're looking forward very, very eagerly to the opening of this production. Some of you may be concerned about going into these minority areas. I think we'll achieve a feeling of goodwill wherever we go." Barring minor incidents (objects thrown onto the stage from kids outside the audience), the mobile tour, playing to large and appreciative audiences, many of whom had never before seen a live performance, was a success. With some cast changes the same production was sent to the schools in the fall. Papp was anxious to have mobile theater casts reflect the racial makeup of the neighborhoods they would be visiting. The following summer he would mount a mobile *Henry V* with Robert Hooks as Henry and Ellen Holly as Katharine, Princess of France.

In every respect 1964 was the biggest summer yet, marking the fullest expansion of the New York Shakespeare Festival as a free summer theater with winter extensions. In the park Papp produced and directed his first *Hamlet*. "I've never done the play before, so I don't have to do it in any different way," he said. "All my feelings about the play and my reading and studying about it for the last ten years will go into it." Alfred Ryder, cast as Hamlet, developed a throat infection which prevented his being heard from the stage, and Robert Burr, who had been standing by downtown for Richard Burton in the Broadway *Hamlet,* was brought in as the hurried and heroic replacement to play opposite Julie Harris as Ophelia. *Hamlet* was followed by *Othello* with James Earl Jones, and *Othello* by the Festival's first non-Shakespearean play, the *Electra* of Sophocles, with Lee Grant in the title role.

By any measure the Festival had grown into an impressive institution. It was the largest employer of actors in the country. Its annual budget was $750,000 dollars and would soon reach $1,000,000. Among the four acting companies the Festival had 250 persons on its payroll.

At the outset of the 1965 season Walter Kerr raised questions about the artistic development of the Festival that related to its seasonal existence—a summer cultural diversion rather than a continually developing artistic institution. "A further impulse is needed," Kerr wrote, "if the project is to become better than a worthy civic service, if it is to become realized art as well as pleasant community activity. Probably what Papp needs is some sort of guaranteed continuity: continuity of actors, continuity of directors. . . . Without continuity of staff, without long-range commitment, it is virtually impossible to inch a production level steadily upward. Growth comes of picking up from where you left off last year. But each year is a beginning year as things now stand. . . ."

Papp has often been chided by critics on artistic grounds, for directorial clumsiness in this or that play. The work has not always been of even excellence and sometimes not even very good. Frequently Papp has been too diverted by financial burdens to give artistic direction and coherence to the enterprise. He himself would never wish to escape artistic judgment or claim exemption on the grounds of altruistic civic aims. To him the work always comes first. "The whole way we make our point is by the quality of the production," he once said. "The social significance of the Festival depends entirely on that." But the general run of critical appraisal omits recognition of his practical accomplishment—not only the creation of a theater, but also the establishment of new patterns of public and private support for a theater institution and the cultivation of a new audience that cuts across economic, social, and racial grounds.

However painful and even gratuitous Kerr's criticism may have seemed to Papp at the time, there was some truth to it, as Papp himself may have been unconsciously aware. The following winter a whole new prospect opened—the possibility not only of an enlargement of the idea, but also of a clear pattern of artistic continuity. Gerald Freedman had been taken on as an associate artistic director in expectation soon of the establishment of a year-round theater. And in January, 1966, the Astor Library on Lafayette Street was acquired as a permanent home. In his search for a building Papp had applied to the city's recently formed Landmarks Commission in hopes of finding an existing structure that might be adapted to theatrical use. After considering two other sites he was told about the Astor Library, a large brownstone and brick building with an impressive Italianate Renaissance façade nearly half a city block in width. The building was begun with funds from John Jacob Astor's estate in 1853 and put up in three sections by three generations of Astors, the last section being completed in 1881, to become the first public library in New York City and at one moment of history the third largest library in the United States. What is now Papp's Anspacher Theater was the main reading room, decorated with columns, balconies, and a glass-domed ceiling. The building is situated in what was at the time of construction one of the finest neighborhoods in New York, standing across cobblestoned Lafayette Street from the handsome marbled colonnaded apartments known as La Grange Terrace, whose few remaining graceful french windows open onto a neighborhood lately gone to factories, garages, and warehouses, south of busy Astor Place.

Since 1920 the building had been used by the Hebrew Immigrant Aid Society as a receiving and relocation center for European arrivals. The Landmarks Commission stepped in when HIAS, running out of immigrants, sold the building to a real estate developer for demolition. Papp responded immediately to the enormous amount of space available, the magnificent lobbies, the great halls upstairs inviting conversion into working theaters, generous storage areas for shops and scenery and costumes. Demolition plans were halted, and the Festival, with an initial anonymous gift of a quarter of a million dollars from a member of the board, bought the building for $575,000 with a promise to preserve the architectural details both inside and out of what the Landmarks Commission considered the most important early Victorian building left standing in the city. It would be called the New York Shakespeare Festival Public Theater. August Heckscher headed a committee to assist in planning its future and in raising needed funds. Giorgio Cavaglieri, the architect who had converted the Jefferson Market Courthouse in the West Village into a branch library, was commissioned to plan the conversion, and Ming Cho Lee, the Festival's regular stage and set designer, to design the theaters.

Enormous added financial obligations were implicit in the new building plan, getting it ready, remodeling the interior to contain theaters, restoring and preserving its decorative detail. Papp plunged ahead, certain in his own mind that the scheme was correct, trusting that financial support would follow. His commitment was to audience and to theater; money would be found. Artistically he needed to move out of the classics in winter and into the contemporary theater. "The classics have their place, but the theater doesn't move forward without new plays. I'm part of the time I live in, and I don't want to be completely cut off from it. Originally, I started out as a director of new work, not classical plays."

In the meantime, with allies all through the Lindsay administration—the mayor himself a declared theater fan, August Heckscher now parks commissioner and administrator of recreation and cultural affairs—Papp unbelievably was having trouble prying free regular city funds to sustain the Festival's normal annual operations. No matter how promising the prospect, Papp was too wary ever to put himself in the pocket of any politician. He has been very adroit in his dealings with successive city administrations. He has shown considerable catholicity in his political friends. When the Conservative Republican James L. Buckley was elected to the United States Senate, Papp lost little time getting to see him to talk particularly about the nature of Buckley's constituency, a section of the public Papp wanted to attract to his theater, and about his long-range plans for a national theater. Papp had his own strong views, but politics on a day-to-day basis was filtered through the needs of his theater. Now he was ready to do battle with the mayor whose administration promised enlightened action on the arts but yearly cut the Festival's appropriation. In 1966 Papp advised the mayor he would fight the $100,000 cut despite the mayor's promise to raise that sum privately. The board listened to Papp and restored $73,000, to be added to the $27,000 the mayor had by then collected on the outside. Papp refused stubbornly to let municipal government off the hook. "New York has been in a financial crisis since the time of Peter Stuyvesant. It all has to do with an attitude toward the arts. Regardless of the financial situation, a concerned mayor will find ways and means of supporting important cultural institutions in the same way as he finds money for all essential services." But his gravest crisis at City Hall was yet to come in the winter of 1970.

The foremost theatrical event of the fall, an event of overpowering importance that reverberated through the theater all season and momentarily diverted Papp from his own problems was the visit of Jerzy Grotowski's Polish Laboratory Theater to New York. Joe Papp was especially interested. In Grotowski Papp could discern the commitment and lifelong dedication required to make a real theater—so rare a thing in this country. Papp had gone abroad for the first time in October, 1964. Traveling with Joseph B. Martinson, the chairman of the board of the Festival, and Bernard Gersten, he saw some of the major theaters of Europe, the Royal Shakespeare Company, the Berliner Ensemble, Walter Fel-

senstein's Komische Oper, the Schiller Theater. The party
also visited Prague, Warsaw, and Cracow. What impressed
Papp most was that everywhere the big government-sup-
ported permanent companies were superior to the random
groups. Now Grotowski brought such a theater, though small
in size, to the United States. The two theater men got to
know one another; they argued and became friends.

In the regular off-Broadway season that fall the rock musical trend continued strong with *Salvation*, one of the first of
the Christ musicals, an attempt to relate religion to the
emerging life-styles of younger people. *A Whistle in the
Dark*, the violent drama of an England-based Irish family
consisting of a demanding and bullying father and his rebellious sons, was sent into town from the Long Wharf Theater
in New Haven, and there was a revival of *Fortune and Men's
Eyes* in a sensationalized and distorted production directed by
Sal Mineo at Stage 73. The three Grotowski productions,
existing on an altogether different plane from anything that
had ever been seen off-Broadway, were *The Constant Prince,
Acropolis*, and *Apocalypse*. Grotowski, who himself attended
each performance, rigidly controlled the size and placement
of the audience each night. About 90 persons were admitted
to the first, between 100 and 120 to the second, and only 40
to the third, lined along narrow benches against two walls of
the Washington Square Methodist Church. For the company's eight weeks in New York in the fall of 1969, Grotowski
was the "hardest" ticket in town. The audience was apt to
read like a Who's Who of the theater. For *Apocalypse* one
evening, for example: Lee Strasberg, Jerome Robbins,
Cheryl Crawford, Harvey Schmidt, Harold Prince, Andre
Gregory, and Stephen Sondheim. There was an obligatory
wait of some forty-five minutes on the inside steps leading
into the church, during which one was asked to read the
detailed program notes. Then the doors were opened; the
audience was led in solemnly in single file and placed tightly
on benches along the church wall. In the dim light robed

figures could barely be discerned lying on the large open floor. Then a shaft of light, a prone figure rising up, and the play began. Grotowski describes his theater as a "poor" theater—a theater stripped of all artifice of lighting, makeup, scenery, sound effects, and costuming. It was a theater reduced to actor and audience, a rigorously trained actor and a carefully circumscribed audience. This was no desire on Grotowski's part to create an elitist theater, only an intensified theater experience. The Polish Lab was a breathtaking sight —never had such technical control by an actor over his movements, facial muscles, and voice been seen or heard on any stage here. Clearly the acting came out of more than training, discipline, and ensemble playing. It came out of a total life commitment to the work. No American theater could touch it. Grotowski had no "method" to promote, but he gave the inspiration of an art form taken to near perfection, granted the narrow terms of reference he insisted upon. Papp said of the work, "It is a fully realized work of art, not merely commentary on the world but set into the world."

At the Public Theater, Papp had taken in a young, untrained company from the South, most of them former University of Texas students, to perform their rock protest musical *Stomp*, in which they acted out theatrically a real-life dropping out of society. A sad and yet joyful musical of alienation of children from homes and towns in which they had grown up, it fascinated Grotowski. He saw it more than once and loved it.

The most interesting new American play of the season was Paul Zindel's *The Effect of Gamma Rays on Man-in-the-Moon Marigolds*, eloquent playwriting of a kind of Tennessee Williams sensibility. First produced by Nina Vance's Alley Theater in Houston in 1965, it was brought to off-Broadway in April by the producer Orin Lehman. In its acting and writing, it justified this faith and became the most highly praised work of the season. Sada Thompson is one of those half dozen hardworking, nonstarred, middle-rank actresses in

New York whose competency is taken for granted. Suddenly the big role comes along, and her really extraordinary capabilities are tested and realized. Her performance was outstanding in any season. The part was that of a distraught mother whose inability to face the world outside her mean and cluttered rooms threatens, but finally does not overbalance, the precarious mental poise of the more sensitive of her two daughters. Miss Thompson in her performance never failed to show that however harsh she may have been on her frightened children, she was always more destructive of herself. Zindel and Sada Thompson divided the year's prizes between them, and the play won the Pulitzer. It was the playwright's second produced play in New York. Fryer and Carr had put on Zindel's *A Dream of Swallows* in 1964, when he was a twenty-seven-year-old high school chemistry teacher on Staten Island.

Several other noteworthy productions came before summer. For years Carmen Capalbo had worked toward a production of the Brecht-Weill work *Mahagonny* as a follow-up to *The Threepenny Opera*. In late April he opened a very large but diffuse production in the enormous Phyllis Anderson Theater on lower Second Avenue. The cast was headed by Barbara Harris as Jenny, in the role Lotte Lenya had once played in Germany in the 1930's, and Estelle Parsons. The unfocused work, despite its magnificent score and the work of these two splendid actresses, went down as a clumsy failure. In May, Tom Eyen's *The Dirtiest Show in Town*, social satire behind a nude foreground, opened a long off-Broadway run, and Zoe Caldwell gave the second remarkable performance of the season in *Colette* at the Ellen Stewart Theater, an evening arranged by Elinor Jones out of the autobiographical writings of Colette.

A growing awareness of ghetto existence brought forth *The Me Nobody Knows* with the actual words of street children incorporated into the book and lyrics. The 1969–70 season then ended with the Circle putting on a new play by Atholl Fugard about Cape Coloreds, *Boesman and Lena*, remarkably played by Ruby Dee and James Earl Jones.

The 1970's are bound to bring a further blurring of the once hard-and-fast distinctions between Broadway and off-Broadway. Some change will come through geographical redistribution. The City Planning Commission's attempts to use building waivers and easements to encourage the construction of theaters of various sizes and uses within office buildings in the Times Square theater district has caused some off-Broadway theaters to forsake their old "gypsy land" locations on the fringe—in Billy Rose's phrase—and move into the center. Circle in the Square has a new 650-seat theater in the Uris building rising at the corner of Broadway and Fiftieth Street, the American Place Theater a 299-seat house in the new Stevens Building complex at the Avenue of the Americas and Forty-sixth Street. The Phoenix Theater operates either on Broadway or off, depending on the nature of its attraction.

Economic forces, as always, come into play. During the actors' strike in the fall of 1970—the grimmest labor crisis in off-Broadway history—two downtown shows, the musical *The Me Nobody Knows* and Kurt Vonnegut Jr.'s *Happy Birthday, Wanda June*, were simply moved into Times Square theaters on Broadway production contracts and managed very well to survive. This step would have been unthinkable five years before. The strike began on November 16, 1970, and lasted thirty-one days. In an arbitration award the actors won a $33\frac{1}{3}$ percent pay boost from $75 to $100, scaled up to $125 in the third year of the contract. The Broadwayization of off-Broadway continued apace.

Broadway more and more became simply a showcase for work that had already been pretested elsewhere. Elsewhere used to be London. Now, more and more, it was the regional theater and off-Broadway, where both the producers and the audiences were more venturesome. Increasingly in the early 1970's the more interesting material was beginning to come out of Joe Papp's big theater.

As off-Broadway's newest and handsomest theater, the Anspacher, with its thrust stage and three-quarter arena staging in the columned old Astor Library reading room, was opened in the fall of 1967. The Public Theater's first season consisted of the history-making *Hair*, from which the Festival still derives royalties; Joseph Papp's mod version of *Hamlet*, for which Galt MacDermot, the *Hair* composer, had written some rock songs; Jakov Lind's *Ergo*, an example of German Expressionism of the 1930's; and Vaclav Havel's *The Memorandum*, a Czech play about bureaucratic gibberish in modern society. The new program was to continue to turn up original and unusual work with an exciting contemporaneity: Adrienne Kennedy's *Cities in Bezique*; Anne Burr's *Huui Huui*, the self-comforting cry of a man in moments of disturbance; and, of course, Charles Gordone's rambling, angry, honest *No Place to Be Somebody*. But it was first in June, 1970, that Papp came uncomfortably close to losing the whole institution, building, Festival, and all.

Papp's worst time was the second week in June, 1970, when all the bills seemed to fall due at once. Four years before, the Festival had put down $215,000 in cash toward the purchase price of the building and had taken out a $360,000 mortgage. The following sums had been spent converting the building: $30,000 for the administrative offices on the ground and second floors; $450,000 for the Anspacher; $10,000 for the Other Stage, the small experimental theater; $1,200,000 for the Newman Theater, the building's second 300-seat house; and $250,000 for the small cinema theater. With the mortgage, all these improvements meant that Papp had put $2,600,000 into the building. Constructing the Newman was especially expensive because the old supports for this earliest of the three sections of the Astor Library, dating back 117 years, had to be taken out and new steel reinforcements introduced. No matter; Papp got a beautiful, long, sloping brick-walled auditorium out of it and a wide, serviceable, prosceniumless stage.

But where was all the money coming from? Papp's figures have always been uncannily accurate, for which his right-hand man Bernard Gersten is due much credit. More than three years earlier, projecting all the costs of conversion, Papp had proposed that the city buy back the building for exactly what would have been put into it. The figure Papp mentioned to Mayor Lindsay was—$2,600,000. The mayor was said to be delighted with the proposal. Instead of the strained expense budget, these funds would come out of the city's far easier capital budget. Once in city hands, the Public Theater, just like the City Center in its Mecca Temple on West Fifty-fifth Street, would be leased back to the Festival for $1 a year.

It was not to be so easy. A steady barrage of follow-up letters and meetings with city officials in the three years had failed to move the plan anywhere. The previous month the proposal had finally reached the City Council, but the council was then enmeshed in a bitter political squabble with the mayor. Council members would have none of the Lindsay-backed plan.

Now, in June, all but the roof of the Astor Library fell in. Papp's patient contractor, owed just under half a million dollars for completed work of a very high standard, was threatening to take out a lien to foreclose on the mortgage and sell the building out from under him. Special appeals had gone out to the major foundations and this week the rejection letters came in from Mellon, from Ford for the umpteenth time. One offer of $500 had come in from a small foundation—about enough, as Papp wryly commented, to keep them in postage stamps. Going to meet last week's $28,000 payroll, he looked into the Festival's bank account and found only $16,000. Fortunately he was able to obtain a hurried loan of $25,000 from one good friend of the Festival, and the paychecks were distributed. For the first time the Festival found itself in arrears to its steady tradesmen—$85,-000 more owed.

On top of all the domestic troubles on Lafayette Street, Papp had sixty actors in Central Park rehearsing the mammoth summer schedule of the *Chronicles of Henry VI* and *Richard III*, with the opening date one week off and $300,000 more tied up in that project. The summer package in all was going to cost $675,000, and only the previous week Papp had heard that the city would appropriate but $350,000. "Never in our fifteen years," Papp wrote City Council President Sanford D. Garelik, "have we faced so massive and unrelenting a crisis."

The visionary attitude Papp assumed was a subject of derision among uptown Broadway producers, who felt he had gone mad falling so heavily into debt building all those little theaters in that remote Astor Library few of them bothered to visit. I remember standing among a group of them on the day the newspapers announced the sums he had spent putting those theaters into the Astor Library. They had no conception of what sort of institution it was, no feeling for the audacity of the man, and they simply smiled with a commercial cynicism, sensing disaster, not realizing that in this moment when he was most vulnerably in debt, Papp had already surpassed the lot of them in his historical importance in the American theater, that in that hour they had been eclipsed, and that Joseph Papp, who charged no admission and whose modest annual salary was a fraction of what they made, was now a more powerful and commanding figure in theater than even the most envied and feared producer among them. The balance of power between Broadway and off-Broadway had shifted, most dramatically in the direction of Joe Papp.

During the height of the trouble I spent one long afternoon with Papp in his large office on the second floor on Lafayette Street. For just a moment he permitted himself to get his head out of the discouraging red ink figures and review some of his artistic problems. Even these were gloomy. But he turned to stagecraft with something like relief. Out in the park the *Henrys* were rehearsing, and he wasn't satisfied, "The fencing is rotten," he said. "It's artificial, clumsy. They don't look like fights to me. They're embarrassing. It's not just the timing, it's the styling. All the personal combats are rotten."

Then he came back to the finances. "We've got just enough money to open the plays. That's all. For a while I felt like closing the whole shop up. But then I realized that was self-pitying. Let them [the city officials] take the responsibility. What we do is all that counts. We'll stand on what we do."

Papp renewed his campaign to get the city to buy the building. The summer crisis was staved off temporarily with bank loans, and creditors were held at bay on the prospect of eventual city action. In December, however, the Board of Estimate turned down his request for a $5,100,000 appropriation which included all the projected future improvements on top of the $2,600,000 purchase price of the building as it stood. One Broadway producer who recognized the importance of Papp's theater and fully appreciated its difficulties was Roger L. Stevens, who, when he was chairman of the National Endowment for the Arts, saw to it that the Festival received its due and who later headed an Emergency Committee to Save the Public Theater which came together in December. As his troubles deepened, Papp seemed to redouble his production efforts. The proof of his worth was in the work, as always. The Newman Theater, designed by Giorgio Cavaglieri with Ming Cho Lee and Martin Aronstein, was opened for the new season in the fall of 1970. Dennis J. Reardon's *The Happiness Cage*, about a man discharged from the Army who finds himself in a Veterans Hospital ward with two terminal cancer patients, although he is suffering only from a broken arm, opened in October. And in

November, at the same theater, Papp presented *Jack Mac-Gowran in the Works of Samuel Beckett,* one of the finest one-man studies ever seen off-Broadway. One remembers MacGowran from the jaunty figure of Joxer Daly he played in an all-too-short-lived Broadway musical, *Juno.* As Beckett's man some years later the jauntiness was gone, and in its place a human being who endured life but howled at the pain of it, seeking some poor comfort from the sucking stones he had distributed among the pockets of his ragged greatcoat and liked to rotate in his mouth so evenly that he could go through the sixteen stones in rotation without once being so careless as to suck the same stone twice over before the whole string had been sampled. MacGowran recited passages from the novels, poems, and plays alone on a stage decorated only with an irregularly sculpted rock that had been there since the beginning of time and a clear blue cycloramic background that suggested infinity. Here were two perfectly matched artistic instruments, the voice of MacGowran and the words of Beckett, discoursing on the most elemental of life's experiences, birth, boredom, and death. A resigned shrug is MacGowran's, and Beckett's, nearest approach to affirmation.

The productions kept coming in rapid succession: Robert Montgomery's brilliantly verbal *Subject to Fits,* a play written "in response to" Dostoyevsky's *The Idiot,* dealing with the outsider in society stepping in and out of a conventional world, on February 14, 1971; *Slag* on February 21, a play set in a private girls' school by a twenty-three-year-old Briton, David Hare; *Here Are Ladies* on February 22, Siobhan McKenna's one-woman show directed and designed by Sean Kenny, taken from the works of the Irish writers O'Casey, Yeats, Shaw (*St. Joan*), Synge (*Riders to the Sea*), Joyce's "Anna Livia Plurabelle" from *Finnegans Wake,* Beckett's *Happy Days*; and after that, *Blood,* March 8, a musical conceived, directed, and designed by Doug Dyer, the young author of *Stomp.*

The Public Theater did not account for all the product of off-Broadway. In October, Kurt Vonnegut, Jr., had come in with his first play. *Happy Birthday, Wanda June* at the de Lys considered what happened in the life of a waiting wife when a modern-day Ulysses, a kind of blustering, gun-happy Hemingway figure, comes home from his adventures with his wartime pilot buddy, Looseleaf Harper. The two roles were played hilariously by Kevin McCarthy and William Hickey, the latter an actor whose talent lives up to the comic expecta- tion of his physical presence. Vonnegut's humor had made it to the stage. Another writer of rare comic gifts was John Guare, who managed to bring off the humorous possibilities in a play of outrageous premise and happenings, but touch- ing real characters, called *The House of Blue Leaves*. And, for acting excitement, two of this season's more interesting productions were the Claire Bloom-Donald Madden appear- ances in *A Doll's House* and *Hedda Gabler* in which Miss Bloom, after a long absence from the New York stage, reestab- lished herself as an actress of the first rank, not only tal- ented, but lovely to look at. There were other interesting revivals, a *Waiting for Godot* directed by Alan Schneider with Henderson Forsythe as Vladimir, Anthony Holland as Lucky, Edward Winter as Pozzo, and Paul B. Prince as Gogo; a *Long Day's Journey into Night* directed by New Haven's Arvin Brown with Robert Ryan, Geraldine Fitzgerald, Stacy Keach, James Naughton, and Paddy Croft; and Pinter's *The Homecoming* directed by Jerry Adler with Eric Berry, Janice Rule, Tony Tanner, and Lawrence Keith. A season ahead of *Jesus Christ Superstar* came the rousingly tuneful musical *Godspell*, based on St. Matthew's account of the life of Jesus, adapted by John Michael Tebelak with the music and lyrics of Stephen Schwartz.

Papp's purchase offer to the city was finally taken up on April 27, 1971, when the council voted 27–10 to buy the

Public Theater building for $2,600,000, the very sum Papp had suggested to Mayor Lindsay three years before.

Papp was able to breathe easier than at any time in the three years since his heavy construction bills began accumulating. For the summer, 1971, he scheduled *Timon of Athens, Two Gentlemen of Verona,* and *Cymbeline,* the middle one an enormous popular success, the other two unfamiliar Shakespeare one suffered through. But they brought the Festival only three plays short of presenting the complete canon of thirty-eight plays attributed to Shakespeare. At the outset of the season, on the Delacorte stage, Mayor Lindsay and Commissioner Heckscher presented Papp with the Handel Medallion, the city's highest award for cultural achievement.

Certainly Joe Papp had never been in a stronger position when in 1971 he opened the new season at the Public Theater. *Pavlo Hummel* was still running on the Newman stage. He had leased an annex across the street in anticipation of having too many new plays for the Public Theater itself to handle, and a musical, *Slaughterhouse Play,* was rehearsing there. Also as part of his Open Stage workshop series, a musical play called *Don't Fail Your Lovin' Daddy, Lily Plum* was giving performances to full houses in the Anspacher. A new David Rabe play, *Sticks and Bones,* was in preparation, there were concerts in Martinson Hall, a new ticket plan, whereby one could buy a "pass" to all the season's productions when seats were available, had been put into effect, and many more projects were ahead. Papp had decided to veer toward doing more specifically black material on his stages. In the early weeks of the season he found his hands full with a new play by Richard Wesley ominously called *The Black Terror.* It was just at the time of Attica, and so much hatred was being acted out in rehearsal that the cast closed the doors and would permit no outsiders, not even Papp, or perhaps especially not Papp, since he symbolized a kind of final authority over them that it was the whole intention of their play to resist and subvert. Papp insisted upon

observing rehearsals not so much to assert his rights as producer and landlord as to draw off their acted-out hatred,
which threatened to become violent. They came to loathe his
presence. They wanted their hatred intact.

Outside his own theater Papp joined another public war,
the fight to save the Forum Theater at Lincoln Center. City
Center had offered to take responsibility for the management
of the expensive Vivian Beaumont Theater provided that
interior areas could be rearranged to accommodate movie
theaters and film archives. That meant destruction of the
Forum. Papp's position in this dispute created an ironic jux-
taposition. Lincoln Center, swelling once with dreams of creating the American National Theater, had started from an
architectural concept for the perfect theatrical structure and
then found that such an elaborate and well-equipped plant
could be sustained neither artistically nor financially. Papp,
starting in the opposite way with an artistic concept and a
company of actors trained over the years in his theater, converted an old existing structure into the kind of artistic home
that wrapped itself around his concept and evolved naturally
in less than five years into exactly the kind of cultural center
Lincoln Center might have hoped to achieve.

But, after all, that was what off-Broadway was all about. It
was what George Cram Cook meant and what Jose Quintero
stood for. It was where David Ross, and Richard Barr, and T.
Edward Hambleton, and Julian Beck and Judith Malina,
and Theodore Mann stood. Place drama first, and the rest
would follow. It was where Joe Papp stood. And today his
Public Theater from its small start has become institutionally
the most powerful and artistically the most promising theater
we have—and off-Broadway's enduring monument.

Off-Broadway Award
Winners—1955-1971

The principal awards in the off-Broadway theater are the Drama Desk-Vernon Rice Awards and the Obies, presented annually in the spring at the end of the theater season.

The Drama Desk is an organization of theater writers, editors, and critics which meets monthly for discussion during the season and determines awards by vote of the membership. Until 1964 the awards, restricted to off-Broadway, were made in the name of the late New York *Post* critic who in his writings gave early recognition to the off-Broadway theater. For the next five years the citations, which were for distinguished contributions in the off-Broadway theater, and not for the "best" of anything, were known as the Drama Desk-Vernon Rice Awards. In 1969, under the leadership of Henry Hewes, the president, the Drama Desk changed its awards policy in order to recognize merit wherever it existed in the theater—prompting the growing notion that the ironclad distinctions between off-Broadway and Broadway, particularly in quality of work, were no longer valid. The Vernon Rice Award was made separately for achievement in the off-Broadway theater.

The Obie (or off-Broadway) Awards were initiated by the *Village Voice* at the end of the 1955–56 season and in 1964 were extended to off off-Broadway. In 1969 the judges altered the form of the awards to eliminate specific categories in favor of general citations for "outstanding achievement," but the use of specific categories was resumed the following year. The yearly selections have usually been made by a panel of three judges, which is changed every year.

1955 Vernon Rice Awards

Proscenium Productions for its productions of *The Way of the World* and *A Thieves' Carnival*

The Shakespearewrights for their productions of *Twelfth Night* and *The Merchant of Venice*

David Ross for Fourth Street Theater productions of *The Dybbuk* and *The Three Sisters*

Nancy Wickwire for her performances in *The Way of the World* and *The White Devil*

Jack Landau for his direction of *The Clandestine Marriage* and *The White Devil*

1956 Vernon Rice Awards

Janine Manatis for her performance in *Village Wooing*

Pernell Roberts for his performance in *Macbeth*

Circle in the Square for its production of *The Iceman Cometh*

Jose Quintero for his direction of *The Iceman Cometh*

1956 Obie Awards

Best New Play: *Absalom* by Lionel Abel

Best Production: *Uncle Vanya*, Fourth Street Theater

Best Actress: Julie Bovasso in *The Maids*

Best Actor: Jason Robards, Jr., in *The Iceman Cometh*
George Voskovec in *Uncle Vanya*

Best Director: Jose Quintero for *The Iceman Cometh*

Best Musical: *The Threepenny Opera* by Bertolt Brecht and Kurt Weill in an adaptation by Marc Blitzstein

Distinguished Performances, Actresses: Peggy McCay, Shirlee Emmons, Frances Sternhagen, Nancy Wickwire

Distinguished Performances, Actors: Gerald Hiken, Alan Ansara, Roberts Blossom, Addison Powell

Sets, Lighting, or Costumes: Klaus Holm, Alvin Colt

Special Citations: The Phoenix Theater, The Shakespearean Workshop Theater (later New York Shakespeare Festival) , The Tempo Playhouse

1957   Vernon Rice Awards

Sada Thompson for her performance in *The River Line*
and *The Misanthrope*
Arthur Malet for his performance in *Volpone* and *The
Misanthrope*
Paul Shyre for his adaptation of Sean O'Casey's *Pictures
in the Hallway* and his production of *Purple Dust*

1957   Obie Awards

Best New Play: *A House Remembered* by Louis A. Lippa
Best Actress: Colleen Dewhurst in *The Taming of the
Shrew, The Eagle Has Two Heads, Camille*
Best Director: Gene Frankel for *Volpone*
Distinguished Performances, Actresses: Marguerite Len-
ert, Betty Miller, Jutta Wolf
Distinguished Performances, Actors: Thayer   David,
Michael Kane, Arthur Malet
Special Citations: Paul Shyre

1958   Vernon Rice Awards

Gerry Jedd for her performance in *Blood Wedding*
George C. Scott for his performance in *Children of Darkness*

1958   Obie Awards

Best New Play: *Endgame* by Samuel Beckett
Best Actress: Anne Meacham in *Suddenly Last Summer*
Best Actor: George C. Scott in *Richard III, As You Like
It, Children of Darkness*
Best Adaptation: *The Brothers Karamazov* by Boris Tu-
marin and Jack Sydow
Best Revival: *The Crucible* by Arthur Miller, directed in
revival by Word Baker
Best Comedy: *Comic Strip* by George Panetta
Best One-Act Play: *Guest of the Nation* by Nell McKenzie

Distinguished Performances, Actresses: Tammy Grimes, Grania O'Malley, Nydia Westman

Distinguished Performances, Actors: Leonardo Cimino, J. D. Cannon, Robert Gerringer, Michael Higgins

Special Citations: The Phoenix Theater, The Theater Club, Lucille Lortel

1959   Vernon Rice Awards

Jane McArthur for her performance in *Our Town*

Hal Holbrook for his performance in *Mark Twain Tonight!*

William Ball for his direction of *Ivanov*

1959   Obie Awards

Best New Play: *The Quare Fellow* by Brendan Behan

Best Production: *Exiles*, Renata Theater

Best Actress: Kathleen Maguire in *The Time of the Cuckoo*

Best Actor: Alfred Ryder in *I Rise in Flame, Cried the Phoenix*

Best Director: William Ball for *Ivanov* (foreign play), Jack Ragotzy for the Arthur Laurents cycle (American plays), Stuart Vaughan for the New York Shakespeare Festival

Best Musical: *A Party with Betty Comden and Adolph Green*

Best Revue: *Diversions* by Stephen Vinaver

Distinguished Performances, Actresses: Rosina Fernhoff, Anne Fielding, Nancy Wickwire

Distinguished Performances, Actors: Zero Mostel, Lester Rawlins, Harold Scott

Sets, Lighting, or Costumes: David Hays, Will Steven Armstrong, Nikola Cernovich

Music: David Amram

Special Citations: Hal Holbrook

1960   Vernon Rice Awards

Edward Albee for his play *The Zoo Story*

Rick Besoyan for his musical *Little Mary Sunshine*

Jack Gelber for his play *The Connection*
Jack Richardson for his play *The Prodigal*

1960   Obie Awards

Best New Play: *The Connection* by Jack Gelber
Best Production: *The Connection*, Living Theater
Best Actress: Eileen Brennan in *Little Mary Sunshine*
Best Actor: Warren Finnerty in *The Connection*
Best Director: Gene Frankel for *Machinal*
Best Foreign Play: *The Balcony* by Jean Genet
Distinguished Plays: *Krapp's Last Tape* by Samuel Beckett, *The Prodigal* by Jack Richardson, *The Zoo Story* by Edward Albee
Distinguished Performances, Actresses: Patricia Falkenhain, Elisa Loti, Nancy Marchand
Distinguished Performances, Actors: William Daniels, Donald Davis, Vincent Gardenia, John Heffernan, Jack Livingston
Sets, Lighting, or Costumes: David Hays
Special Citations: Brooks Atkinson

1961   Vernon Rice Awards

Joan Hackett for her performance in *Call Me by My Rightful Name*
Tom Jones and Harvey Schmidt for their musical *The Fantasticks*
Richard Barr and Clinton Wilder for their Theater '61 productions of new playwrights, especially Edward Albee and Jack Richardson
Boris Tumarin for his direction of *Montserrat* and *The Idiot*
Theodore J. Flicker for *The Premise*

1961   Obie Awards

Best New Play: *The Blacks* by Jean Genet
Best Production: *Hedda Gabler*, Fourth Street Theater
Best Actress: Anne Meacham in *Hedda Gabler*
Best Actor: Khigh Dhiegh in *In the Jungle of Cities*

Best Director: Gerald A. Freedman for *The Taming of the Shrew*

Best Off Off-Broadway Production: *The Premise*, produced and directed by Theodore J. Flicker

Distinguished Performances, Actresses: **Joan Hackett**, Gerry Jedd, Surya Kumari

Distinguished Performances, Actors: Godfrey **M. Cambridge**, James Coco, Lester Rawlins

Music: Teiji Ito

Special Citation: Bernard Frechtman

1962   Vernon Rice Awards

Arthur Kopit for his play *Oh Dad, Poor Dad, Mamma's Hung You in the Closet and I'm Feelin' So Sad*

Barbara Harris for her performance in *Oh Dad, Poor Dad, Mama's Hung You in the Closet and I'm Feelin' So Sad*

Cicely Tyson for her performance in *Moon on a Rainbow Shawl*

Geoff Garland for his performance in *The Hostage*

Association of Producing Artists for its entire repertory season

1962   Obie Awards

Best Actress: Barbara Harris in *Oh Dad, Poor Dad, Mama's Hung You in the Closet and I'm Feelin' So Sad*

Best Actor: James Earl Jones, New York Shakespeare Festival, *Clandestine on the Morning Line, The Apple, Moon on a Rainbow Shawl*

Best Director: John Wulp for *Red Eye of Love*

Best Foreign Play: *Happy Days* by Samuel Beckett

Best American Play: *Who'll Save the Plowboy?* by Frank D. Gilroy

Best Musical: *Fly Blackbird* by C. Jackson, James Hatch, and Jerome Eskow

Distinguished Performances, Actresses: Sudie Bond, Vinnette Carroll, Rosemary Harris, Ruth White

Distinguished Performances, Actors: Clayton Corzatte, Geoff Garland, Gerald O'Loughlin, Paul Roebling

Sets, Lighting, or Costumes: Norris Houghton
Special Citations: Ellis Rabb; *The Hostage*

1963   Vernon Rice Awards

Oliver Hailey for his play *Hey You, Light Man!*
William Hanley for his plays *Whisper into My Good Ear* and *Mrs. Dally Has a Lover*
Murray Schisgal for his plays *The Typists* and *The Tiger*
The Boys from Syracuse for best overall production
The Coach with the Six Insides for best overall production

1963   Obie Awards

Best Production, Play: *Six Characters in Search of an Author*, Martinique Theater
Best Production, Musical: *The Boys from Syracuse*, Theater Four
Best Actress: Colleen Dewhurst in *Desire Under the Elms*
Best Actor: George C. Scott in *Desire Under the Elms*
Best Director: Alan Schneider for *The Pinter Plays*
Distinguished Performances, Actresses: Jacqueline Brooks, Olympia Dukakis, Anne Jackson, Madeleine Sherwood
Distinguished Performances, Actors: Joseph Chaikin, Michael O'Sullivan, James Patterson, Eli Wallach
Special Citations: Jean Erdman, *The Second City*

1964   Drama Desk-Vernon Rice Awards

Gloria Foster for her performance in *In White America*
Imelda De Martin for her performance in *The Amourous Flea*
Lewis John Carlino for his plays *Cages*, *Telemachus Clay* and *Double Talk*
In White America for best overall production
The Streets of New York for best overall production

1964   Obie Awards

Best New Play: *Play* by Samuel Beckett
Best Production, Play: *The Brig*, Living Theater

Best Production, Musical: *What Happened*, Judson Poets
   Theater
Best Performance: Gloria Foster in *In White America*
Best Director: Judith Malina for *The Brig*
Best American Play: *Dutchman* by LeRoi Jones
Distinguished Plays: *Funnyhouse of a Negro* by Adrienne
   Kennedy; *Home Movies* by Rosalyn Drexler
Distinguished Performances, Actresses: Joyce Ebert, Lee
   Grant, Estelle Parsons, Diana Sands, Marian Seldes
Distinguished Performances, Actors: Philip Bruns, David
   Hurst, Taylor Mead, Jack Warden, Ronald Weyand
Distinguished Direction: Lawrence Kornfeld
Sets, Lighting, or Costumes: Julian Beck
Music: Al Carmines
Special Citations: Judson Memorial Church

1965   Drama Desk-Vernon Rice Awards

Robert Lowell for his play *The Old Glory*
Harold Willis for *A Sound of Silence*
Ulu Grosbard for his staging of Arthur Miller's *A View
   from the Bridge*
James Earl Jones for his performance in *Othello*
Barbara Ann Teer for her performance in *Home Movies*
Susan Towers for *Shout from the Rooftops*

1965   Obie Awards

Best New Play: *The Old Glory* by Robert Lowell
Best Production, Musical: *The Cradle Will Rock*, Theater
   Four
Best Performance: Roscoe Lee Browne, Frank Langella,
   Lester Rawlins in *The Old Glory*
Best Director: Ulu Grosbard for *A View from the Bridge*
Distinguished Plays: *Promenade* and *The Successful Life
   of Three* by Maria Irene Fornes
Distinguished Performances, Actresses: Margaret De Priest,
   Rosemary Harris, Frances Sternhagen, Sada Thompson
Distinguished Performances, Actors: Brian Bedford, Rob-
   erts Blossom, Joseph Chaikin, Dean Dittmann, Robert
   Duvall, James Earl Jones

Sets, Lighting, or Costumes: Willa Kim
Special Citations: The Paper Bag Players, Caffe Cino and
Cafe La Mama

1966   Drama Desk-Vernon Rice Awards

Douglas Turner Ward for his plays *Day of Absence* and
Happy Ending
William Alfred for his play *Hogan's Goat*
John Arden for his play *Serjeant Musgrave's Dance*
Kevin O'Connor for his performance in *Six from La
Mama*
Irene Dailey for her performance in *Rooms*
The Living Theater for its work abroad

1966   Obie Awards

Best New Play: *The Journey of the Fifth Horse* by Ronald Ribman
Best Actress: Jane White in *Coriolanus* and *Love's Labor's Lost*
Best Actor: Dustin Hoffman in *The Journey of the Fifth
Horse*
Distinguished Plays: *Good Day* by Emanuel Peluso; *Chicago, Icarus's Mother* and *Red Cross* by Sam Shepard
Distinguished Performances, Actresses: Clarice Blackburn,
Mari-Claire Charba, Gloria Foster, Sharon Gans, Florence Tarlow
Distinguished Performances, Actors: Frank Langella,
Michael Lipton, Kevin O'Connor, Jess Osuna, Douglas
Turner
Distinguished Direction: Remy Charlip, Jacques Levy.
Sets, Lighting, or Costumes: Lindsey Decker, Ed Wittstein
Special Citations: Joseph H. Dunn, H. M. Koutoukas,
Peter Schumann, Theater for Ideas, Theater in the
Street

1967   Drama Desk-Vernon Rice Awards

Jean-Claude van Itallie for his three one-act plays *America Hurrah*
Lanford Wilson for his play, *The Rimers of Eldritch*

Dustin Hoffman for his performance in *Eh?*

Stacy Keach for his performance in *MacBird!*

Joseph Hardy for his direction of *You're a Good Man, Charlie Brown*

Bill Hinnant for his performance in *You're a Good Man, Charlie Brown*

Will Lee for his performance in *The Deer Park*

1967   Obie Awards

Best Actor: Seth Allen in *Futz*

Best Director: Tom O'Horgan for *Futz*

Distinguished Plays: *La Turista* by Sam Shepard; *Futz* by Rochelle Owens

Distinguished Performance, Actress: Bette Henritze

Distinguished Performances, Actors: Tom Aldredge, Robert Bonnard, Alvin Epstein, Neil Flanagan, Stacy Keach, Terry Kiser, Eddie McCarty, Robert Salvio, Rip Torn

Sets, Lighting, or Costumes: John Dodd

Special Citations: La Mama Troupe, The Open Theater, Tom Sankey, The Second Story Players, Jeff Weiss (Joseph Cino Memorial Award)

1968   Drama Desk-Vernon Rice Awards

Helen Hayes, best performance by an actor or actress in a repertory company for her performance in the APA Repertory Company's production of *The Show Off*

Ron Cowen for his play *Summertree*

Israel Horovitz for his play *The Indian Wants the Bronx*

Ed Bullins for his plays presented originally as *The Electronic Nigger and Others* and subsequently as *The Ed Bullins Plays*

Donald Driver for his adaptation *Your Own Thing*

Joseph Papp's Public Theater

The Negro Ensemble Company

Al Carmines for the music for *In Circles*

Tom O'Horgan for his direction of *Tom Paine*

Galt McDermott for his music for *Hair*

Robert Moore, for his direction of *The Boys in the Band*

1968   Obie Awards

Best Actress: Billie Dixon in *The Beard*
Best Actor: Al Pacino in *The Indian Wants the Bronx*
Best Director: Michael A. Schultz for *Song of the Lusitan-
ian Bogey*
Best Foreign Play: *The Memorandum* by Vaclav Havel
Distinguished Plays: *Muzeeka* by John Guare; *The In-
dian Wants the Bronx* by Israel Horovitz; *Forensic
and the Navigators* and *Melodrama Play* by Sam Shepard
Best Musical: *In Circles* by Gertrude Stein and Al Car-
mines
Distinguished Performances, Actresses: Jean David, Marl
Gorman, Peggy Pope
Distinguished Performances, Actors: John Cazale, James
Coco, Cliff Gorman, Moses Gunn, Roy R. Schneider
Distinguished Direction: John Hancock, Rip Torn
Sets, Lighting, or Costumes: Robert La Vigne
Special Citations: The Fortune Society, The Negro En-
semble Company, San Francisco Mime Troupe, El
Teatro Campesino

1969   Drama Desk Awards

Commencing this season, in opening up its awards to the
entire theater, the Drama Desk adopted a new form of voting.
The vote was restricted to those critics, editors, and reporters
who had attended a majority of the season's productions. A percentage system was used to tabulate the votes so that a candidate
heavily favored by only half the voters had a chance to win
against a candidate seen by all. The Broadway awards are here
marked with an asterisk. Candidates are listed in order of the
percentage they received.

The Best Performances:
*James Earl Jones, *The Great White Hope*
*Jane Alexander, *The Great White Hope*
*Al Pacino, *Does a Tiger Wear a Necktie?*
James Coco, *Next*

*Alec McCowen, *Hadrian VII*
*Donald Pleasence, *The Man in the Glass Booth*
*Nicol Williamson, *Hamlet*
 Ron O'Neal, *No Place to Be Somebody*
 Joseph Wiseman, *In the Matter of J. Robert Oppenheimer*
*Marian Mercer, *Promises, Promises*
 Bernadette Peters, *Dames at Sea*
*Dustin Hoffman, *Jimmy Shine*
*Dorothy Loudon, *The Fig Leaves Are Falling*
 Nathan George, *No Place to Be Somebody*
 Linda Lavin, *Little Murders*
*Ron Leibman, *We Bombed in New Haven*
 Douglas Turner Ward, *Ceremonies in Dark Old Men*
*Jerry Orbach, *Promises, Promises*
*Brian Bedford, *The Misanthrope*
 Frank Langella, *A Cry of Players*

The Best Direction:
*Edwin Sherin, *The Great White Hope*
 Gordon Davidson, *In the Matter of J. Robert Oppenheimer*
 Tom O'Horgan, *Futz*
 Neal Kenyon, *Dames at Sea*
 Alan Arkin, *Little Murders*
*Michael A. Schultz, *Does a Tiger Wear a Necktie?*

The Best Scene Designers:
*Ming Cho Lee, *Invitation to a Beheading* and *Billy*
*Boris Aronson, *Zorba*

The Best Costume Designers:
*Tanya Moiseiwitsch, *The House of Atreus*
*Patricia Zipprodt, *1776* and *Zorba*

The Best Composers:
 Al Carmines, *Peace*
*Burt Bacharach, *Promises, Promises*

The Best Lyricists:
George Haimsohn and Robin Miller, *Dames at Sea*
*Fred Ebb, *Zorba*

The Best Choreographer:
*Grover Dale, *Billy*

The Best Musical Book Writer:
*Peter Stone, *1776*

The Most Promising Playwrights:
Charles Gordone, *No Place to Be Somebody*
Lonne Elder III, *Ceremonies in Dark Old Men*
Elaine May, *Adaptation*

1969   The Vernon Rice Award:
Joseph Chaikin

1969   Obie Awards

General Citations for Outstanding Achievement:
The Living Theater *Frankenstein*
Jeff Weiss, *The International Wrestling Match*
Julie Bovasso, *Gloria and Esperanza*
Judith Malina and Julian Beck, *Antigone*
Israel Horovitz, *The Honest-to-God Schnozzola*
Jules Feiffer, *Little Murders*
Ronald Tavel, *The Boy on the Straight Back Chair*
Nathan George and Ron O'Neal, *No Place to Be Somebody*
Arlene Rothlein, *The Poor Little Match Girl*
Theatre Genesis (sustained excellence)
The Open Theater, *The Serpent*
OM Theater, *Riot*
The Performance Group, *Dionysus in '69*

1970   Drama Desk Awards

For Outstanding Performance:
Zoe Caldwell, *Colette*

Sada Thompson, *The Effect of Gamma Rays on Man-in-the-Moon Marigolds*
*Fritz Weaver, *Child's Play*
*Frank Grimes, *Borstal Boy*
*Lauren Bacall, *Applause*
*Melba Moore, *Purlie*
Ryszard Cieslak, *The Constant Prince*
*Lewis J. Stadlen, *Minnie's Boys*
*Stacy Keach, *Indians*
*Cleavon Little, *Purlie*
*Tammy Grimes, *Private Lives*
Colleen Dewhurst, *Hello and Goodbye*
Stephen Elliott, *A Whistle in the Dark*
*Niall Toibin, *Borstal Boy*
Ron Leibman, *Transfers*
Christopher Walken, *Lemon Sky*
Austin Pendleton, *The Last Sweet Days of Isaac*
*Brian Bedford, *Private Lives*
Sandy Duncan, *The Boy Friend*
*James Stewart, *Harvey*
*Ethel Merman, *Hello, Dolly!*

Outstanding Director:
*Harold Prince, *Company*
Jerzy Grotowski, *The Apocalypse*
Alan Arkin, *The White House Murder Case*
*Joseph Hardy, *Child's Play*
*Ron Field, *Applause*

Outstanding Scene Design:
*Boris Aronson, *Company*
*Jo Mielziner, *Child's Play*
Fred Voelpel, *The Memory Bank*

Outstanding Costume Design:
*Freddy Wittop, *A Patriot for Me*
Willa Kim, *Promenade, Operation Sidewinder*
Theoni V. Aldredge, *Peer Gynt*

Outstanding Choreographer:
*Ron Field, *Applause*

Outstanding Composer:
*Stephen Sondheim, *Company*
Kurt Weill, *Mahagonny*

Outstanding Lyricist:
*Stephen Sondheim, *Company*
Bertolt Brecht, *Mahagonny*

Outstanding Book Writer for a Musical:
*George Furth, *Company*

Most Promising Playwrights:
Paul Zindel, *The Effect of Gamma Rays on Man-in-the-Moon Marigolds*
Stanley Eveling, *Dear Janet Rosenberg, Dear Mr. Kooning*
Susan Yankowitz, *Terminal*

Most Promising Musical Writers:
C. C. Courtney and Peter Link, *Salvation*
Nancy Ford and Gretchen Cryer, *The Last Sweet Days of Isaac*
Gary William Friedman and Will Holt, *The Me Nobody Knows*

1970   Vernon Rice Award:
No award

1970   Obie Awards

Best New Play: *The Effect of Gamma Rays on Man-in-the-Moon Marigolds* by Paul Zindel, *Approaching Simone* by Megan Terry
Best Performance: Sada Thompson in *The Effect of Gamma Rays on Man-in-the-Moon Marigolds*
Best Foreign Play: *What the Butler Saw* by Joe Orton
Distinguished Plays: *The Deer Kill* by Murray Mednick,

The Increased Difficulty of Concentration by Vaclav
Havel

Best Musical: *The Last Sweet Days of Isaac* by Gretchen
Cryer and Nancy Ford, *The Me Nobody Knows* by
Robert Livingston, Gary William Friedman, and Will
Holt

Distinguished Performances, Actresses: Rue McClanahan,
Roberta Maxwell, Fredericka Weber, Pamela Payton-
Wright

Distinguished Performances, Actors: Beeson Carroll, Vincent Gardenia, Harold Gould, Anthony Holland, Lee
Kissman, Ron Leibman, Austin Pendleton

Distinguished Direction: Alan Arkin, Melvin Bernhardt,
Maxine Klein, Gilbert Moses

Special Citations: Chelsea Theater Center, Gardner Comp-
ton and Emile Ardolino, *Elephant Steps*, Andre Gregory, The Ridiculous Theatrical Company, Theater of
the Ridiculous

1971 Drama Desk Awards

Performances:

*Ralph Richardson, *Home*

*John Gielgud, *Home*

*Cliff Gorman, *Lenny*

Claire Bloom, *A Doll's House* and *Hedda Gabler*

Jack MacGowran, *MacGowran in the Works of Beckett*

Ruby Dee, *Boesman and Lena*

*Alec McCowen, *The Philanthropist*

*Brian Bedford, *The School for Wives*

Siobhan McKenna, *Here Are Ladies*

*Marian Seldes, *Father's Day*

Madeleine Renaud, *L'Amante Anglaise*

*Alexis Smith, *Follies*

Mildred Dunnock, *A Place Without Doors*

*Anthony Quayle, *Sleuth*

*Helen Gallagher, *No, No, Nanette*

*Keith Baxter, *Sleuth*

*James Earl Jones, *Les Blancs*

*Colleen Dewhurst, *All Over*

*Maureen Stapleton, *The Gingerbread Lady*
*Paul Sand, *Story Theatre and Metamorphoses*
Roberta Maxwell, *Slag*

Directors:
*Peter Brook, *A Midsummer Night's Dream*
*Harold Prince and Michael Bennett, *Follies*
*Paul Sills, *Story Theatre* and *Metamorphoses*
Robert Wilson, *Deafman Glance*
Andre Gregory, *Alice in Wonderland*
*Tom O'Horgan, *Lenny*

Scene Designers:
*Boris Aronson, *Follies*
*Sally Jacobs, *A Midsummer Night's Dream*
*Robin Wagner, *Lenny*

Costume Designers:
*Florence Klotz, *Follies*
*Raoul Pene du Bois, *No, No, Nanette*

Choreographers:
*Michael Bennett, *Follies*
*Donald Saddler, *No, No, Nanette*

Composer:
*Stephen Sondheim, *Follies*

Lyricist:
*Stephen Sondheim, *Follies*

Best Book for a Musical:
*Burt Shevelove, adaptation of *No, No, Nanette*

Most Promising Playwrights:
Kurt Vonnegut, Jr., *Happy Birthday, Wanda June*
David Rabe, *The Basic Training of Pavlo Hummel*
Robert Montgomery, *Subject to Fits*
A. R. Gurney, *Scenes from American Life*

Most Promising Composers:
Stephen Schwartz, *Godspell*
Itsuro Shimoda, *Golden Bat*

Most Promising Lyricists:
Stephen Schwartz, *Godspell*
Yutaka Higashi, *Golden Bat*

Most Promising Directors:
Jeff Bleckner, *The Basic Training of Pavlo Hummel*
John-Michael Tebelak, *Godspell*
Russell Treyz, *Whitsuntide*

Most Promising Scene Designer:
Eugene Lee and Fran Newman, *Alice in Wonderland*

Most Promising Costume Designer:
Susan Tsu, *Godspell*

1971 Vernon Rice Award:
To the cast of *Long Day's Journey into Night*—Paddy
Croft, Geraldine Fitzgerald, Stacy Keach, Robert Ryan,
James Naughton—and to the director, Arvin Brown

1971 Obie Awards

Best Play: *House of Blue Leaves* by John Guare
Best Performance by an Actress: Ruby Dee in *Boesman
and Lena*
Best Performance by an Actor: Jack MacGowran in
Beckett
Distinguished Playwriting: Ed Bullins for *The Fabulous
Miss Marie* and *In New England Winter*; David Rabe
for *The Basic Training of Pavlo Hummel*
Distinguished Production: *The Trial of the Catonsville
Nine*
Distinguished Foreign Plays: *Boesman and Lena* by Athol
Fugard, *AC/DC* by Heathcote Williams, *Dream on
Monkey Mountain* by Derek Walcott

Distinguished Performances: Susan Batson, Margaret
Braidwood, Hector Elizondo, Donald Ewer, Sonny Jim,
Stacy Keach, Harris Laskawy, Joan MacIntosh, William
Schallert, James Woods
Consistent Excellence of Performance: Kirk Kirksey
Special Citation: *Orlando Furioso*
Best Set: John Scheffler
Distinguished Direction: John Berry for *Boesman and
Lena*, John Hirsch for *AC/DC*, Gordon Davidson for
The Trial of the Catonsville Nine, Jeff Bleckner for
The Basic Training of Pavlo Hummel, Larry Kornfeld
for *Dracula: Sabbat*

Index

RY